AF541799

SAFFRON
versus
GREEN

Saffron versus *Green*

COMMUNAL POLITICS IN THE CENTRAL PROVINCES AND BERAR 1919–1947

Kanchanmoy Mojumdar

MANOHAR
2003

First published 2003

ISBN 81–527–5

Published by

Ajay Kumar Jain for
Manohar Publishers & Distributors
4753/23 Ansari Road, Daryaganj
New Delhi 110 002

Typeset at

Digigrafics
New Delhi 110 049

Printed at

Lordson Publishers Pvt. Ltd.
Delhi 110 007

To
Moni,
my brother

Contents

Preface

Saffron and green are but two colours. But Saffron *Versus* Green symbolizes the acutely conflictual relations between Hinduism and Islam in modern India. The growth of the conflict was coeval with the British colonial rule, and its course and character correlated to the British policy of playing off one community against the other to meet the challenge of the nationalist forces to the colonial rule.

Communalism, meaning for the present purpose, the feeling of hostility between the Hindus and Muslims, was an inescapable fact in the political development of the Central Provinces and Berar, though not the keynote of its political life in the late colonial period.

Underlying communalism were both a determination to defend religious and cultural rights and a bitter competition for political power. Consequently, it represented a clear political outline of a religious discord and a clear religious overtone in the political conflict between the Muslim minority and the Hindu majority.

The development of the conflict was influenced by the pace, extent, and character of administrative changes effected by constitutional reforms. Communalism in this context became for the Hindus and Muslims alike both a binding and blinding faith for ensuring cultural security and achieving political progress.

The social fall-out of the problem of communalism in the province were the riots that raged after 1920 between the Hindu and Muslim riffraffs. The riots bred insecurity among both the Hindus and Muslims leading to the former organizing a unity movement and the latter seeking the colonial government's protection. The result, in the context of the intensifying nationalist movement, was that the Muslim minority in the province became branded as a group playing into the hands of the colonial government and in the process turning hostile to the nationalist aspirations of the majority Hindus. The anti-Muslim spirit encouraged by the Hindu Mahasabha and Rashtriya Swayamsevak Sangh provoked a strong Muslim reaction both at the mass and elitist levels; and this was manifested in communal violence.

It was in such a situation that the Muslim League deepened its influence in the province—a development which no doubt pleased the colonial government. It formed a strong anti-Congress force during the Second World War with Muslims and many anti-Congress Hindu political groups, both keen on receiving the favours of the government.

With a brief history of the political development of the province in the first half of the twentieth century as the background I have traced the origin and growth of the conflict of the two creeds resulting in political bitterness and social tension for their followers. I have analysed the deeds and mis-deeds of both the commoners and elites in creating an atmosphere of inter-communal distrust, hate, and fear when constitutional and administrative changes were on course.

I have sought to examine how the colonial government's policy itself created an intractable political issue out of what had earlier been only a routine law and order problem easily amenable to local solution. The level of the regional communal trouble was determined by the state of relations between the elites at the national scene, representing not only differing political ideologies but clashing social groups as well.

The history of the CP and Berar in the last fifty years of the colonial rule has a lot to write about. No full-length study exists on the role of the Muslims in the evolving political life of the province in modern times. Herein lies the reason why I decided to work on the theme. I hope some others would work more extensively on it. I leave it to them to say the last word on the theme, and to say it more convincingly and perhaps differently.

Generally speaking, I have tried to see the long past scene through the eyes of those who enacted it. Compulsions of circumstances existing at the time, and not the notions of right and wrong prevailing now, have been taken into account while examining whether the political actors of the time played their role wisely or not. Necessarily, therefore, I have drawn largely on contemporary source materials; for, indeed, a phrase struck at the time when the event took place is worth much more than the many coined years later.

Such materials I have collected mostly from repositories of official documents and old newspapers; to their authorities and in particular to those of the National Archives of India and the Nehru Memorial Museum & Library, New Delhi I owe a heavy debt of gratitude. I was allowed access to the rich collection of old books and periodicals preserved in the Nagpur University Library, Hindu Dharma and Sanskriti Library, Nagpur, Jawaharlal Nehru University Library and the Library of the Indian Council of World Affairs, New Delhi. At Norlin Library, University of Colorado at Boulder, USA, I could get many books published from Pakistan having a bearing on Hindu-Muslim relations in British India.

I am thankful to Professor Jai Prakash Mishra, Dr K.S. Kshirsagar and Dr (Mrs) Shubha Johari whose personal collection of copies of official documents I have used. Dr Sheikh Shabbir, once my colleague and a very dear friend, has helped me in numerous ways; he got me in touch with Dr Sharafuddin Sahil whose book on the Muslims of Vidarbha in Urdu has a lot to commend itself. I thankfully recall the help extended to me by Dr Muhammad Ilyas Quddusi and his brother Dr Yasin Quddusi, officers at the Archaeological Survey of India (Arabic and Persian Inscription—Epigraphy branch), Nagpur; they translated into English the Urdu books I have used.

With the nonagenerian, Shri R.K. Patil, who resigned the Indian Civil Service to plunge into the Indian nationalist movement and who served the CP and Berar as a Congress Minister, I often discussed events in which he was personally involved and of which he still has a vivid recollection. The octogenerian Muhammad Zahir Warsi of Kamptee, once a prominent Muslim League leader of the province, favoured me with first-hand information on his former colleagues in the party and their activities.

My friend, Dr David Baker, who did pioneering work on the politics of the CP and Berar in the colonial period and is an acknowledged authority on the history of central India under British rule, took a keen interest in what I consider to be my foray into his preserve.

Nagpur KANCHANMOY MOJUMDAR

Abbreviations

AIML	All India Muslim League
ARCP	*Report on the Administration of the Central Provinces*
ARCPB	*Review of the Administration of the Central Provinces and Berar*
CCCP	Chief Commissioner, Central Provinces
CDM	Civil Disobedience Movement
CID	Criminal Investigation Department
Commr.	Commissioner
CP	Central Provinces
CPB	Central Provinces and Berar
CPDG	*Central Provinces District Gazetteer*
CPLA	*Central Provinces Legislative Assembly Proceedings*
CPLC	*Central Provinces Legislative Council Proceedings*
CS	Chief Secretary
CSCPB	Chief Secretary, Central Provinces and Berar
CSUP.	Chief Secretary, United Provinces of Agra and Oudh
CWC	Congress Working Committee
DC	Deputy Commissioner
Dep	Deposit
DIB	Director, Intelligence Bureau
Dn	Division
DPI	Director of Public Instruction
DSP	District Superintendent of Police
Dy SP	Deputy Superintendent of Police
EAC	Extra-Assistant Commissioner
ED	Education Department
FPC	Foreign Political Consultations
FR	Fortnightly Reports
GG	Governor-General
GOI	Government of India
HD	Home Department
HP	Home (Political) Department
HP Dep	Home (Political) Department Deposit
ICC	Indian Central Committee
IDC	Indian Delimitation Commission

IFC	Indian Franchise Committee
IG	Inspector General
IGP	Inspector General of Police
IRTC	Indian Round Table Conference
ISC	Indian Statutory Commission
LP	Linlithgow Papers
MA	Maharashtra Archives
MAGAD	Maharashtra Archives General Administration Department
MAHD	Maharashtra Archives Home Department
MAPM	Maharashtra Archives Political and Military Department
Med. Dept.	Medical Department
MLA	Member of Legislative Assembly
MLC	Member of Legislative Council
MPSRR	Madhya Pradesh Secretariat Record Room
NAI	National Archives of India
NRC	Nagpur Residency Correspondence
NRR	Nagpur Residency Records
Offg.	Officiating
PIHC	*Proceedings of the Indian History Congress*
Pol.	Political
Prog.	Proceedings
RACP	*Report on the Administration of the Central Provinces*
RACPB	*Review of the Administration of the Central Provinces and Berar*
Resd.	Resident
RIN	*Report on Indian Newspapers*
RSS	Rashtriya Swayamsevak Sangh
RTC	Round Table Conference
SC	Scheduled Castes
SDM	Sub-Divisional Magistrate
Secy.	Secretary
SP	Sinha Papers
Telg.	Telegram

Glossary

akhada	wrestling ground
bakr-id	a Muslim religious festival
bania	a caste of Hindu money lenders
chaprasi	office attendant
darbar	court
deshmukh	revenue collector turned landowner
deshpande	revenue collector turned landowner
dhoti	male lower garment
diwali	a Hindu festival
dusserah	a Hindu festival
fakir	Muslim mendicant
farman	rescript, an order
goonda	a hooligan, a criminal
hakim	Muslim physician
hartal	strike; closure of markets and business establishments
holi	a Hindu festival
jagir	assigned estate
jagirdar	one with assigned estate
jamat	association, organization
jihad	holy war waged by Muslims against heretics
kafir	non-believer
kayasth	a Hindu caste of scribes
kaji	Muslim officer to dispense justice
khatib	one who delivers religious discourse in mosques
kunbi	a Maratha caste
lathi	a club; a stuff
muharram	a Muslim religious observance
nikah	Muslim marriage
panchayat	village council of five members to settle local disputes
pardanashin	a lady under veil
pargannah	a sub-division of a district
patel	village head
patwari	village record keeper
pesh imam	one who leads the prayer in mosque
pir	Muslim holy man

prabhat pheri	a procession taken out in the morning
purdah	veil
ramzan	Muslim month for fasting
sabha	association
sahukar	moneylender
sanad	a charter
sangathana	organization; Hindu unity movement
sarpanch	head of the *panchayat* (village council)
satyagraha	application of the soul or force of Truth; the use of moral force applied by Gandhi for the political purpose
shia	a sect of Islam
shuddhi	a movement for re-conversion of non-Hindus to Hinduism
sunni	the main sect of Islam
swadeshi	made at home; a movement supporting Indian industry
swaraj	self government
tabligh	the preaching of Islam
taluk	administrative unit within a district
tanzim	a reform movement of the Indian Muslims
tazia	a float taken in procession during *muharram*
tehsil	sub-division of a district
watan	rent-free tenure

Introduction

Primarily four factors determine the genesis, growth, and intensity of majority-minority syndrome in the political life of a plural society: the numerical strength of the minority communities in the local population, the depth and dimension of their feeling of deprivation and denial, the success of the minority leaders in articulating the feeling and converting it into a force for political reckoning with the majority community, and the reaction of the majority community to the discontent in the minority communities and the means they adopt to redress their grievances. Judged by these counts, the Hindu-Muslim conflictual relations in the Central Provinces and Berar was, by and large, a rather tame phenomenon compared with such relations in other provinces of British India.

Barring Orissa, of all the provinces, the CP and Berar had the smallest number of Muslims—not even five per cent ever. Not until the 1920s did the men smart under any apparent bitter feeling of being wronged by the majority Hindus; the feeling, when it grew, was more imagined than real, considering the absence of two important factors which generated such feeling in other provinces. For example, through the years the Muslims in the CP and Berar had made the most of the available opportunities for education and public employment, reaching a position better than not only their co-religionists in several other provinces but also the local Hindus. And this position they retained till the very end of the British rule. In fact, unlike in the UP and Bengal, the general Muslim grievances in the CP and Berar against the Hindus initially developed more by external stimuli than by any spontaneous internal impulsion.

CP and Berar with its large tribal population was a politically backward province. Created in 1861, it stayed downgraded as a Chief Commissioner's charge till 1921; it had no legislature till late 1913; no elections took place there till 1921; it had no second chamber of the legislature, which further restricted the scale and scope of political activity. The political inertia of the local people was often referred to in official papers.

Slow to grow, the political leadership in the province stayed stunted for long: its Hindi and Marathi speaking leaders functioned as political wards of Allahabad and Poona stalwarts respectively; intense rivalry between local public men of the two linguistic groups and later the bitterness between caste groups further weakened the thrust of the Hindu solidarity movement in the province which was started to counter what some elements of the Hindu leadership perceived as Muslim aggressiveness.

More apparent was Muslim political backwardness. The Muslim middle class constituted a very small community; the men went not to Aligarh or Lahore for education but to Amravati, Nagpur, Jabalpur, and at best Hyderabad—a fact which was to have had a bearing on their mind-set when reacting to Hindu communalism. Only a few of these men, mostly lawyers, joined politics, working till the late 1930s, as junior colleagues of important local Hindu leaders; most others preferred the security of government service.

Historically and generally speaking, middle India's proneness to communalism had been less than that of most of north India, the process of inter-community interaction resulting in integration, having fewer impediments. Compared to northern India, distinctive Islamic culture was less apparent in the CP and Berar where there were no educational and cultural institutions like Deoband. Here a fair number of Muslims spoke Hindi and Marathi as their mother tongue, not Urdu, and they were far less nostalgic about the glories of Islamic rule, remote or recent.

The Raj Gonds, rulers of the Nagpur tract before the Bhonsles, retained most Hindu traditions in their family, even after adopting Islam as but a means of political expediency. In the Gond rule the Muslims had no privileged position any more than in the Bhonsle rule the Hindus had.

Above all, there were no meddlesome and powerful Ulema class to influence Muslim public opinion in the CP and Berar, although, like in other provinces, in the 1940s particularly, the Muslim League used local mosques as pulpits for political propaganda besides bringing in the *maulanas* and *maulavis* from the UP, Bombay and Delhi to propagate its cause. Compared to north India, *tabligh* and *tanzim* in the CP and Berar were a rather low-key movement, for not much different was the Hindu *Shuddhi* and Conversion Movement, going by its actual outcome. All in all, Muslim consciousness of being a separate community was not as keen as it was in northern

India; it had, besides, a far shorter history and much slower development.

The Nagpur and Berar region had no pre-British history of inter-community bitterness culminating in riots. The Bhonsles, ruling the tract for more than a hundred years, faced no problem created by the fury of faiths any more than the Nizams did when collecting revenues from Berar conjointly with the Bhonsles.

Muslims of the CP and Berar were in fact, less 'fanatic' than those of northern India, as observed by the first governor of the province with an unmistakable sense of relief. Neither the bitter Urdu-Nagari controversy nor the prolonged Cow Protection movement, which sparked off riots in parts of the UP, Bihar, and Bombay in the 1880s and 1890s, affected the inter-community relations in the CP and Berar, although Nagpur, its capital, was for long a stronghold of the Cow Protection Movement. The Hindu and Muslim revivalist movements of the time also did not lead to any communal violence. The first four decades of British rule in the Central Provinces passed off with hardly any reported case of such violence.

Unlike in northern India again, CP and Berar authorities were never worried over Muslim disaffection except during the Khilafat–Non-Cooperation Movement days. When pan-Islamism made the government wary in northern India, the CP and Berar government was confident about the continued loyalty of the local Muslims.

Going by official records and the local press, initially the Muslims of central India had a much narrower trans-Indian perspective of their interests than those of north India. Later, however, the Muslim leadership, in widening the perspective, created in the general Hindu mind the image of the Muslims having extra-territorial affinity. The Muslim League, in drawing the Muslims closer to the government and keeping them away from the Congress-led nationalist movements made them appear as anti-national. This impression was fully exploited by Hindu communal groups to fuel the communal fire in the province.

The leadership factor had much to do with the character of communalism in the province. The Hindu leadership eventually outgrew its tutelage of the Allahabad and Poona leadership; as Congressmen, in particular, the leaders gave the government no small trouble. Individually, some prominent Congressmen, a few Marathi speaking men among them having also had close association with the Hindu Mahasabha and the RSS of the province were all for upholding Hindu interests, but as a party, the Congress in the province, as elsewhere in the country, projected its non-communal image.

The Congressmen were, of course, bitterly anti-Muslim League, particularly opposed to its Pakistan scheme; but the Congress, as a party had no love lost either for the Hindu Mahasabha—which, however, did not deter the League from branding it as no different from the Mahasabha.

As for the Muslim leaders, even a sympathetic governor dismissed them in the late 1930s as being not out of a top drawer. The men had little political clout and far less national political standing, unlike Muslim leaders elsewhere in the country. They were even ill-suited as playable pawns on the political chessboard of the province. Even then the fact that the men were so used by the local authorities at the time indicated less their intrinsic worth than the authorities desperately grabbing whatever means they could to meet the political crisis created by the Congress.

Unlike in the UP and Punjab, there was no affluent and ambitious landed aristocracy in the CP and Berar to influence provincial politics. There were only a few rich Muslim landowners who served the government before entering politics.

There was no Muslim political party in the province to articulate Muslim identity consciousness and political awareness that grew slowly both as a fall-out of events outside the province and as a reaction to communal riots in it. The provincial Muslim League did exist but, as elsewhere in the country, merely on paper till the late 1930s; in it individual rivalry for power and prominence was far more evident than collective efforts to further the party's objectives. There were, of course, Jinnah loyalists and Shafi supporters as also those determined to boycott the Simon Commission and others bent on welcoming it.

Excepting the Bohras, there was in the province no affluent Muslim business community to which the promoters of the cause of the community could turn as financiers. The Bohras maintained aloofness from any active political involvement in politics, although from the late 1930s they began showing some support to the League and later turned very enthusiastic about the party's Pakistan scheme like the rest of the Muslim community.

M.A. Jinnah himself viewed the CP and Berar Leaguers no very differently from the governors: utterly mediocre men. In his reorganized League of the late 1930s, its CP and Berar unit counted for little by way of its inputs in the party's policy decisions. He, of course, gave representation to the CP and Berar Leaguers in the highest bodies of the party, but that indicated more his adherence to the democratic norm than any recognition of those men's political worth.

The Congress-League equation in the CP and Berar was different from that in the UP. The League was a far smaller party in the CP and Berar and figured no prominently in the provincial Congress calculations. The Congressmen viewed the Leaguers as no political force by themselves, far less as a potential or actual counterweight to the Congress clout in the province. Such a party and such men the Congress saw no reason to woo. Therefore, unlike in the UP, there was no tacit understanding between the two parties after the 1937 elections let alone any talk of sharing power with it in a coalition ministry after the elections.

In fact, Muslims as a community and the League as a party were made politically important first by the governors and then by Dr N.B. Khare and his small anti-Congress group who wanted to cobble up a pliant, pro-government non-Congress ministry to help the governor in smoothly conducting war operations.

But then, compared to most other provinces, the CP and Berar proved for Jinnah an easy province to spread his influence among the local Muslims and to stay unchallenged as the supreme leader of the entire community, not just of the party which he had virtually recreated. Here there were neither strong Muslim parties to rival the League nor any Muslim group fit enough to share power with, let alone to thwart Jinnah's personal ambitions. The Momins, Ahrars, and Khaksars made only shrill noises till the early 1940s when they acquiesced in Jinnah's primacy; they were never any real threat to his authority.

Jinnah's hold over the CP and Berar Muslims stayed firmer than that over Muslims in many other provinces where some strong Muslim leaders successfully fought his fiat or obliged him to defer to the views different from his own. Here in the CP and Berar there were no Sikandar Hyat Khans, no Fazlul Haqs, no Sadullah Khans, and no Khan Sahebs to contest his claim as the sole spokesman of the entire Muslim community and his League as the only party to preserve, protect, promote, and project Muslim interests.

Nor among the CP and Berar Muslims were any elements like those who formed in the UP the Nationalist Agriculturist Party, fit enough to form a short-time ministry and be attacked by the Congress and the League alike. As for the government in the province, it suspected no disloyalty in any section of the local Muslims; the provincial League, in fact, was most steadfast in its attachment to the government.

Jinnah was far surer of his flock in the CP and Berar than in the UP, in particular. Yusuf Shariff and Abdur Rauf Shah, successive Presidents of the provincial League, vexed him no doubt, but they were no nagging worries as Khaliquzzaman and Hafiz Ibrahim had been in the UP by their propensity to hobnob with the Congress. There were no suspected crypto-Congressmen in the League's CP and Berar unit. Nationalist Muslims and Muslim Independents counted for little. Above all, there were in the CP and Berar no Rafi Ahmad Kidwais to serve as a link between the Congress-leaning and power-seeking Leaguers and Congressmen believed to be soft towards the League; unlike in the UP again, here there were no left-leaning Leaguers to bother Jinnah.

Excepting Yusuf Shariff, no important League leader in the CP and Berar deserted to the Congress whereas in the UP several Leaguers did so; rather the few Muslim leaders who were still in the CP and Berar Congress, left for the League in the late 1930s. Of course, their being in the party or going out of it made little difference to the widening popularity of the Congress, which anyway had never drawn to itself any considerable number of Muslims except during the Khilafat–Non-Cooperation days. But then, it served the League's propaganda purpose: no genuine Muslim could be in the Congress, a Hindu party out to harm the Muslim interests.

To gladden Jinnah all the more, the League won all the post-1937 bye elections for the Muslim reserved constituencies in the CP and Berar; in the UP, the League had to concede some of such seats to the Congress.

The fate of Yusuf Shariff and Rauf Shah deterred all Leaguers in the CP and Berar from falling out with Jinnah. Unlike Hafiz Ibrahim in the UP, Shariff had to quit his ministership very soon, and that under a cloud; as a Congress MLA he utterly failed to drum up any Muslim support for the party; he found himself consigned to virtual political insignificance, shunned by his own community and suspected no less by his erstwhile Congress friends.

As for Rauf Shah, he really made no move to be a Congress Muslim; he only wished to make it to a non-Congress ministry by piggy-backing on the governor's support. Whether or not Jinnah knew it, the governor was aware of Rauf Shah's lack of enthusiasm for the Pakistan scheme; this enhanced his acceptability to his Hindu colleagues in the legislature with whom, the King's Party, the governor wanted to set up a make-shift ministry when the Congress demitted the office. However, Rauf Shah's wish remained just a pipe dream; Jinnah scotched his ambition with ease.

The CP and Berar was far more peaceful than northern and eastern India in the tumultuous two years, 1946–7. Here the partition left no deep scar on the Muslim life and psyche; it was a far lesser tragedy than elsewhere. Here broken homes and sundered families were far fewer; so were atrocities, the level of violence being far lower. Here women were spared traumatic experiences.

Muslim exodus from the province did take place but far more to Bhopal and Hyderabad than to the new Muslim homeland created by Jinnah. The few Muslim grandees and League leaders who went away to Pakistan soon returned home, disillusioned and perhaps wiser. Some of these men forged friendship with Hindu public men and all gave out their fullest support to the measures taken by the Congress government for refugee rehabilitation. Some ambitious Muslims teamed up with Congress leaders to win elections as corporators in municipalities; some made ample hay as elements in local and regional Congress party set up.

The new ethos of the administration after 1947 with constitutional provision for democracy and adult suffrage for all citizens made minority communities politically far more important than they were in colonial India. The Congress party ruling the CP and Berar (renamed M.P. in 1956) for long made the most of the minority communities' growing attachment to it.

CHAPTER I

Muslims of the Central Provinces and Berar

The Central Provinces and Berar was constituted in two stages, two extensive territories merged into its making. In 1861, the Saugar and Nerbudda Territories, wrested from the Peshwa of Poona and the Bhonsle of Nagpur in 1817–18,[1] and the Nagpur Territories, which lapsed to the British in 1854, were brought together to form the Central Provinces to which was added in 1902 Berar, coded by the Nizam of Hyderabad to the British government on perpetual lease. Berar was brought under the CP administration in 1903.

A Chief Commissioner headed the administration till 1920, when the CP and Berar was upgraded into a Governor's province. Hindi, with regional variations, was the principal language in the Saugar and Nerbudda Territories while majority of the people in the Nagpur territory and Berar spoke Marathi. The vast tribal population living in the hilly midland areas spoke their own languages.

The province had a small Muslim population—never more than 4.6 per cent—the men being mostly converts from local low-caste Hindus and immigrants from neighbouring tracts when held by Muslim rulers. Muslim Gond rulers of Deogarh,[2] which formed a part of the later Nagpur state of the Bhonsles, welcomed Muslim immigrants as did Muslim rulers of Khandesh who ruled Nimar for about three hundred years. Then there was the inflow of Muslims from Berar ruled by the Nizams. Many Muslim *deshmukhs* (*pargana* officials) were originally Hindus who embraced Islam during the rule of the Mughal Emperor, Aurangzeb (1658–1707) to retain their hereditary offices.[3] Trade and a variety of other occupations brought in more Muslim immigrants who raised families among local women.

The increase in the Muslim population of Berar was partly due to their 'superior fecundity' and partly due to the 'proselytizing efforts' in the last decade of the nineteenth century.[4] In 1911–12, there were 5,85,000 Muslims in the province, half of them living in Berar. The more Muslim-populated districts were Nimar (9.8 per cent), Amravati (8.3 per cent), Akola (8.8 per cent), and Buldana (8.2 per cent).[5]

The Nagpur region saw great days when ruled by the Gond rulers, Bakht Buland and Chand Sultan, in particular. Nagpur received its first immigration of expert Hindu farmers and artificers whom Bakht Buland 'tempted away from their homes' by liberal land grants.[6] His son, Chand Sultan, made Nagpur his capital, linking it by roads with far off regions. Career in Gondwana, as the Gond-ruled kingdom was called, was indeed open to talent, and so flocked to Nagpur, in particular, many Muslims from the Deccan besides western and northern India.[7]

Under the Bhonsles, Muslims in general had a recognized place in the society and the Muslim nobility an enviable position in the administration. Muslim grandees served the rulers well, enjoying their trust and patronage. Sheikh Muhammad Ali, holding the 'domestic station about the person of the Raja', Raghuji II, and being a 'companion of his amusements',[8] headed the civil court of justice in the city of Nagpur. Dealing with the East India Company's emissaries to the Nagpur court was his additional responsibility; his courtly manners and impressive personality were highly spoken of by the Company's men dealing with the Bhonsles.[9] Raghuji II's troops fighting the Pathan chief, Amir Khan, in Bhopal, were led by the 'much employed' Sadiq Ali Khan[10] whom the British Resident, Richard Jenkins, viewed as the only person fit to function as the Minister of the State when its administration was taken over by the British in 1818 following Bhonsle's defeat in the third and the last Anglo-Maratha War.[11]

However, the Governor-General disapproved the idea for 'the nomination of a Mussalman to that station in a Maratha government was not an arrangement likely to operate successfully'.[12] And this, inspite of the Resident reporting that Sadiq Ali enjoyed the Raja's 'partiality and confidence' when some of his other Muslim officers were guilty of treacherous correspondence with Amir Khan, the Pathan chief.[13] Sadiq Ali helped Jenkins in reorganizing the administration and in recovering the personal property of the deceased King,

Raghuji II.[14] Alafuddin, once the head of the state camel department, led the opposition to Raghuji's Ministers, mostly Hindus; he wielded 'considerable influence on the mind of the Raja' who rewarded him with a ministership.[15] Raghuji II left his health to the care of his personal physician, Hakim Fazil Khan and his colleagues.[16]

Pathans, Arabs and Muslims of northern India served in the Bhonsle army which had Muslim commanding officers. Raghuji II had four thousand Arabs and a number of Pathans as his elite corps. The Berar cavalry, rated the best in the Deccan, was largely Muslim in composition.[17] 'The fixed military population' of Nagpur city in 1854 was almost entirely Muslim and Rajput—some eight thousand men.[18] In Chhattisgarh, ruled by the Bhonsles, there were, in 1818, three thousand Muslims, mostly sepoys and revenue peons. Many Muslims hailing from Bengal settled down in Chattisgarh as traders and farmers, giving up their earlier military occupation.[19]

In the Bhonsle judicial administration there were Muslim *kazis* to interpret the Islamic law. Haji Rasul was the principal *maulavi* of Nagpur, who Raghuji III wanted to act as a *sarpanch* in a case involving Muslim law when members of the *panchayat* were not Muslims themselves.[20] The Muslim Gond rulers of Deogarh, ousted by the Bhonsles, received from them both respectful treatment and a substantial maintenance allowance.[21]

Karim Khan, a famous architect, built Raghuji II's palace while Ahmadbhai worked as the farmer of town duties. Famous Muslim singers, Alam Shaheen, son of Zafar Khan, Mithumian of Lucknow and Karim Khan regaled the connoisseurs of music at the Bhonsle darbar.[22] Maulavi Qasim and Saiyad Ibrahim were two lawyers sent to London by the dowager Bhonsle Queens to seek justice from the British government.[23]

The Bhonsles provided for no exclusive education for their Muslim subjects but they allowed private schools to function for instruction in Arabic and Persian. Muslim tutors imparted free education 'under the impression that so meritorious an act will be taken into consideration in a future state'.[24] Their pupils were wards of respected families in whose homes the teachers lived. There were fifty six such teachers of whom twenty eight taught only Persian and Arabic. Of the 1,259 Muslim pupils in all, 181 read Persian and Arabic.[25] At this time (1826), when Jenkins was the Resident, there were 1,076 Muslim slaves out of a total of 3,500 in the Nagpur state, the Raja having more than 500 himself.[26]

Through the years there grew a local Muslim landed aristocracy, loyalty, and service to the rulers facilitating its growth. Muhammad Amin Khan held an extensive tract which earned him an annual income of Rs. 3 lakh. Muhammad Zaman Khan, a zamindar of Seoni, helped Raghuji II quell a mutiny in his regular troops, of mostly Muslims. Vilayat Khan Pathan, Zainuddin Pathan, and Muhammad Umma Khan were the other Muslim zamindars of Seoni.[27]

The British sternly dealt with the Muslims who opposed their rule while amply rewarding those who cooperated with it. Thus, two Muslim notables, Nawab Kadar Ali Khan, and Vilayat Mian, were executed for their suspected complicity in the abortive mutiny of the Nagpur Irregular Force in 1857; another grandee, Muhammad Jalaluddin, had to suffer a protracted trial before aquittal.[28] Captain Tuffasul Hussain Khan's 'personal exertions' for effecting the 'tranquillity of the native capital', Nagpur, during the 1857 revolt earned him official approbation.[29] The British drove away from the state service a horde of 'mischievous and turbulent' Muslims, descendants of the Arabs and Rohillas who for generations had served the Bhonsles.[30] The Nagpur Irregular Force, consisting of mostly Muslims and raised in 1854, was disbanded in 1862.[31]

But then, the early British government raised and reared a Muslim professional elite more in recognition of their educational attainments, economic affluence, and social standing than as a political counterpoise to the local Hindus. The earliest Indian employees in the C.P. medical department were Muslims as were the Extra-Assistant Commissioners in the judicial service and corporators nominated on municipalities.[32] Till almost the end of the nineteenth century Muslims outnumbered Hindus as Deputy Commissioners of districts.

The new British government recognized and made use of the local influence of the Muslim landed aristocracy. Till about the first decade of the twentieth century, in some districts like Seoni, in particular, Muslims vied with the kayasths as the predominant land owning class[33] which paid the government a nominal quit rent and at places no rent at all. With the years, however, constant litigation and consequent indebtedness compelled some Muslims to sell off their land to local Hindu *banias* and kayasths. Some old Muslim land owning families suffered due to the general British policy of recognizing tenures held by officers for life and not in perpetuity.[34]

Muslims who served in the British Indian army during the First World War, were rewarded with land grants tenable for life.[35]

The rate of growth of the Muslim population[36] compared to that of the Hindus was not invariably higher. Thus, while the Hindu population increased by 16 per cent between 1881 and 1911, the Muslim population increased by 24 per cent; but then, in the decade 1901–11, the Hindu population increased by 16 per cent while the Muslim population increased by 13 per cent—and that despite Berar's inclusion in the province in 1902–3.[37] In fact, as reported in the 1911 Census Report, the Muslim growth rate in the C.P. and Berar, compared to that in other provinces, had been slower partly because of the want of 'some of the conditions which are held to favour extra-fecundity in Muhammadans'.[38] Besides, some Muslims—the polygamous Bohras, Kachhis, and Khojas, for example—were temporary sojourners in the province as itinerant merchants, not living with their wives.[39] In the decade 1911–21, the Muslim population fell by 5 per cent due to high infant mortality and epidemics.[40] Emigration and immigration caused fluctuations in the local Muslim population of Berar. In the 1860s many Hindu *koshtis* (weavers) migrated to and settled in Berar where labour was more remunerative and food cheaper than at their old habitation elsewhere. These men became Muslims in large numbers.[41]

Most Muslims lived clustered in towns and thinly spread over vast rural areas.[42] Of farmers only 2.5 per cent were Muslims; but they outnumbered the Hindus as weavers and traders in cloth as also in timber and furnishing business. Hindus dominated in most other occupations, although there were a large number of Muslim dyers, shoe makers, traders in metals, bangles, and building materials, besides carpenters, vegetable sellers, and mendicants. There were Afghan and Pathan moneylenders, some engaged by Hindu *sahukars* and landlords for either recovering loans or collecting delayed rents. Muslim *kazis* and *khatibs*, keen on keeping their community members steady on the customary moral keel, interpreted ecclesiastical rules, arbitrated in disputes and dispensed justice.[43] Some Muslim landlords—as in Buldana—did moneylending business apart from serving on local boards, wielding both social and political influence.[44]

There were some occupations neither exclusively Hindu nor entirely Muslim, but shared by both. Thus there were Hindu butchers, called *khatiks* or *bakr kasais* (goat-killers) and Muslim butchers or *gai kasais* (cow-killers); due to Hindu influence on them, some Muslim butchers of Berar did not slaughter cows nor inter-dined and inter-married with Muslim *gai-kasais*. Sellers of glass bangles (*manihars*) were mostly Muslims while their makers were generally Hindus. The *bafnas* and *pinjaras* (cotton carders), half-Hindu and half-Muslim, practised customs common to both the faiths.[45] A large number of the Bhils of Nimar becoming only 'nominally Muslims'—perhaps after forcible conversion by the Muslim rulers of Khandesh—held on to their traditional animistic customs and practices, refusing to marry outside their community. They served mostly in the local Muslim army.[46]

Not more than some three per cent of the Muslims of the province were *Shias*, the rest being *Sunnis*. The Sheikhs, rather an 'indefinite tribe', were mostly Hindus converted to Islam who registered themselves in census operations under no caste names.[47] There were Muslim *deshpandes* and *deshmukhs* in Berar, some hereditary *patwaris* and *patels*; there were even some 'Muslim kayasths and rajputs'.[48]

Conversion of Hindus to Islam in the nineteenth century in the Central Provinces was motivated by the hope of freedom from social oppression and economic insecurity. But for most, conversion resulted in no change in either accustomed lifestyle or social practices, let alone in occupations; and this was accepted by the local Muslims. *Sari*—not *salwar*—clad Hindu women converted to Islam not only cleansed their homes with cow dung but secretly performed the Hindu *bhaiwar* ceremony in marriage before the *kazi* made his appearance to solemnize the *nikah*.[49]

Some Muslims even retained their original caste names, denoting their hereditary occupations, e.g. atari, fakir, gaoli, bhat, pinjari, bhisti, kagadi, jokhara, kunjara and kasai. However, in many cases caste distinctions did not survive change in occupations.[50]

The Muslim *bafnas* and *pinjaras* were indistinguishable from low caste Hindus whose social customs they continued to follow even after conversion. There were Muslim endogamous groups who married in their respective castes only. In fact, some rural Muslims were as caste conscious as the local Hindus were; they would not take water to drink from low caste Hindus nor their women would eat from the plate used by Muslims who originally were low caste Hindus. Town living Kachhis and Bohras, the most educated and advanced sections of the Muslims, would not eat food given by any non-Muslims other than high caste Hindus. The Muslim *momins* (weavers) and *satranjwallahs* (carpet makers) and *bagwans* (gardeners) of Amravati retained a few Hindu marriage customs; they would not only refuse food cooked by low caste Hindus, but even throw away their own earthen cooking pots if defiled by the touch of such Hindus. A Hindu invited to a Muslim marriage ate the food cooked by himself, the host providing him with all the materials needed. Since the converts carried their castes into their new faith, the customary ban on inter-caste marriages in Hindu society was also carried over into the neo-Muslim families.[51] Some Muslims' reluctance to marry widows reflected Hindu influence on them.[52]

Many Muslims followed the Hindu law of succession, their women were denied any right to inherit property. Wine was no taboo for some Muslims while beef was so for some others. Poor Muslim mendicants received alms from Hindus and Muslims alike during the holi festival in particular; some Muslim *pirs* had as many Hindu followers as some Hindu deities in villages had Muslim devotees.[53]

The vanishing border line between Hindus and Muslims made British officers wonder over the 'backsliding of lower caste Muhammadans'; the *kachera* and the *pinjara*, in particular, they saw, were 'lost to Muhammad', having drifted irrevocably 'far from the faith'.[54] The Muslim *bafnas* were, the officers lamented, practically Hindus, while the Muslim *manihars* made no effort to conceal their fondness for Hindu festivals.[55] Like the Hindus, many Muslims gave their caste names to census enumerators, convincing them that there indeed was 'very little real distinction between the lower class of Muslims who had adopted the caste system and the Hindus'.[56]

Nearly fourteen per cent of the Muslims being originally Hindus it was probable that 'more than half the followers of Islam in these provinces' did not belong to 'any genuine Muhammadan race'.[57]

Even in Muslim-ruled Berar, Hindu influence on local Muslims surprised serving British officers. Originally, Berar Muslims had an 'excessive veneration of dead hermits and martyrs'; they worshipped at the tombs of men who 'preached and fought against idolatry'.[58] But through the years, Hindu influence, imperceptibly working in Muslim society, caused a great change in the way *urs* or annual commemoration of some local Muslim saints was observed; in Buldana particularly, they had 'degenerated into much that is mere carnal traffic and pagan idolatry, a scandal to the rigid Islamite', as a British officer ruefully observed.[59] Any protest against 'such soul-stirring abuses' was likely to be opposed by the local 'loose living Mussalmans', and particularly Muslim shopkeepers, who being 'no more than Ephestian silversmiths' would cry down 'an inconvenient religious reformer'.[60]

British officers found only a few good Muslim families in Buldana district who were once 'somewhat very favourable specimens of their creed and race'. But due to their constant interaction with the local Hindus, they had gradually absorbed 'the sympathetic feeling of surrounding superstitions', best manifested in their pompous celebration of Muharram.[61] Most of these Muslims had Hindu ancestors, and so their 'continued reverence for the old Hinduism'.[62] Thus some Muslim *deshmukhs* and *deshpandes* of Buldana professed Islam in public while engaging Brahmins in the sly to worship their family deities. They consulted astrologers before finalizing marriages and fixing dates for any celebration. 'Usually fatalists of the extreme type', these men kept their women secluded 'as an integral part of their religion'.[63] Poor Muslim women, however, did not observe purdah while out to earn their living as daily labourers and vendors at market places.

Apparent Muslim influence accounted for the Hindu kunbis of the Yeotmal district burying their dead instead of cremating them. They begged during Muharram and gave a part of their earnings in cereals to Muslim beggars.[64] There were also evidences of mingling of Hinduism and Islam in some local cults—as in that of Shah Dawal, for example. Dawal, a Mahar (untouchable Hindu) and Shah Malik, an itinerant Muslim fakir, lived together like Nanak and Farid, the Hindu and Muslim disciples of Kabir. At their death, Dawal and Shah Malik were entombed together at Uprai in the Daryapur taluk of Amravati district. The kunbis, telis, bhois and dhangars, all low caste Hindus of Berar, worshipped at the shrine of Shah Dawal; newly married mahar couples never failed to visit the shrine.[65]

A similar syncretic faith was popular among the low caste Hindus of Nimar, its founder being one Muhammad Shah Dullah, a Muslim saint. He revered the Hindu god, Vishnu, as the Supreme Deity and founded a sect, naming it *Nishkalanki*, the sinless one. The holy book of the sect was a compilation of Hindu and Muslim scriptures.[66]The Pirzada was yet another such local sect whose followers, though calling themselves Muslims, were to all intents and purposes Hindus, observing caste rules.[67] The *urs* at Rasulpura in Khandesh, commemorating a local saint, drew many devout Hindus.[68]

In the Hoshangabad district the Ghori kings of Malwa attained 'divine dignity'; a Hindu in difficult times would as reverently invoke the blessings of the 'Ghori Badshah' as of any other supernatural power.[69] Muslim saints of Nimar, known as Panchon Pirs, were venerated by Muslims and Hindus alike.[70] Opposite to the Ramtek hill, where the Bhonsles built the Rama temple, lay the tomb of a Muslim saint, Sheikh Farid, revered by both Muslims and Hindus. The Bhonsles regularly visited the tomb and never failed to provide for its maintenance.[71] Hindus and Muslims participated in each other's religious functions—Diwali and Muharram in particular. In Chhindwara the two communities celebrated Muharram together. The Bhonsles took part in the celebration of Muharram, visiting *tazias* on the occasion. They also attended marriages in the Nizam's family.[72]

Hindu-Muslim societal relations in the province were generally free from strain till about the 1920s when political developments in the country at large and their impact on the province bred in the two communities a growing identity consciousness. Customs and usages so long observed peacefully—and some jointly—were now flaunted as *rights* of the two communities to be forcefully asserted and violently fought over. And thus developed the communal problem in this otherwise peaceful province.

NOTES

1. The Bhonsles, a Maratha family, ruled the Nagpur state for a little more than one hundred years from 1743, when it was founded by Raghuji I. His successors were Janoji (1755–72), Sabaji (1772–4), Mudhoji (1775–88), Raghuji II (1788–1816), Appa Saheb (1816–8) and Raghuji III (1818–53). During 1817–8 took place the third and last Anglo-Maratha war. Appa Saheb lost his war with the British and coded to them all his territories northward of the river Narmada and the whole of Berar.
   In their heydays, the Bhonsles ruled over a vast tract in central and eastern India, including most of the present Madhya Pradesh, the whole of Berar and parts of western and coastal Orissa besides a portion of southern Bengal. The Nagpur state was annexed by the British in December 1853, when its last ruler, Raghuji III died leaving no natural heir. *Report on the Nagpur State by George Ramsay, 1845*. Charles Grant, *The Central Provinces Gazetteer,* 1871, pp. 303–14. R.M. Sinha, *Bhonsles of Nagpur The Last Phase, 1818–1854* (New Delhi, 1967).

2. The Muslim Gonds of Deogarh ruled much of what later went into the making of the Nagpur state. Raghuji I, exploiting the quarrels in the Gond ruling family, ended its rule in 1737 and gradually took over the Gond kingdom before he died in 1755. Ramsay, *Report of the Nagpur State*, p. 3. Grant, *The Central Province*, pp. xxviii, cx. C.U. Wills, *The Raj Gond Maharajahs of the Satpura Hills: A Local History* (Nagpur, 1923). FPC, 6 Nov. 1939, no. 105: Grome, Asst. Resident, Nagpur, to Govt., 25 May 1838.
3. RACPB, 1921–2, p. 30.
4. W.W. Hunter, *The Imperial Gazetteer of India,* vol. VII, *Berar*, Oxford, 1908, p. 380.
5. RACPB, 1911–12, p. 42.
6. Grant, *The Central Province*, p. lxxiv.
7. Ibid., pp. 322–3, 345. Eyre Chatterton, *The Story of Gondwana* (London, 1916), pp. 44, 46.
8. 'Forester's Account of Nagpur in 1788', C.U. Wills, *British Relations with the Nagpur State in the 18th century,* Nagpur, 1926, p. 95.
9. 'Journal of a Route to Nagpore by the way of Cuttack', Burrosumber, Dangur Ghur and the Southern Bunjare Ghaut in the Months of March, April, May to the 3rd June, 1790', by C.F. Leckie, C.U. Wills, *Early European Travellers in the Nagpur Territories*, Nagpur, 1930, p. 70; 'A Narrative of Journey from Mirzapore to Nagpore', by H.T. Colebrook, ibid., pp. 206–7.
10. *Supplement to the Report on the Territories of the Raja of Nagpore submitted to the Supreme Government of India by Richard Jenkins, 1827*, Nagpur, 1923, p. 29.
11. The state was administered by the Resident till 1829, when the minor ruler, Raghuji III, came of age. Jenkins, *Report*, pp. 67–73, FPC, 13 Nov. 1839, no. 63, Ramsay, *Report of the Nagpur State*, p. 24.
12. NRR, vol. 41, pt. III, no. 328: J. Adams, Secy. Pol. Dept., to Jenkins, Resident, Nagpur, 5 Sept. 1818.
13. Ibid. vol. 25, no. 419.
14. Jenkin's *Report*, p. 23. R.V. Russell and Hira Lal, *The Tribes and Castes of the Central Provinces of India*, vol. I, Indian edn., Delhi, 1975, p. 248.
15. NRR, vol. 25, no. 284. NRC (unindexed), Apr.-Dec. 1818: Jenkins to Lord Hastings, GG, 1 July 1818.
16. *Escheat of the Nagpur State, the Arrangements for the Administration of the New Province and the Settlement of the Bhonsle Family*, Nagpur, 1920, p. 3.

    Raghuji II wanted Bande Ali, a noted physician of Delhi, to come to Nagpur to treat his only son. NRR, vol. 28, no. 23: Jenkins to C.T. Metcalfe, Resident, Delhi, 2 Dec. 1815. Also NRR, vol. 25, no. 284.

    The Nizam sent two Muslim hakims, Muhammad Shah and Mir Altaf, to attend to an ill Raghuji II. P.L. Saswadkar, 'Nagpur at the end of the 18th century', *PIHC*, 1969, p. 412.
17. Wills, *The Raj Gond*, pp. 113, 188.

18. *The Escheat of the Nagpur State*, p. 84.
19. *A Report on the Subah or Province of Chattisgarh by Major P. Vanasagnew, 1820* (Nagpur, 1922), pp. 5–6.
20. NRC (unindexed), 1845–48: George Ramsay, Resident, Nagpur, to Perry, 21 Dec. 1848.
21. Wills 'Forester's Account', p. 90.
22. Saswadkar, 'Nagpur at the end of the 18th century', p. 412.
23. The queens were sore over the outright annexation of the state, the British non-recognition of their adopted son as the new ruler of the state, the inadequacy of the maintenance allowance provided to them and the expropriation of the Bhonsle family property and its sale by public auction. C.G. Mansel, Commissioner of Nagpur, proposed to leave with the queens the private treasure of the Bhonsle family consisting of some Rs. 20 lakh besides jewellery worth Rs. 50 lakh to 75 lakh. Government of India under Lord Dalhousie not only rejected the proposal but, for recommending a lenient treatment of the queens, removed Mansel from his post. The Government, after giving the queens a part of the property, turned the rest into cash, thus creating the Bhonsle Fund. The Fund was extinguished in 1864. *The Settlement of the Affairs of the Ranees of Nagpore and the Course of Events after the Escheat of the state,* Nagpur, 1920, pp. 54–65. *The Escheat of the Nagpur State*, pp. 108–9, MAPM, File 1–3/1933.
24. Jenkins, *Report*, p. 37.
25. Ibid. pp. 36–7.
26. Ibid. p. 33.
27. Ibid. p. 132.
28. Bundle Correspondence, Judicial, no. 10 of 1862. Grant, *The Central Provinces*, p. 315. *Administration of the Nagpore Province by G. Plowden, Commissioner from 1855 to 1959*, Nagpur, 1920, pp. 47–50.
29. Ibid. p. 51. Tuffasul Husain Khan was the *Risaldar* or the 'Native Commandant' of the Nagpur Mounted Police.
30. Richard Temple (Offg. Chief Commissioner, CP), *Report on the Administration of the Central Provinces for 1862*, Nagpur, 1923, p. 10.
31. Ibid. p. 82.
32. In 1854 Sheikh Ali Baksh, a Muslim doctor served at the British army camp at Sonegaon, near Nagpur. At the same time another Muslim doctor, Subhan Ali was attached to the British Residency in Nagpur. Jamaluddin was a *Munshi* at the office of the Commissioner of Nagpur when the office was set up in 1854. NRC (unindexed), 1853–6: E.K. Elliot, Commr. Nagpur, to J.T. Maule, Supdt. Surgeon, Kamptee, 31 March 1855: C.G. Mansel, Resd. Nagpur, to J.E. Williams, Commanding Officer, Kamptee, 19 May 1854: Elliot to Williams, 17 Jan. 1855.

    Among the earliest Indian Extra Assistant Commissioners, II class, in the CP were Mohib Hussain Khan, Sheikh Imdad Khan and Agha Muhammad Shastri, who distinguished himself as 'a prompt and efficient civil judge of Nagpore'. Temple, *Report on the Administration*, p. 102.

    Maulavi Mazhar Jamil was Extra Asstt. Commr. of Harda in

Hoshangabad district during the revolt of 1857. For his services to the Government he was rewarded with an estate in Damoh district having sixty five villages in it. Khan Bahadur Syed Aulad Hussain was DC Damoh in 1871. R.V. Russell, CPDG, Narsingpur, Bombay, 1908, p. 105. Russell, *CPDG*, *Damoh*, Allahabad, 1906, p. 73.

In the Nagpur Local Fund Committee (1863), there were two Muslim nominated members, Agha Muhammad Shastri and Mohib Hussain. In 1864, when the Nagpur municipality was set up, there were two Muslim elected members in it, Muhammad Aminchandbhai and Mir Khairat Ali, out of seventeen non-official members. Abdul Fateh, Abdul Hussain, Abdul Rasul alias Lakkad Shah, Nawab Hussain Ali Khan, Khan Manbelah and Muhammad Hassanji were some members of the municipal committee in Nagpur before the 1870s. P.L. Joshi, *Nagpur Nagar Sanstha Satabdi Grantha*, Centenary volume of Nagpur municipal corporation, Nagpur, 1964 (in Marathi).

33. Leckie's Account, Wills, *The Raj Gond*, p. 77. Jenkins, *Report*, p. 132. Muslim zamindars once held half of the Seoni district. There were several Muslim families in the district who, in 1907, held about 250 villages. R.V. Russell, *CPDG*, *Seoni*, Allahabad, 1908, p. 70. At the same time, in Amravati district also important jagirdars were Muslims, some holding estates which earned them five lakh rupees annually. S.V. Fitzerald and A.E. Nelson, *CPDG*, Amravati, Bombay, 1911, p. 172.
34. Russell, *Seoni*, p. 70; *Damoh*, p. 73.
35. MAPM, File 35–28 of 1923. The CP and Berar provided 5,491 combatants and 10,414 non-combatants for the war. Ibid, File 69 of 1922.
36. In 1825, when the Nagpur state was under British management, Muslims were 2.36 per cent of the local population. Jenkins, *Report*, p. 12.

    In 1872, 1881, 1891 and 1901, the Muslims in the CP were, respectively, 2.8 per cent, 2.47 per cent and 2.25 per cent of the local population. *Census Reports* of the CP, 1872, p. 20; 1881, vol. II, p. 28; 1901, p. 26.
37. J.T. Marten, *Census of India, 1911*, vol. X, *CP and Berar*, pt. I, *Report*, Nagpur, 1912, p. 92. In the decade 1891–1901, the Muslim population decreased by about seven per cent. In 1881–91 their number increased by about 8 per cent—at a slightly lower rate than the general population. *Census, CP and Berar, 1901*, p. 96.
38. Marten, *Census of India*, p. 65.
39. Ibid. Russell and Hira Lal, *The Tribes and Castes*, p. 248. In Berar Muslims in 1891 were 7.1 per cent of the population, and in 1901, 7.6 per cent. Hunter, *Imperial Gazetteer of India*, vol. VII, *Berar*, Oxford, 1908, p. 380.
40. N.J. Roughton, *Census of India, 1921*, vol. XI, *CP and Berar*, pt. 1, *Report*, Nagpur, 1923, p. 59.
41. J.W. Neill, *Census of India, 1872, The Central Provinces*, p. 48. R.V. Russell, *Census of India*, vol. XIII, *1901*, pt. 1, *Report*, p. 191.
42. In 1881, 1,10,375 Muslims, out of a total of 2,85,687, lived in towns (that is 38 per cent). Only 5,46,766 Hindus, out of a total of 87,03,110 lived in towns (that is 6.28 per cent). *Census, CP, 1881*, vol. II, p. 161. In 1901,

44 per cent Muslims were living in towns. *Census, CP, 1901*, pt. I, *Report*, p. 26. In 1916, 37 per cent. Muslims lived in towns though the general percentage of urban population in the province was only 7. Russell and Hira Lal, *The Tribes and Castes*, p. 248.

43. A.E. Nelson, *CPDG*, *Buldana*, Calcutta, 1910, p. 151. Russell and Hira Lal, *The Tribes and Castes*, p. 248. Roughton, *Census, CPB, 1921*, p. 168.
44. Nelson, *Amraoti*, pp. 176, 230.
45. Russell, *Seoni*, p. 51. Marten, *Census*, 1911, pp. 228, 230.
46. Ibid., p. 220. Russell and Hira Lal, *The Tribes and Castes*, p. 248.
47. Marten, *Census, 1911*, p. 233.
48. C. Brown and R.V. Russell, *CPDG, Yeotmal*, Calcutta, 1908, p. 49.
49. Russell, *Seoni*, p. 51. Fitzerald and Nelson, *Amraoti*, p. 125. A rural Muslim was 'more than three parts of a Hindu'. Russell, *CPDG, Nagpur*, Bombay, 1908, p. 70.
50. Russell, *CPDG, Nimar*, Allahabad, 1908, p. 64. Nelson, *Buldana*, p. 142. Russell and Hira Lal, *The Tribes and Castes*, p. 248. About 8 per cent Muslims returned their caste names during the 1901 census, *Report*, p. 97. In 1911, about 14 per cent of Muslims did so. *Census, 1931*, *Report*, p. 331. Russell and Hira Lal, ibid., p. 248.
51. Hunter, *Berar*, p. 380. Russell, *Narsingpur*, p. 56: *Nimar*, op. cit., p. 64. Russell, *CPDG*, *Chhindwara*, pp. 53, 54; *Sagar*, p. 48. Fitzerald and Nelson, *Amraoti*, p. 125. A.E. Nelson, *CPDG*, *Jabalpur*, Bombay, 1909, p. 96.
52. Ibid. p. 253.
53. Russell, *Seoni*, p. 51; *Nimar*, p. 63; *Sagar*, p. 48.
54. Russell, *Seoni*, p. 52. Respectable Muslim families contracted no marriage relations with the *Pinjaras*. Russell, *Nagpur*, p. 70. Like the Hindus, *Pinjaras* had their caste panchayats; *Census*, *1901*, p. 97.
55. Russell, *Damoh*, p. 43; *Narasingpur*, p. 56; *Chhindwara*, p. 43. 'Bafnas are subjected to considerable ridicule on account of their curious mixture of Hindu and Muhammadan ceremonies, amounting in some respects practically to a caricature of the rites of Islam'. 'Primitive bafnas', besides performing Hindu rites in marriages and celebrating Hindu festivals, fed brahmins on the tenth day after a death. When respectable Muslims looked down upon the bafnas as being not pure Muslims, they retaliated by refusing to accept food or water from any Muslim who was not a bafna. Russell and Hira Lal, *Castes and Tribes*, vol. II, p. 73.
56. Russell, *Census of India*, *1901*, p. 97.
57 *RACPB*, 1911–12, p. 42. Russell and Hira Lal, vol. I, *Castes and Tribes* p. 248.
58. Nelson, *Buldana*, quoting A. Lyall, *Berar Gazetteer* (1870), p. 92.
59. Nelson, *Buldana*, p. 93.
60. Ibid.
61. Ibid., p. 94.
62. Ibid., p. 95.
63. Ibid.
64. Brown and Russell, *Yeotmal*, p. 66.

65. Fitzerald and Nelson, *Amraoti*, pp. 123–4.
66. Russell, *Nimar*, p. 63. Nelson, *Buldana*, p. 96.
67. Ibid.
68. Russell, *Nimar*, p. 83.
69. Grant, *The Central Provinces*, p. cxxviii.
70. Russell, *Nimar*, p. 59.
71. Jenkins, *Report*, p. 28.
72. T.S. Sejwalkar, *Nagpur Affairs*, vol. I, Nagpur, 1954, pp. 284, 380. Colebrook, p. 152. NRR, vol. I, no. 17: Colebrook to GG, 25 June 1799.

CHAPTER II

Muslim Identity Consciousness and Political Awakening

Identity consciousness among the Muslims in the CP and Berar preceded their political awareness which was the result of education and closer communication links with the world outside. The emergence of the Muslim press and political elite were a rather slow development, the latter measured by their active involvement in politics either regional or national.

Identity consciousness among the local Muslims had its first manifestation in their feeling that as a minority community they deserved more educational and employment opportunities than the government had given them. This feeling was externally induced; Aligarh provided the impulse. In 1882 the National Muhammadan Association of Aligarh represented to the viceroy Lord Ripon that Muslims under the British rule had been denied their due in respect of public services and educational opportunities; it urged the government to 'restore the balance of state patronage' between the Hindus and Muslims.[1] The CP government's enquiry, however, established that the Muslim grievance was unfounded: in educational institutions and provincial public services Muslims held a far better position than Hindus though they were only about 2.5 per cent of the population of the province.

The ratio of Muslims and Hindus employed by the government was ten times as great as the ratio of Muslims to the Hindus in the local population.[2] The ratio of Muslims to the Hindu population was only 3.4 per cent, but the ratio of Muslim government employees to the Hindu government employees was as high as 36.70 per cent. There were 5,111 Muslims in government service with their salary ranging between less than Rs. 10 a month and more than Rs. 200;

the number of Hindu government employees in the same salary range was 13,924.[3] The Muslims numbered 2,75,773 in the population and the Hindus 79,71,254.[4]

In respect to education as well, Muslims were better placed than Hindus; the ratio of school going Muslim pupils to the total Muslim population was larger than that of Hindu school going pupils to the total Hindu population, the figures respectively being 1.9 and 0.8 per cent. The total number of pupils in government and aided primary, secondary, and high schools in the province was 74,266 of whom 5,483 were Muslims and 65,660 Hindus, the rest being Europeans and Indian Christians. Thus, the ratio of Muslim pupils to Hindu pupils was 8.35 per cent. Of the total number of school boys in the province, Muslims constituted about 34 per cent, while one in every hundred school going girls was a Muslim. In proportion to their number, three times as many Muslim boys were at school as those belonging to all other religious communities, excepting the animist aboriginals. The percentage of Muslim boys and girls going to schools to the total number of Muslim boys and girls of school going age (5 to 19 years) was 8.11; the corresponding figure in respect of the Hindus was only 2.83.[5]

The Berar authorities too had given a 'very fair recognition' to local Muslim claims to the 'distribution of Government patronage'.[6] Of the seven Assistant Commissioners, III class, five were Muslims; of twenty two Tahsildars, eight were Muslims. There were more Muslim Honorary Magistrates than Hindus in similar position.[7] And Muslims were a little more than just seven per cent in the population of Berar.[8] Muslims outnumbered Hindus 'enormously in the police and to some extent . . . in the forest department and in the ranks of tehsil chaprassies'.[9] And all this despite the Muslims' inadequate knowledge of English, the official language.[10] As for education, the proportion of Muslim school going children to the Muslim population of Berar was 2.18 per cent as against 1.01 per cent in respect to the Hindus.[11]

Muslim grievances were thus wholly unjustified, and consequently, neither the CP nor the Berar authorities needed to do anything to redress them. The CP government held that the 'experience of this province tends to show that the Muhammadan can quite well hold his own with the Hindu in the battle of life when he enters in that battle on equal terms and in manly spirit'.[12]

The Berar authorities also established that in respect to both education and public services, the local Muslims' position had been 'an improving one rather than the reverse'.[13]

High class Muslims in particular could further improve their position if, instead of scornfully turning away from Marathi, the local language, they equipped themselves with its knowledge.[14] The Aligarh representation to the Viceroy was indeed an example of what the Indian Education Commission headed by Sir W.W. Hunter, himself a champion of the Muslim cause, reported at the time that except in higher education, there existed 'a tendency to exaggerate the backwardness of the Muhammadans'.[15]

Besides, it was not just educational opportunities that the Muslims wanted; they also demanded for decades an education which would facilitate the preservation of their cultural distinctiveness: Muslim denominational schools with Urdu as the medium of instruction and a curriculum to infuse Muslim pupils with Islamic values.

The government met this demand as well. Following the Hunter Commission's recommendations, orders went out for opening Arabic and Persian classes in all district schools; the government closely monitored the progress of Muslim education, as evident from the annual administrative reports. The government also set up a Muslim high school at Amravati and two more came up in Jabalpur and Nagpur partly aided by the government. 'Hindustani public schools' in Berar provided for special curricula for Muslim pupils.[16]

Till the end of the British rule in the province, the Muslim demand for denominational education persisted, its justification being their fear, whether real or imagined, of absorption in the Hindu cultural fold. Muslims were determined not to lose their distinctive existence. This was despite the fact that local Muslims retained their educational superiority over the Hindus till almost the end of the British rule.[17] Loss of cultural identity was really a bogey which, in rallying the Muslims together, deepened in later years the Hindu-Muslim political divide.

Also externally induced—and by Aligarh again—was the feeling among local Muslims that they better kept themselves away from any political organization either potentially or pronouncedly anti-government, and that they stayed loyal to the British government. Political organizations in the 1880s were almost wholly Hindu-led which was the additional reason for Aligarh to dub them as intended to promote only Hindu interests. In 1888, just before the Indian National Congress session was held in Allahabad, Muslims of

Nagpur gathered at a meeting convened by Anjuman-i-Hami-Islam where Sir Syed Ahmad Khan was congratulated on having formed the United Patriotic Association at Aligarh.[18] In the meeting resolutions were passed blaming the Congress for fanning disloyalty and disaffection towards the government and for pursuing a policy detrimental alike to the interests of the Indian people in general and the 'welfare and prosperity of the Muhammadans' in particular. Local Muslims were warned against attending the Allahabad session of the Congress on pain of being ostracized as 'renegades from the Muslim community'.[19]

From the British loyalist Syed Ahmad's point of view such a fatwa was perhaps called for because the Congress message had already reached a section of the small Muslim intelligentsia, if not the Muslim mass. One of the four CP delegates to the Congress session in Calcutta in 1886 was a Muslim pleader, Abdul Aziz, who made an impressive speech in Urdu at the session.[20]

But then, it was not so much the Aligarh directive as the general inertia of the local Muslims which accounted for their apathy to politics till about the beginning of the First World War. Till then, politically a listless community, Muslims had no leader wielding province-wide influence. Even the ongoing pan-Islamic movement failed to stir them, although events such as those in Morocco and Persia in the first decade of the twentieth century received some notice in the small fitfully existing Urdu press.[21] This was made clear in a confidential communication of the local government to the government of India, stressing in particular, the improbability of the local Muslims turning against the government, and for the purpose making a common cause with the 'dissident party', the Bengalis and the Maharashtrian Brahmins, the two working in tandem. The small Muslim community was then in 'quite a distinct camp' and likely to remain so till the All India Muslim League could weld the men into an anti-government force; so far as the CP and Berar was concerned such a fear was then groundless, the League being of no influence whatsoever.[22]

Militant nationalism, then sweeping other parts of the country, had no impact on the Muslims of the province. Barring a very few who attended some meetings of protest against the partition of Bengal in 1905, Muslims of the CP and Berar were unconcerned about the event. The local Hindu press vainly appealed to the Muslims to boycott foreign sugar, saying that it was 'mixed with the blood of cows and other animals that are not *hallaled* (killed as prescribed by the ecclesiastical law)'.[23] As for the Swadeshi Movement, its only effect on the Muslims lay in a few of them joining some factories launched by the Hindus and a fewer still setting up some small factories themselves.[24] Shivaji festival, then an annual celebration by the Marathi population of the province, made no impression on the Muslims.[25]

To draw the Muslims to this celebration, Dr B.S. Moonje, then a prominent extremist leader and later a more prominent Hindu Mahasabhite,[26] specially invited Hyder Ali Raza from Delhi who spoke in large gatherings on swadeshi and boycott. Addressing meetings to celebrate the Tilak *jayanti*, Raza described him as the 'preceptor . . . of the whole of India' while expressing his own sorrow and shame over Muslim indifference to the ongoing political movements in the country.[27] Moonje's Rashtriya Mandal, a political body, set up to infuse nationalism among the people, and *Hind Kesri*, an influential newspaper run by the Tilakites, entertained Raza with *pan-supari*, the traditional Maharashtrian way of welcoming a guest.[28] However, the only reaction of the community to Tilak's transportation to Burma in 1908[29] was a few Muslims closing their shops.

The provincial government, keeping track of extremist activities in Nagpur and some other places was happy that Hyder Raza failed to 'enliven the drooping spirits of Nagpur';[30] even the foremost Tilakite of the province, Ganesh Srikrishna Khaparde's exhortations, punctuated by his followers' full-threated cry 'Allah ho Akbar', left his Muslim admirers unmoved.[31]

Thus, in the troubled times of militant nationalism, the government had no fear of any Muslim activity against the established authority, let alone any Hindu-Muslim combination for the purpose. On the contrary, there were some signs of strain in Hindu-Muslim relations. Hindu and Muslim students had come to blows at a college hostel in Nagpur over the Muslim non-participation in the Swadeshi Movement.[32] Music playing Hindu religious processions passing by mosques worked up Muslim feelings while an official ban on such processions that followed angered the Hindus.[33] Raja Raghuji Bhonsle vented the Hindu anger most vehemently when refusing to bring out the customary dusserah procession, 'a great national function' annually held since the very establishment of the Bhonsle rule in the region and regarded as a part of the local socio-religious tradition.[34] The press urged the Hindus to boycott Muharram, so long celebrated by both the communities, and to participate instead in the Ganapati worship in larger numbers to register Hindu unity. That unity was the object of the Hindu Rashtriya Mandal set up by Moonje with which later the Bhonsle family was also associated.[35]

The political moderatism of the Indian Muslims came in for caustic comments in the provincial Hindu press: it was 'unbecoming to nationality'.[36] The press, however, hoped that the Muslims of the province would soon get over their fear of the government and their accustomed deference to Aligarh; then they would see for themselves that the Morley-Minto reforms (1909) of which the Indian Muslims had been 'bewitched and elated'—for having provided separate electorates to them—were actually hollow.[37] The Hindu press also referred to the oppressive Muslim rule in medieval India and the extra-territorial loyalty of the Muslim community.[38]

The provincial Muslim press countered this by strongly condemning Lala Lajpat Rai's communal speeches and the proneness of some local Hindu officers to deprive the Muslims of their due share in public employment.[39] *The Nagpur and Berar Times*, edited by an Englishman, reported that Muslims of Jabalpur had supported their correligionists' campaigns in Lucknow against attempts at the replacement of Urdu by Devanagari.[40]

As for the government, it had the fullest faith in the local Muslims' 'long-held tradition of conspicuous loyalty',[41] nurtured by the pro-government Urdu press and the small Muslim elite obliged to the government for its patronage in the form of land grants and official jobs.

II

However, active collaboration between the Hindu and Muslim elites marked the growth of moderatism in the political life of the province in the first decade of the twentieth century; the government had no reason to discourage the growth. The two elite groups had in fact much in common: ownership of extensive landed estates and flourishing business, service in the government before foraying into politics, acceptance of government patronage, titles and honours, and adherence to liberal political views which made them comfortable conservatives in politics; for both steadfast loyalty to the government was prudent and profitable.

Hindu and Muslim notables' involvement in public affairs at the time cut across communal lines. They worked in close concert on many public bodies to promote the common cause; they made no conscious attempt at building up their personal image as community leaders. In the Hindu-led political organizations, the small Muslim elite had an assured place. Khan Bahadur H.M. Malak, the leading Muslim notable of the province,[42] was the Vice-President of the first political conference of the province which, meeting at Nagpur in April 1906, resolved that the CP and Berar be given representation in the Central Legislative Assembly besides being upgraded into a Governor's province.[43] In another provincial conference held at Jabalpur in the same year, a committee was formed to arrange meetings with a view to politically educating the public and making representations to the government on matters of public interest; in the committee there were four Muslims besides Malak.[44] Seth Yusuf Ali Kothawala, a merchant was the Vice-President of the seventh CP and Berar Annual Political Conference held in 1919.[45]

There were other instances of collaboration among the Hindu and Muslim elites. The Hindu gentry recognized the need for Muslim representation on both the central and provincial legislatures, though differing on the size of the representation. In 1917 the CP deputation and the CP and Berar Graduates Association submitted a scheme of reforms of the provincial government to the Secretary of State for India and the Viceroy, suggesting that the central legislatures should have two elected Muslim members, one each from the CP and Berar. As for the provincial legislature having one hundred members, there should be twelve Muslims in it, nine from the CP and three from Berar.[46] The Nagpur District Council in its scheme of reforms submitted to the government at the same time proposed that out of the fifteen elected members from the province to the central legislature, there should be two Muslims, while in the provincial legislature, out of a total of sixty members, there should be nine Muslims representing the CP and three Muslims from Berar.[47] However, the Central Muhammadan Association, Calcutta wanted Muslim representation in the provincial legislature to be no less than 15 per cent of the total elected membership as agreed upon by the Congress and the Muslim League at Lucknow in 1916. And this in later years was to influence the Muslim political elite of the province considerably.

Cordiality between the elite groups of the two communities was more conspicuous in Berar. Ganesh Khaparde, who spoke Urdu fluently and was elected President of the Muhammadan Association of Amravati, counted among his friends and beneficiaries many prominent Muslims of Berar. Muslim and Hindu notables of Amravati jointly felicitated him when he became a Senator of the University of Allahabad.[48] Abdul Kadir was a member of the Berar Vidya Prasarak Mandal (Society for the spread of Education) of which the leading members were Khaparde and Sir Moropant Joshi, the foremost liberal leader of Berar.[49] Muhammad Yusuf Khan Merchant of Berar was elected a delegate to the Congress session in 1901.[50] Above all, Muslims winning elections to municipal and other local bodies for years from predominantly Hindu areas[51] was a testimony to their popularity being wholly unrelated to the communal composition of the electorate, there being no reserved constituencies for the Muslims in such elections.

Muslim and Hindu gentry's patronage to the educational development of the local people did not follow any communal lines either. Rai Bahadur Rajaram Dixit's contribution to the Nagpur Anjuman high school fund set up by the Muslims was reciprocated by Malak's donation to the projected Banaras Hindu University.[52] Moropant Joshi, when an MLC and later the first Home Member in the Governor's Executive Council, strongly pleaded for separate Urdu schools for Muslims in Berar.[53] Most prominent local Hindus attended in 1919 the sixth session of the Berar Muslim Educational Conference at Yeotmal. The priest of a Hindu religious establishment, Shri Dutt Sansthan of Shikar near Mahur was one of the several Hindus who contributed to scholarships for needy Muslim students.[54] Malak and some other Muslims fully shared the general Hindu gentry's concern over the condition of Indians in South Africa and the flood stricken people of Burdwan in Bengal; they donated to funds raised for the alleviation of the distressed people.[55]

In fact, the scope for any rivalry between the Hindu and Muslim elites at the time was far less than in later years because opportunities for a career in politics with power and pelf accompanying it were far fewer. There was no electoral politics worth the name till 1920 when the Montford reforms were implemented in the province. The CP and Berar legislative council was set up in 1914, but for six years it had only twenty four members, of whom only seven were elected by a miniscule electorate of landholders and rate payers to municipalities and district boards; all the rest were government nominees, official and non-official. Nawab Salimullah Khan, a landholder of Amravati, was the only Muslim nominee.[56]

Thus, with an extremely limited franchise and without any communal constituencies provided for the provincial Council elections till 1920, there was no fear of moderate Hindu and Muslim public men turning into rabid communal leaders, using religion for political gains.

III

For the Muslims of the province the first important political event was the fourth session of the All India Muslim League at Nagpur in December 1910;[57] it enabled the first most conspicuous involvement of the local Muslim elite in an all-India political organization of the community, linking them with the national political leadership of the Muslims. The one point most vigorously made at the session was that the minority Muslim community in the province deserved special consideration to safeguard their interests; both the government and the local Hindu political elite were expected to take note of the Muslim feelings. Hindu-Muslim relations in later years were influenced most by how the government and the Hindu elite addressed themselves to the issue of special consideration for the Muslim minority.

Malak was the moving spirit behind the League session; he was eminently fitted for the role he played. He had been a member of the Agha Khan's delegation to Viceroy Lord Minto at Simla in 1906 and had attended the inaugural session of the League at Dhaka. Along with Khan Saheb Muhammad Amir Khan, a pleader of Nagpur, Malak had served on a committee set up by the League to frame the constitution of the party. At the party's first session at Aligarh in March 1908, he was elected a member of its Central Committee. In January 1910 he was elected one of the sixteen Vice Presidents of the party.[58] Above all, just before the Nagpur session of the party, Malak had set up its provincial branch and its units in all the districts of the province.[59] Malak was a pioneer in Muslim education in the CP and Berar; he set up an Urdu press besides a library. A religious leader,[60] he was also a committed public man, for years serving the Nagpur municipality as a member.[61] Malak had a grave grace about him; the

Hindu elite held him in high respect; the government valued his loyalty.

By holding the League session at Nagpur, 'an out of the way place' having no direct railway link with any large Muslim-inhabited town in the country,[62] Malak catapulted the town to the attention of the Muslim national elite. What with the Agha Khan, Prince Ghulam Muhammad, a scion of the old ruling family of Mysore, the Consul-General of Persia in Calcutta and the firebrand Muḥammad Ali, all attending the League session at Nagpur, the town acquired an importance as never before.[63] To add to it Malak at the same time organized the annual session of the All India Muslim Educational Conference,[64] suggesting the interdependence between educational development and political awakening of the Muslim community.

The League leaders' expression of loyalty to the government pleased it as did their condemnation of 'anarchical crimes' committed by militant nationalists. While expressing his gratitude to the Chief Commissioner, Reginald Craddock, for his sympathy and consideration for the Muslims of the province, Malak pointed out that the men were still in 'distress', awaiting 'regeneration'. For introducing communal electorates for elections to legislatures, Lord Minto deserved 'undying gratitude' of the Muslim community; Malak pleaded that such electorates be extended to municipalities as well so as to benefit Muslims living in small towns.[65]

Muslims of Nagpur heard Barrister Nabiullah, the President of the League session, professing Muslim cooperation with the Hindus but condemning their 'suggestively aggressive celebrations' and the 'sinister deification of Shivaji' which provoked the Muslms.[66] Leaguers regretted the raging Nagari-Urdu controversy in the country, Muhammad Ali referring particularly to the attack on Urdu in the UP, and Nabiullah dismissing Hindi as no language in itself but only 'Urdu degraded and vulgarised'.[67] Resolutions were passed demanding more government jobs for the Muslims and representation of the province in the central legislature.[68]

In fact, however, Muslims of the province at the time could have no grievance in respect either of government jobs or educational opportunities. They had retained their erstwhile over-representation in the jobs and superiority over the Hindus in respect of literacy. In the army and police, they held 27 per cent and 38 per cent of jobs respectively as against 24 per cent and 59 per cent held by the

Hindus. There were in the province 78 Muslim and 367 Hindu gazetted officers; in the administrative service Muslims held 19 per cent of the posts and the Hindus 77 per cent; of managers of factories, there were 19 Muslims and 140 Hindus.[69]

Five years later, Muslim position in government jobs was no worse; they held 37 per cent of jobs in the police and 20 per cent in other services. Even in medical and teaching professions, their number was 'comparatively large'.[70] Though as clerks the Muslims, due to their deficiency in the local Hindi and Marathi languages, may have failed to compete on equal terms with the Hindus, in executive posts they more than held their own.[71]

The level of literacy among the Muslims continued to be higher than that among the Hindus. As against 64 literate Hindus per mile, there were 94 literate Muslims.[72] The Muslim population, by the 1911 census was 3.5 per cent, the Hindus being more than 80 per cent.[73]

Politically, the Nagpur session of the League was a tame affair; although it brightened the image of the local Muslim elite—Malak particularly—ensuring their place in the national setup of the League.[74] As for the Muslim masses, they were treated to a spectacular pageant; it filled them with pride of belonging to a great community.

The provincial government had no cause to worry over the growing Muslim political awareness any more than the Hindu elite did. The *Nagpur and Berar Times*, in fact, welcomed the establishment of the Muslim League provincial and district branches;[75] it also published a series of letters written by 'A Patriot' urging the Muslims to stay loyal to the British government, making the most of western education provided by the government besides organizing themselves politically 'as a distinct entity' under the Muslim League.[76] The *Marwari* and *Hitakarini*, Hindu papers, also welcomed the formation of the League in the province.[77]

Until the First World War broke out in 1914, Muslim loyalty to the government appeared to outweigh their sympathy for Turkey which fought the British—a fact reinforced further by large Muslim recruitment in the British Indian army and unstinted support assured to the government by Muslim notables, Malak and Salimullah in particular.[78] The provincial government was confident that the Muslims could not be shaken off their loyalty until the militant Young Muslim party operating elsewhere in the country spread its influence in the province and incited the local Muslims.[79] And this precisely happened in the years 1916–22.

IV

The Young Muslim party led by the Ali brothers, Shaukat Ali and Muhammad Ali, and later the Congress led by Mohandas Karamchand Gandhi, acting in concert with the Ali brothers, drew the Muslims into the maelstrom of agitational politics. The Ali brothers, while interned at Chhindwara, urged the local people not to co-operate with the British government, the enemy of Turkey. Shaukat Ali, officiating as the *pesh imam* of the local mosque, offered special prayers for Turkey's victory in the war while Muhammad Ali kept up his correspondence with the League leaders, besides entertaining the Congress leader, Abul Kalam Azad, at Chhindwara itself. A worried Viceroy Lord Hardinge, pulled the local government up for their apparent laxity in dealing with the two 'dangerous fanatics with ill-balanced minds',[80] who seemed to have cast a spell on the local Muslims. Stricter control on the two brothers followed; Gandhi was not permitted to see them.[81]

For about four years after the war, Muslim political activity in the province was correlated to and commensurate with such activity of the Hindus. This was evident in their joint agitation against the Rowlatt acts and Jallianwala Bagh massacre, the Khilafat and Non-Cooperation Movements. Besides, both Hindus and Muslims heartily participated in the Congress and League sessions held in Nagpur in December 1920. An unprecedented fraternization between the two communities marked the years 1919–22. Protesting against the Rowlatt Acts, Hindus, Muslims, and Sikhs at Chhindwara observed 6 April 1919 as 'a day of purification', invoking the divine blessings of a local Hindu deity to enable them to bear the government's repression with courage and fortitude. The town observed a total hartal, all shops staying shut.[82] In late 1921, some Muslims joined the Hindus in Nagpur boycotting the visit of the Prince of Wales.[83]

Gandhi's influence among the Muslim middle class and professionals spread through the efforts of the Ali brothers, his close associates in the Central Khilafat Committee. Samiullah Khan and Maulana Abdul Hasan Natiq, the two fledgling leaders of Nagpur[84] brought into the Congress party many *momins* (Muslim weavers) then rendered unemployed due to the mechanization of cotton mills.[85]

More than one thousand Muslims attended the Nagpur Congress in December 1920, making it 'almost a Muslim session of the Congress';[86] they jeered at Muhammad Ali Jinnah for opposing Gandhi's resolution on non-cooperation. Hakim Ajmal Khan, Dr M.A. Ansari and the Ali brothers backing Gandhi to the hilt, Jinnah left the *pandal* in a huff, peeved and dejected.[87] Muslim delegates to the Congress session were 'exceedingly bitter' in their speeches, the Ali brothers demanding complete independence of the country followed by the establishment of a republic.[88]

The Khilafat Movement struck the high water mark of Hindu-Muslim political cooperation in the CP and Berar as everywhere else in the country. The Nagpur Congress fully endorsed Gandhi's policy of using the Khilafat Movement as a mass mobilization technique, despite the initial misgivings of some Congress leaders about the propriety of the course adopted by the party.[89] Gandhi and the Ali brothers addressed several meetings at Nagpur, Jabalpur, and Seoni, Muhammad Ali in particular, speaking most violently.[90] Shaukat Ali helped the Khilafat committees being set up at many places in the province;[91] the provincial Khilafat Committee sent a delegation to Allahabad to attend the Central Khilafat Committee meeting held there in June 1920.[92] Some volunteers from Aligarh addressed meetings in villages to explain the objects of the Khilafat and the Non-Cooperation Movements.[93]

Both the movements were strongly supported at the thirteenth session of the Muslim League in Nagpur in December 1920. Speeches at the League session were 'considerably more violent' than those made at the Congress session; the speeches made by the Ali brothers, being practically veiled threats of rebellion, roused the local Muslims to a 'temporary feeling of frenzy'.[94]

Dr Ansari, presiding over the League session, exhorted the Muslims to remember that non-cooperation with the colonial government was for them 'not only a political and moral necessity', but 'a religious obligation' as well.[95] The League resolved to intensify the swadeshi and boycott movements, attainment of swaraj being the ultimate aim of all Indians.[96]

During the Non-Cooperation Movement some Muslim lawyers suspended their practice, some resigned their government jobs and some gave up their position as Honorary Magistrates.[97] The Ali brothers threatened moderate Muslims and Muslim government employees with social boycott which demoralized them.[98] Muslims joined the temperance movement besides picketing foreign liquor and cloth shops.[99] In December 1920, some Muslims withdrew as candidates for the provincial Council elections,[100] while in October next year, forty students left their studies at the government Muslim high school at Amravati.[101] Even the moderate Malak joined the Khilafat Movement, assuming its leadership in the province.

Samiullah Khan of Nagpur, Abdul Qadir Siddiqui of Burhanpur, and Tajuddin of Jabalpur worked hard for the Congress, exhorting the Muslims to wear only Khadi during Ramzan 'if they desired the Khilafat wrongs to be rectified'.[102] Local Khilafat committees were urged to open shops to sell *khadi*. Still, the government was not worried, although taking note of the fact that during the province-wide condolence over the death of Tilak in August 1920, the local Muslims were 'particularly respectful' to the memory of the dead extremist leader.[103] Muslims were a poor community besides being very small in number; they were 'not perhaps so fanatical as in north India'—so believed Sir Frank Sly, the Governor, considering it unlikely that the men would turn troublesome unless some serious events elsewhere in the country greatly agitated them.[104] Nevertheless he took some steps: Malak was pressurized to resign his presidentship of the provincial Khilafat committee; some influential Hindu and Muslim notables were engaged in counter-propaganda against the Khilafat and Non-Cooperation Movements;[105] the government sternly warned Muslim *watan* holders against any involvement in the movements.[106] Soon, almost all Muslim students returned to the school they had left earlier;[107] in August 1923, even some leading Khilafatists waited on the Governor visiting Bilaspur.[108] Sly had reasons to feel relieved.

V

Just as at the mass level, at the elitist level too, provincial politics in the war years and immediately after were free from inter-communal bitterness. This was evident in the way Hindu and Muslim legislators discussed and debated issues such as cow slaughter and Muslim education, for example. The Hindu Cow Protection Movement launched in the province in the 1880s was supported by some influential Muslims like Muhammad Murtiza Khan of Seoni and Malak who urged their cerreligionists to give up beef eating in deference to Hindu sentiments.[109] As for the government, it had for years noted the strong Hindu religious overtone of the movement but feared no political fall-out from it, least of all any Hindu-Muslim tension as a result.[110]

When the CP Slaughter of Animals Bill was passed in the Council in 1915, the sole Muslim MLC, Nawab Salimullah Khan, did not oppose it despite references in course of discussion of the bill to cow slaughter hurting Hindu sentiments and affecting agricultural interests in general. The Select Committee itself suggested some relaxation in the restrictions on animal slaughter originally provided for in the bill so as to enable both Hindus and Muslims killing animals during Dussehra and Bakr-Id respectively.[111]

The bill became an Act soon; the Act was avidly discussed in the Council several times in later years when Hindu MLCs demanded amending it with a view to more strictly implementing it to control trade in beef and cow hide. Muslim MLCs expressed concern over the hardship caused to Muslim butchers by the closure of slaughter houses following strict implementation of the Act at Sagar and Damoh in particular.[112] The government itself disfavoured any more restriction on cow slaughter, fearing a 'great economic loss' from the diminution in beef and hide trade; the Minister, Shankarrao Madhavrao Chitnavis, a high caste Hindu himself, saw no 'need for the legislature to impose the scruples of one community on others who do not share them'.[113]

In fact, the Act after amendment, embodied provisions recommended by a special committee of which a Hindu, Rai Bahadur R.N. Mahajani and a Muslim, Khan Bahadur Zakir Ali were members. The committee had also considered the opinion of Fakir Muhammad, Veterinary Advisor of the government and his colleagues before recommending that no animal less than nine years old should be killed in any slaughter house. The government had widely publicized the rules regulating animal slaughter, Chitnavis himself discussing them with many Muslims; none opposed the rules restricting cow slaughter and the licensing of slaughter houses under the Act to prevent indiscriminate killing of young animals.[114]

The Hindu press projected the Cow Protection Act as an acid test of Hindu-Muslim unity, the *Pranaveer* (Nagpur) wondering 'if Hindus and Muslims cannot jointly solve this cow problem, how can they win *swaraj*'?[115] It urged the Hindus not to make much of the Muslim opposition to the Act and leave the matter to the Muslims 'in whose good sense and patriotism' the press had full confidence.[116] The press rather blamed the government for exploiting the Act to divide the Hindus and Muslims at a time when their unity had become a 'settled fact', the Khilafat and the *swaraj* being 'interdependent and indissolubly connected with one another'.[117] The *Karmaveer* praised the Muslim League and the Khilafat committee for supporting the Cow Protection Movement, while the *Lok Mitra* reported that even the Amir of Afghanistan and the Nizam of Hyderabad had prohibited cow slaughter to register their solidarity with the Khilafat Movement and to gain Hindu goodwill.[118]

Gandhi himself testified to the Ali brothers giving up beef eating at their home 'for the sake of their countrymen'.[119] Pandit Sundarlal, President, CP Provincial Congress Committee, appealed to all Hindus, particularly Congressmen, to 'remain perfectly indifferent towards the question of cow protection and to leave it to the Muhammadans to solve it in the best way they can'.[120] There were exhortations in some Hindu papers for communal amity, Hindus being urged to 'fraternise with the Muslims and to cease to make a fetish of cow protection'; Muslims were advised to renounce their religious intolerance, cultivate nationalist sentiments, respect Hindu feelings, and 'consider India as their mother country'.[121]

With all this, and in view of the Khilafat spirit then running high, the Muslim MLCs though objecting to some provisions of the amended Animal Slaughter Act, refrained from making it an issue affecting their community interests; they knew that Muslim commoners at Sagar had themselves come to an agreement with the local Hindus for restricting cow slaughter.[122] Ultimately, when the motion of further restricting cow slaughter was carried unanimously in the Council no Muslim legislator spoke anything on the motion, let alone oppose it.[123]

Even later in 1925, when the Khilafat spirit had disappeared and several communal riots had taken place,[124] a Hindu MLC's move to further restrict cow slaughter was withdrawn in deference to the advice of the Swarajist leader, Ravi Shankar Shukla, to respect the Muslim sentiments on the issue.[125] Shukla was supported by Moonje, a fellow Swarajist and Hindu unity activist, who, in 1927 effected the withdrawal of another bill to further restrict the slaughter of cattle, as a Muslim MLC had opposed the bill which he feared would hit the Muslim butchers all the more.[126]

Good relations between the Hindu and Muslim political elite in the Khilafat days were further indicated by Hindu MLCs strongly supporting their Muslim colleagues' demand for Urdu schools while some other Muslim MLCs opposed such schools, contending that the Muslims should learn Hindi and Marathi, the two languages of the province, instead of insisting on education through Urdu alone, thus suggesting their 'separatist tendencies'.[127] A Muslim MLC's resolution that Nagpur University should provide for special representation of Muslims on its boards was opposed by a fellow Muslim legislator on the ground that since education benefited all communities alike, there lay no justification for any communal differentiation in the matter, no matter if some Muslims considered it necessary to promote the interests of the minority community.[128] Even years later, in 1931, a Muslim MLC's resolution that the government create professorships in Persian and Sanskrit was opposed by some Muslim MLCs.[129]

Some Hindu MLCs even supported their Muslim colleagues' contention that in respect to funds for education, the 'lion's share should not be in the hands of the majority community', for it was the 'bounden duty' of the community to safeguard minority interests, Hindu-Muslim unity being as essential for the country's 'peaceful life' as 'food is to life itself'.[130]

That the Hindu and Muslim legislators' opinion was not yet polarized on communal lines, was further evidenced by the former's urging the government to increase the number of Muslim gazetted holidays[131] and to amend the new Arms Act which provided that gun licences could be renewed only after their users displayed to the authorities the bones of animals they killed. Seth Mojilal, the Hindu MLC, pleaded that the provision offended the religious feelings of the brahmins, vaishyas, and the Muslims alike, for all of them had 'objection to touching the pigs of any kind'.[132] All of this suggested that the political elite then functioned as custodians of public interest, not as promoters of their respective faiths.

The situation changed from about 1923 when Gandhi rather suddenly called off the Non-Cooperation Movement and Kemal Pasha abolishing the Caliphate, the Khilafat Movement petered out. By then, consequent on Muslim Moplah atrocities on the Hindus in Malabar,[133] communal tension had built up at many places in India. The Moplah outbreak 'exposed the hollowness of the concordat between the Hindu and Muslim leaders',[134] the Moplahs persecuting the Hindus after ceremonially hoisting Khilafat flags and holding many Khilafat meetings.[135] The myth of Hindu-Muslim unity for the national cause lay shattered.

In fact, even before 1923 some rifts in the lute had surfaced despite the generally amicable relations between the two communities. In 1918 some Muslim Home Rule League activists in the province had drawn away from the movement offended by Bipin Chandra Pal's insinution against the Muslim community, branded by him as 'extra-territorial Indians' having scant regard for national interests.[136] Muslims in the Jabalpur municipality, who were involved in the Non-Cooperation Movement, grudged being sidelined by their Hindu colleagues who allegedly monopolized most plum official positions.[137] Some Muslims also resigned from the Jabalpur District Congress Committee;[138] some others threatened bloodshed if cow killing was interfered with.[139] At Bhandara clashes took place between Muslims supporting the Non-Cooperation Movement and those opposing it.[140] The large Muslim butcher community in Sagar and Hoshangabad got restive when Hindu *sangathana* zealots stepped up propaganda against cow slaughter and justified reconversion of Muslims to Hinduism.[141] The coincidence of the Muharram and Ganapati festivals created law and order problem at places in the Nimar, Chhattisgarh, and Berar districts where some riots broke out.[142] In November 1923, Hindu-Muslim relations became tense in Nagpur where Hindus, agitated over reports of beef flung into some temples and idols broken by suspected Muslim miscreants, demonstrated for several days on end and courted arrests.[143]

Some Hindu newspapers demanded that Muslims respect Hindu feelings about cow protection as a *quid pro quo* for Hindu support to the Khilafat Movement. Some Hindus pointedly asked why the Khilafat committees which swore by Hindu-Muslim unity did not do anything to check the Moplahs from attacking the Hindus. The Hindu press advising the Muslims to subordinate their fanaticism to patriotism offended the Muslims.[144]

In such circumstances the combined efforts of the Congress and Khilafat committees to restore communal unity did not succeed even with visits of national leaders, Hakim Ajmal Khan, Motilal Nehru, Shaukat Ali and his mother, Vithalbhai Patel, and Dr Ansari.[145] A leading Muslim of Nagpur wrote to Hindu leaders regretting on behalf of the Muslim community the desecration of Hindu temples and offering rewards for the apprehension of the culprits. Local Hindu and Muslim leaders made at places arrangements for night patrolling of temples and mosques by volunteers and the police.[146]

However, all this failed to stem the rot that had developed in Hindu-Muslim relations. Little wonder, Shaukat Ali and his mother did not succeed in impressing on the Muslims of Jabalpur the need to maintain calm when the men vehemently condemned the *Shuddhi* Movement as having 'broken the last link in Hindu-Muslim unity'.[147] At places Muslims killed more cows during Bakr-Id than before, ignoring a widely circulated appeal by the Bombay Khilafat Committee against cow slaughter.[148] In such a situation C.R. Das' Congress-Khilafat-Swaraj Party and his Bengal Pact making concessions to the Muslims enraged the Hindus.[149] The Congress was warned being hoodwinked by the communal Khilafatists who stoked Muslim fanaticism.[150]

Hindu-Muslim rift was both reflected and aggravated by the virtual war of words in their press; Hindus were exhorted to set up organizations to counter Muslim aggressiveness while the Muslims were urged to unite under a single political party to take on Hindu chauvinism. The Hindu press was alarmed by the spectre of Pan-Islamism sweeping all the Muslims in the country, blaming the Khilafat agitation for the Moplah outrage on the local Hindus.[151] For the government all these were good omens. It heaved a sigh of relief: 'There was practically no sign of fraternisation between the two communities such as occurred last year'.[152]

Even the Nagpur Flag Satyagraha,[153] instead of forging Hindu-Muslim unity, rather exposed the developing fissures between Congressmen and Khilafatists who for some years had worked hand in hand. Most Muslims were indifferent to the satyagraha,[154] though a few like Abdur Rahim Khan took part in it and suffered in consequence. Kept in jail without food for two days, his plight provoked MLCs to demand that the government lift the ban on peaceful processions in some areas of the city.[155] Abid Ali was another Muslim to suffer imprisonment for participation in the satyagraha.[156] However, the resolution moved in the Council, condemning the government's repression of the satyagraha, saw the Muslim MLCs divided on the issue; three of them supported the resolution and two opposed it.[157]

Significantly, the Provincial Khilafat Committee, meeting in Nagpur in July 1923, though expressing a general sympathy for the satyagrahis, held that since the movement did in no way concern the Islamic religion, no amount from the Khilafat fund be spent on it.[158]

The intended message went home: Muslims 'as a class should have nothing to do' with the satyagraha, it being 'essentially a Hindu movement'.[159] The Hindus were aware that at a Khilafat meeting in Nagpur, *maulanas* had recited verses from the Koran containing references to jihad against the *kafirs*.[160]

Hindus also grudged what to them appeared as the government's partiality for the Muslims. Muslims were allowed to celebrate the peace treaty with Turkey by taking out processions through the same places and routes which had been closed to the Congress Flag Satyagrahis.[161] Whatever impact the Provincial Khilafat Conference at Raipur might have created on the local Hindus and Muslims,[162] an incident at another such meeting in Nimar left the latter bitter. At the meeting some Gandhians heckled Muslim delegates so much as to leave them wondering 'what have we to deal with idol worshippers and what idol worshippers have to do with successors to the Prophet'?[163] Around this question revolved both Hindu and Muslim religious extremism in later years, bedevilling the societal and political relations of the two communities. The Hindu feeling at the time was best vented through a section of their press when the Caliphate was abolished by Kemal Pasha: good riddance. There now lay some hope for the end of pan-Islamism and Muslim religious fanaticism.[164]

NOTES

1. MPSRR, Civil Secretariat, 1882, ED, File 125(C): Muslim Education.
2. *Report of the Indian Education Commission* (Hunter Commission), Calcutta, 1883, p. 504.
3. MPSRR, Civil Secretariat, 1882; Col. C.A. Grace, Offg. Commr. Jabalpur Dn., to Secy. CCCP, 11 May 1882; Neill, Offg. Commr., Nagpur Dn., to Secy. CCCP, 27 June 1882; Secy. CCCP to Secy. to GOI (HD), 4 Sept. 1882.
4. Ibid.
5. Ibid: *Report* of the Hunter Commission, cited in HD File 11/37, 3 Nov. 1883; IG (ED), CP to Secy. to CCCP, 25 Nov. 1885. *Report of the Central Provinces Provincial Committee (Howell Committee) with Evidence taken before the Committee and Memorials addressed to the Education Commission* (Calcutta, 1884), pp. 69, 74.
6. NAI, HD (ED), Prog. for July-Dec. 1885: Major G.H. Trevor, Secy. (for Berar) to the Resident, Hyderabad, to Secy. GOI (HD), 14 Nov. 1882.
7. Ibid.

8. W.W. Hunter, *Imperial Gazetteer of India*, vol. VII, *Berar*, Oxford, 1908, p. 380. R. Nathan, *Progress of Education in India, 1897–98 to 1901–02, Fourth Quinquennial Review*, vol. II, Calcutta, 1904, p. 370.
9. Trevor to Secy. GOI (HD), 14 Nov. 1882.
The 'authorised proportions' of various classes in the Berar police were 40 per cent Muslims and 20 per cent Hindus of northern India, and 40 per cent Hindus and other classes of the Deccan, Hunter, *Berar*, p. 414.
10. Trevor to Secy. GOI (HD), 14 Nov. 1882.
11. MPSRR, Berar Education and Medical Dept., VI-I, File 73 of 1883, p. 24. In Berar the Muslims kept up their superiority over the Hindus in literacy. There were 0.03 per cent. Muslims in secondary schools in 1881, 1.46 in 1891 and 1.24 per cent in 1901. The corresponding figures for the Hindus were 0.08, 1.36 and 1.13 respectively. In respect of primary education the figures for the Muslims were 17.7 per cent (1881), 25.91 per cent (1891) and 19.91 per cent (1901); for the Hindus the figures were 9.45 (1881), 12.28 (1891) and 10.00 (1901). In 1891, the Muslims were 7.1 per cent of the population of Berar and the Hindus over 87.3 per cent. In 1901, the Muslim population in Berar was 7.6 per cent and the Hindu population 86.7 per cent. Hunter, *Berar*, pp. 380, 418.
12. MPSRR, Civil Secretariat, 1882: Neill to Secy. to CCCP, to Secy. to GOI (HD), 4 Sept. 1882, Extracts from the progs. of GOI, HD (ED), 15 July 1885.
13. Trevor to Secy. GOI (HD), 14 Nov. 1882.
14. MPSRR, Civil Secretariat, 1882, Neill to Secy. to CCCP, 27 June 1882; Offg. Asst. Secy. to CCCP to Secy. to GOI (HD), 30 June 1882.
Urdu was introduced as the official language in the judicial administration of the CP when the province was constituted in 1861. Although the people of Berar understood Urdu, 'Berar has always had the Marhatta as the official language'. Richard Temple, the CC, strongly pleaded for the adoption of Marathi as the court language of the CP. CC's Letters to the GOI, 1866: Secy. to CCCP to Secy. to GOI (FD), 31 March 1866. Temple ordered all British officers and non-Marathi Indian ministerial staff (mostly Hindi speaking men from north India) employed in Marathi speaking tracts to qualify themselves in Marathi. Richard Temple, *Report on the Administration of the Central Provinces for 1862*, Nagpur, 1923, p. 18.
15. *Report* of the Hunter Commission, p. 483.
16. MPSRR, Berar Ed. and Med. Dept, VI-I, File 73 of 1883, p. 24; Ed. Dept. File 125 (F), 1884–86: Offg. Asst. Secy. to CCCP to IG (ED), CP, 14 March 1885. Nathan, *Progress of Education in India*, p. 379. The Muslim High School at Amravati set up in 1910 was the first of its kind in India.
In 1910 the All India Muslim League described Urdu as 'the chief bond of union between the Muslims of different parts of India after their religion'. Rafiuddin Ahmad, *The Bengal Muslims, 1871–1906: A Quest for Identity* (2nd edn. Delhi, 1988) p. 131.
17. In 1931, 156 Muslims out of every 1,000 were literate while only 50 out of every 1,000 Hindus were literate. *ISC: Interim Education Report, Review*

of the Growth of Education in British India (London, 1930). *Census of CPB, 1931*, pp. 278, 284.

Muslims in all educational institutions in the CP and Berar in 1917 numbered 32,356, representing 5.7 per cent of the population. In 1937–40, there were 54,204 Muslims in all educational institutions, representing 6.91 per cent of the community. Bohras among the Muslims were the most literate, 546 out of 1,000 of them were literate. In 1917, Muslim students comprised 9.2 per cent of the total student community in the province; in 1940, they were 9.8 per cent. Ibid., p. 187. *Review of the Administration of the Central Provinces and Berar, 1937–40*, p. 67.

18. It was set up in 1885 at the initiative of Amir Khan, a Muslim notable, who served on the Nagpur municipal committee for many years. Muhammad Sarafuddin Sahil, *Nagpur Ka Muslim Maashara (Ahd-e-Bartaniya Mein, 1857–1947* (in Urdu), Nagpur, 1997, p. 87.
19. Ram Gopal, *A Political History of the Indian Muslims*, New Delhi, 1988, p. 71.
20. B.K. Bose, *Stray Thoughts on some incidents in my life*, Madras, 1923, p. 186. Sir Bipin Krishna Bose (1851–1933) was a great public figure in central India. An educationist, a legislator, and a liberal leader, he was one of the architects of modern CP and Berar.

    Sir Bipin was the President of the CP National Liberal Association when it was formed in April 1919. *Hitavada*, Nagpur, 19 Apr. 1919. See also P.J. Jagirdar, 'A Moderate of Moderates: Sir B.K. Bose', P.L. Joshi, ed., *Political Ideas and Leadership in Vidarbha*, Nagpur, 1980, pp. 01--11.
21. Some Urdu papers of the late nineteenth and early twentieth centuries were *Tarjuman-i-Nagpur*, Nagpur, *Manj-i-Narbada*, Hoshangabad, *Tablig*; Jabalpur, *Lahr-i-Tapti*, Burhanpur, *Safr-i-Berar*, Amravati, *Khadim*, Amravati, *Mashwara*, Jabalpur, and *Sair-i-Alam*, Khandwa. The papers were weekly and monthly.
22. SP 280132, File 18 of 1912, Note by CCCP. The provincial branch of the League had only recently been set up. HP Dep. June 1909, File 3: Report on Disloyal Party in Nagpur, by C.R. Cleveland, IG Police, CPB.
23. *Subodh Sindhu*, Khandwa, 14 Feb. 1906, *RIN*, 1906. In August 1905, Muslims took part in a meeting where an anti-partition and boycott resolution was passed. At Lakheri (Yeotmal district) Muslims attended a meeting where foreign goods were burnt and people vowed to use *swadeshi* only. *Hari Kishore* (Yeotmal), 6 Nov. 1905, *RIN*, 1905; *Pramod Sindhu* (Amravati), 1 Sept. 1905, *RIN*, 1905. A Kachhi Muslim, Walibhai Suleman, presented Aurobindo Ghosh, the extremist leader of Bengal, with a gold ring, a *dhoti* and a *shawl* when the latter addressed a meeting at Nagpur on 1 February 1908. SP 280133, Notes from the Report on Extremists in Nagpur, by C.R. Cleveland from Aug 1900 to Dec. 1908, p. 7.

    In February 1908 a public meeting was held at Amravati to express sympathy for Muslim leaders, Maulavi Liaqat Hussain and Dr Ghafoor of Calcutta, held prisoners for participating in the swadeshi movement. *Hari Kishore*, 10 Feb. 1908, *RIN*, 1908. The Urdu monthly, *Mashwara*, supported swadeshi but not boycott in an aggressive form. Feb. 1911, *Subodh Sindhu* reported Liaqat Hussain's appeal for swadeshi. 14 June 1911, *RIN*, 1911.

24. *Desha Sewak*, Nagpur, 2 May 1910, *RIN*, 1910.
25. Shivaji Festival became popular in the Marathi region of the CP and Berar from the last years of the nineteenth century. Hindu papers urged all people to celebrate it as a national event. Although in certain quarters some apprehension was expressed that Hindu-Muslim ill feelings could be caused by the celebration, no such ill-feelings actually resulted. Government officers like Bapurao Kinkhede and Gangadharrao Chitnavis participated in the celebration. Pictures of Shivaji used to be hung up between two portraits of Queen Victoria. *Desha Sewak*, 30 Apr., 21 May 1900, *RIN*, 1900.

    Later, however, Reginald Craddock, the Chief Commissioner, saw a clear political objective behind the Shivaji festival. While sternly putting down militant nationalism in the province, he banned Shivaji processions carrying Tilak's portraits and the singing of *Vande Mataram* by the processionists. SP 280132, File 18 of 1911: Note by CCCP.
26. Balkrishna Sivaram Moonje (1872–1948) was an opthalmologist who served in the British army at the Boer War in South Africa. A Congressman and an ardent Tilakite between 1904 and 1920, he joined later the Swaraj party and became its leader in the provincial legislature. In 1926 he won the election to the Central Legislative Assembly.

    For years both a Hindu Mahasabhite and a Congressman, Moonje resigned the Congress in 1932, becoming the foremost Hindu Mahasabha leader in the province and the strongest critic of the Congress in later years. For his life see Balashastri Hardas, *Dharmaveer Dr Balkrishna Sivaram Moonje Yanche Charitra* (in Marathi), Pune, 1966. His personal papers are available at the National Library, Calcutta.
27. *Hind Kesari*, Nagpur, 25 July 1908, Also Ibid., 15 June 1907, *RIN*, 1907; 19 Sept. 1908, *RIN*, 1908. *Desha Sewak*, 27 July 1908, *RIN*, 1908. Cleveland's Report on Extremists.
28. *Desha Sewak*, 20 July 1908, *Hind Kesari*, 19 Sept. 1908, *RIN*, 1908. The Rashtriya Mandal was set up by Moonje in 1907. It was broken up by Cleveland as 'a dangerous political society'. SP 280132, File 18 of 1912.
29. *Hind Kesari*, 25 July, 5 Sept. 1908, *RIN*, 1908.
30. SP 280133, Cleveland's Report on Extremists, 24 June 1908. The extremists were active in Berar, politically a far more active region than other parts of the province. SP 280132, File 18 of 1912.
31. SP 280133, Cleveland's Report, Oct. 1906.

    Ganesh Srikrishna Khaparde (1854–1938), a lawyer of Amravati, was a close associate of Tilak and the foremost political leader of the province during his life time. He organized the 1897 session of the Indian National Congress at Amravati and attended the Surat session of the party in 1907. A radical nationalist, he visited London in 1909 when Tilak's case came up before the Privy Council, and again in 1919 as a member of Tilak's Home

Rule League. He was elected to the Central Legislative Assembly in 1917. Adhering to Tilak's responsive cooperation with the Government, he opposed the Gandhian programme and policy. After 1920, when Tilak died and Gandhi dominated the Congress, Khaparde withdrew from active politics, though retaining undimmed interest in its course. For details of his life see his biography in Marathi by his son, B.G. Khaparde. The Senior Khaparde's diaries are at the National Archives of India, and some other private papers are in the Maharashtra Archives (Vidarbha), Nagpur. Khaparde's Diaries have been published by the Govt. of Maharashtra.

32. SP 280133, Cleveland's Report, Oct. 1906. Craddock addressed students of the Muslim Anjuman school in Nagpur, praising their avoidance of politics. *Hind Kesari*, 5 Sept. 1908, *RIN*, 1908. Khaparde Papers: Diary, 28 Sept. 1905.
33. *Hari Kishore*, 28 Aug. 1905, *RNA*, 1905, *Gao Raksha* (Nagpur), March 1904; *Sudha Varahadi* (Akola), 25 Sept. 1904, *RNA*, 1904.
34. *Desha Sewak*, 5 Oct. 1903, *RIN*, 1903, *Gao Raksha*, Oct. 1904, *RIN*, 1904. Hindus were so upset that they thought of stopping financial support to many poor Muslims and their institutions. Ibid. Also *Desha Sewak*, 7 Sept., 3 Oct. 1904, *RIN*, 1904. The Bhonsle family was closely involved in the Hindu unity movement. Chapter IV.
35. *Desha Sewak*, 7, 28 Sept. 1904; *Gao Raksha*, Mar. 1904, *RIN*, 1904. Muslims and Parsis at Amravati used to celebrate the Ganesh festival along with the Hindus. Khaparde, *Life of Dadasaheb (G.S.) Khaparde*, pp. 95–6.
36. *Desha Sewak*, 3 Jan. 1910, *RIN*, 1910. The paper urged the Muslims to join the swadeshi movement and to start their own factories. 21 March 1910, *RIN*, 1910.
37. Ibid., 3 Jan. 1910, *RIN*, 1910. *Pramod Sindhu*, 29 Sept. 1905, *RIN*, 1905. Communal electoral system was not introduced in the CP and Berar till 1920. Local Muslims expressed happiness over the introduction of the system in other provinces by the Morley Minto Reforms.
38. *Sudha Varahadi*, 23 Aug. 1906, *RIN*, 1906.
39. *Mashwara*, May and June 1911, *RIN*, 1911; *Sudha Varahadi*, 23 Aug. 1906, *RIN*, 1906; *Safr-i-Berar*, 8 Dec. 1910, *RIN*, 1910. Sir Andrew Fraser, the CC, knew of one Hindu officer, a Kayasth, being 'notoriously anti-Muslim'; he was assassinated by a Muslim for having used the stones of an old mosque to construct a bathing *ghat* on a river. A.H.L. Fraser, *Among Indian Rajahs and Ryots . . . in the Central Provinces and Bengal*, London, 1912, p. 48.
40. *Nagpur and Berar Times*, Nagpur, 1 Sept. 1900, *RIN*, 1900. T. Bailey was the Editor of the paper; its circulation was 600 per month.
41. SP 280132, File 18 of 1912, CC's Note.
42. On Malak see his biography in Urdu: *Swanesh Umari Khan Bahadur Badr-ud-din Ghulam Hussain Saheb* by Syed Abdur Razak, Nagpur, 1929.
43. *Report of the First Provincial Conference, CP and Berar* held at Nagpur on 22–3 April 1906.
44. Khan Bahadur Syed Ali Ahmad Khan (Jabalpur), Amanat Khan, Salim Khan

and Ghulam Ahmad (all representing west Berar). *Papers Connected with the Report of the Council's Committee*, Calcutta, 1907.

45. *Hitavada*, 1 Feb. 1919.
46. *A Scheme of Reforms of the CP and Berar Government submitted to the Secretary of State and the Viceroy, by the CP Deputation* (1917); *Scheme of Reforms submitted by the Graduates Association, Nagpur*. R.N. Mudholkar, a Liberal leader of Berar, wanted a legislative council for Berar with at least 27 members (21 elected and 6 nominated) in it, there being three elected Muslim members. Ibid.
47. *A Scheme of Reforms submitted to the Secretary of State and Viceroy on behalf of Nagpur District Council (held in a meeting on 7 Nov. 1917).*
48. Khaparde, pp. 94, 153, 199.
49. *Hari Kishore*, 27 Nov. 1905, *RIN*, 1905. Joshi was the Vice-President of the CP National Liberal Federation which was set up in 1919. In 1928 he became the President of the Liberal Party.
50. *Desha Sewak*, 16 Dec. 1901, *RIN*, 1901.
51. Bose, pp. 137–38. In 1864–1900, 18 Muslims had served on Nagpur municipal committee as against 103 Hindus. Some Muslims had a very long record of such service—for example, Malak (1908–25), Samiullah Khan (1915–46; he was twice Mayor of Nagpur municipality, 1931–4 and 1934–7 besides being Deputy Mayor once, (1942–6); Maulavi Abdul Hussain Natiq (1921–50) and Abdul Majid Leader (1934–57). P.L. Joshi, *Centenary Volume of Nagpur Municipality*.
52. *The Marwari*, Nagpur, 19 Sept. 1911, *RIN*, 1911. *Hitavada*, 30 Aug. 1913. Rajaram Dixit was a barrister who was later associated with the Hindu unity movement. The *Hitakarini*, Jabalpur, deplored the scheme of separate Hindu and Muslim universities. Sept. 1911, *RIN*, 1911. The Government issued a circular prohibiting its employees from taking any part in meetings held for the cause of either a Hindu or a Muslim university and joining any fund raising drive for the purpose. *Kartavya*, Amravati, 11 Oct. 1911, *RIN*, 1911.

    Malak raised Rs. 30,000 as contribution of the province to the Aligarh Muslim University fund. Sahil, *Nagpur Ka Muslim*, p. 96.
53. MPSRR, ED Dept. Progs. Aug. 1917, Nos. 18–19: Joshi to DPI, CPB, 28 June 1916.
54. *Hitavada*, 3, 17 May 1919.
55. Ibid. 6 Sept. 1913, 22 Nov., 6 Dec. 1914. Malak also donated to the depressed classes fund. Ibid., 13 Sept. 1914.
56. Ibid., 14 Nov. 1913, 17 Aug. 1914. Salimullah Khan's forefathers migrated from Hyderabad to Buldana. They rendered valuable service to Arthur Wellesley in the second Maratha war (1803) and were rewarded with an extensive *jagir* in the district. Salimullah was made a Khan Bahadur in 1858 and given the title of Nawab in Deolgarh Rajah in the district in 1891. He was a Special Magistrate I class and 'a polished and unassuming gentleman, universally respected and liked'. Nelson, *Buldana*, p. 170.

57. Syed Sharifuddin Pirzada, *Foundations of Pakistan All India Muslim League Documents*, vol. I, *1906–1924*, Karachi, 1969, pp. 128–216.
58. Ibid. pp. 12, 33, 128.
59. The provincial branch of the League was set up in 1910 itself as also all its district units, Muhammad Yusuf Khan helping Malak considerably. Maulavi Muhammad Aziz Mirza Shah, Honorary Secretary, AIML, inaugurated the provincial branch of the party at Nagpur on 27 Oct. 1910; it was attended by representatives of all the district units of the party. *Nagpur and Berar Times*, 25 June, 2 July, 20 Aug., 17 Sept., 15 Oct., 29 Oct., 12 Nov. 1910. *Berar Samachar*, Akola, 11 July, 22 and 29 Oct. 1910, *RIN*, 1910.
60. Malak headed a break-away Shia Bohra sect, 'Atba-e-Malak'.
61. He was a member of the Nagpur municipal committee from 1908 to 1925.
62. Pirzada, *Foundations of Pakistan*, p. 140.
63. Ibid., pp. 140–1.
64. Nawab Salimullah Khan presided over the conference which was attended by more than two hundred delegates from Calcutta, Bombay, Madras, Dhaka, Hyderabad, and Kashmir. At the conference a resolution was adopted to set up a Muslim university for which Malak toured the province to raise funds. Hafiz Muhammad Wilayatullah, EAC, Nagpur, did a lot for the success of the conference. He was instrumental in making the Nagpur Anjuman a high school. The Nizam provided scholarships for students of the Anjuman-Hami-Islam, Nagpur. *Nagpur and Berar Times*, 11 March 1911, *RIN*, 1911.

    Malak was a trustee of the Muhammadan Anglo-Oriental College, Aligarh, a member of the Muslim University Constitution Committee and Vice-President of the Muslim University Federation Committee. He was also associated with Muslim educational institutions in Bombay and Lucknow. In March 1918 he organised in Nagpur the 17th annual conference of the Nadamat-ul-Ulema, Lucknow. Sahil, *Nagpur Ka Muslim*, pp. 87–9, 92, 96, 100–2.
65. Pirzada, *Foundations of Pakistan*, pp. 144–50.
66. Ibid., p. 164.
67. Ibid., pp. 195, 199. In September 1900, a meeting of the Urdu Defence Association was held at Jabalpur in which support was extended to a similar association in Lucknow fighting against the replacement of Urdu by Nagari. Some leading Hindu gentlemen attended the Jabalpur meeting. *Nagpur and Berar Times*, 1 Sept. 1900, *RIN*, 1900.
68. At this time, of the 106 Deputy Collectors in the province, 24 were Muslims; of the 131 Munsiffs, and Sub-Judges, 6 were Muslims; of the 12 Dy. SPs, 3 were Muslims; of the 9 Supdts of Post Offices, one was a Muslim; of the 14 Educational Officers, one was a Muslim; of 90 Tehsildars, 16 were Muslims. There was no Muslim Asst. Surgeon or Engineer in the province. Pirzada, *Foundations of Pakistan*, pp. 212–13.

    At this time, Muslims, being only 3.5 per cent of the population held

28 per cent of the executive posts and 3.9 per cent of the judicial posts; of the total government jobs, they held 19.9 per cent. Hindus, forming 82.62 per cent of the population, held 53 per cent, 88.2 per cent and 64.9 per cent of the executive, judicial and total number of jobs, respectively.

In Madras, Muslims, forming 6.67 per cent of the population, held 6.6 per cent of the total (executive and judicial) jobs under the government. In Bombay, Muslims, who were 20.32 per cent of the population, held 3.7 per cent of the government jobs. In Bengal, Muslims were 52.74 per cent of the population but held only 10.6 per cent of the government jobs. In Assam they held 16.9 per cent of the government jobs though forming 50.25 per cent of the local population. In Bihar and Orissa they were 10.63 per cent of the population, and held 22.7 per cent of the government jobs. In UP, their number was 14.11 per cent of the population and their percentage in the government jobs was 34.7. In the Punjab, Muslims were 54.85 per cent of the population and held 38.6 per cent of the government jobs. *Report of the Public Service Commission, 1912*, vol. I, Calcutta, 1917, p. 191, quoted in David Page, *Prelude to Partition: The Indian Muslims and the Imperial System of Control, 1920–1932*, New Delhi, 1982, p. 8.

69. Marten, *Census, 1911*, pp. 253, 256.
70. Russell and Hira Lal, *The Tribes and Castes*, p. 248. 'The Muhammadans have a much larger share of all classes of administrative posts under Government than they could claim if these were awarded on the basis of population'. Ibid., p. 277.
71. Russell, *Nagpur*, p. 70.
72. Marten, *Census*, pp. 173, 175. In 1911–12, the Muslim literacy rate per mile was 91 persons in vernacular and 8 in English; the Hindu literacy figures were 32 and 2 respectively, Hindus not including the aboriginal animists. *RACPB, 1911–12*.

    Of the total number of students learning English in colleges in the province, Muslims formed 4.6 per cent. Of the total number of students learning English in schools, they were 3.7 per cent. In Madras, Muslims were 1.8 per cent and 5.00 per cent of the total number of students learning English in colleges and schools respectively. The figures for Bengal were 6.6 per cent (colleges) and 9.8 per cent (schools); for Bombay, the figures, respectively, were 3.7 per cent and 7.4 per cent; for Punjab, the figures, respectively, were 24.5 per cent and 24.9 per cent; for the U.P., the figures respectively, were 23.2 per cent and 10.8 per cent. Quoted in Page, *Prelude to Partition*, p. 12.
73. Marten, *Census*, p. 61.
74. At the seventh session of the League (Dec. 1913), Malak was elected an office bearer. At the next session (Dec. 1915–Jan. 1916) he became a member of a committee to suggest constitutional reforms. At the ninth session of the party he was elected one of the 13 vice-presidents. Pirzada, *Foundations of Pakistan*, pp. 323, 351, 391.
75. The paper promoted the cause of the Muslim community. It regularly published appeals for contribution to the Muslim university fund. Abdullah

Yusuf Ali and S.M. Chitnavis, both DCs, attended the League session and the Muslim Educational Conference. Sahil, *Nagpur Ka Muslim*, p. 94.

76. *Nagpur and Berar Times*, 25 June, 2 July, 17 Sept., 15, 22 and 29 Oct. 1910, *RIN*, 1910. The paper urged the Muslims to follow the lead given to the community by the Aligarh movement.
77. *The Marwari*, 28 Dec. 1910, *RIN*, 1910. *Hitakarini*, March 1911, *RIN*, 1911.
78. *Hitavada*, 14 Nov. 1914, 16 Jan. 1915.
79. SP 280132, File 18 of 1912, CC's Note.
80. HP Dep. Jan. 1916; File 55: Note by Hardinge, 7 Jan. 1916. Ibid., Sept. 1916, File 23: Dept. Notes, 14 Jan. 1916. Ibid., Oct. 1818, File 5.
81. Ibid., Jan. 1916, File 55: Extract from FR, 1st half of Jan. 1916. Ibid., March 1916, File 38.
82. David Baker, 'The Muslim Concern for Security: The Central Provinces and Berar, 1919–1947', Mushirul Hasan, ed., *Communal and Pan-Islamic Trends in Colonial India*, New Delhi, 1981, p. 234.
83. HP FR, 2nd half of Jan. 1922.
84. Natiq was a Khilafatist and a follower of Gandhi at first. Later he joined the League. He was a renowned poet too. Samiullah Khan was a prominent Congressman of the province till 1937 when he joined the League.
85. D.E.U. Baker, *Changing Political Leadership in an Indian Province: The Central Provinces and Berar, 1919–1939*, Delhi, 1979, pp. 70–3. D.P. Mishra, *Living An Era*, vol. I, *India's March to Freedom*, Delhi, 1975, p. 75.
86. Chaudhri Khaliquzzaman, *Pathway to Pakistan*, Lahore, 1961, p. 57. Mishra, op. cit., pp. 34–35. M.B. Neogi, 'Glimpses of Political Awakening in Nagpur', *Souvenir, The Indian National Congress, 64th Session*, Nagpur, 1958, p. D-3.
87. K. Mojumdar, 'Nagpur, 1920–23: The Changing Political Scene', *Journal of Indian History and Culture* (Chennai), Sept. 1997, pp. 84–6. D.P. Mishra, ed., *History of the Freedom Movement in Madhya Pradesh*, Nagpur, 1956, p. 302.
88. HP Dep. May 1921: Note by the Intelligence Bureau on the Nagpur Congress. Ibid., no. 77. Ibid., Jan. 1921, no. 55: Frank Sly, Governor, to GG, 1 Jan. 1921. Ibid., Feb. 1921, no. 77.
89. C. Vijayaraghavachariar, President of the Nagpur Congress, himself had misgivings about the matter. Ramgopal, *A Political History*, p. 146. D.P. Mishra, however, says that the Congress President had doubts about the efficacy of Gandhi's non-cooperation policy. *Living an Era*, p. 35.
90. Home Pol. A Progs. Sept. 1920, Nos. 100–3. HP Dep. File 41 of 1921, FR, 1st half of Jan. 1921.
91. Mishra, *Living an Era*, p. 71. By the end of 1921, 68 Khilafat committees had been set up in the province. Baker, 'Muslim Concern', p. 235.
92. Ibid.
93. The provincial Khilafat conference was held at Chhindwara which the Ali brothers and their mother attended. HP FR, 2nd half of Apr. 1922. Also HP Dep. Oct. 1920, File 53. HP A progs. Sept. 1920, nos. 100–3.

94. HP Dep. Jan. 1921, no. 55: Sly to GG, 14 Jan. 1921.
95. Pirzada, *Foundations of Pakistan*, p. 547.
96. Ibid., pp. 533, 554.
97. K. Mojumdar, 'Muslim Factor in the Politics of the Central Provinces and Berar (1880–1937)', *The Indian Archives*, New Delhi, XLVI, nos. 1–2, Jan.-Dec. 1997, p. 109. MAPM, File 1 of 1920, File 2 of 1921/1922.
98. When a Muslim MLC died in Nagpur, his corpse had to be taken to Raipur, his home town, for burial. *Maulanas* in Nagpur refused to do the last rites in local mosques and no place was provided for in burial grounds in Nagpur. This had a demoralising effect on Muslim government servants, in particular. HP Dep. Jan. 1921, no. 55: Sly to GG, 14 Jan. 1921.
99. Ibid., Oct. 1920, no. 53; Feb. 1921, no. 77. Baker, 'Muslim Concern', p. 235.
100. MAPM, File 1 of 1920. *CPLC*, Aug. 1923, p. 792.
101. MAPM, File 1 of 1920; File 21 of 1921: K.W. Kulkarni, Offg. Inspector of Schools, Berar, to DPI, CPB, 21 May 1921.
102. *Taj*, Jabalpur, 16 June 1922, *RIN*, 1922.
103. HP File 111 of 1920, FR, 1st half of Aug. 1920.
104. HP Dep. Jan. 1921, no. 55: Sly to GG, 1, 14 Jan. 1921.
105. MAPM, File 74 of 1921, File 2 of 1921: CSCPB to Commr. Berar, 9 July 1921.
106. Ibid. File 74 of 1921. *Watan* was a rent-free land holding.
107. Ibid., File 1 of 1920.
108. HP FR, 1st half of Aug. 1923.
109. See also Chapter IV.
110. The cow protection movement was a purely religious movement till after 1906 when it was 'coloured with swadeshi politics by Moonje and others', militant nationalists. The *Gao Raksha*, a monthly paper brought out by the organizers of the movement, urged Tilak to help intensify the movement, and Tilak agreed to do so. SP 280133, Report on the Extremists by Cleveland, op. cit. The *Gao Raksha*, June 1906, *RIN*, 1906. At Ganapati festival the message of cow protection was disseminated. Ibid., Sept. 1903, *RIN*, 1903.

    The cow protection movement had the support of 'most Hindus without any political bias', so noted the Chief Commissioner. SP 280132, File 18 of 1912.
111. *CPLC*, 11 Jan., 26 Aug. 1915.
112. Sagar and Damoh had a virtual monopoly in the supply of jerked meat to Burma; together the two districts held a 48 per cent share in the total value of hides exported from the province to different parts of the country. Of the 95,000 maunds of dry beef received at the Howrah station in the first six months of 1920, about 33,000 maunds were supplied by the CP towns. In 1915–20, 4,41,151 heads of cattle were slaughtered at Sagar alone, mostly agricultural and milch cows. Ibid., Aug. 1921, vol. II, pp. 780–4, 816.

113. Ibid., Any ban on the export of beef from the province involved an immediate loss of Rs. 15 lakh to the government. Ibid. See also Mojumdar, 'Muslim Factor', pp. 107–8.
114. *CPLC*, Aug. 1923, pp. 497–8.
115. *Pranaveer*, Nagpur, 15 Aug. 1922; *Prani Rakshak*, Akola, 5 Aug. 1922, *RIN*, 1922, pp. 137, 405.
116. *Karmaveer*, 17 June 1922, *RIN*, 1922.
117. Ibid.
118. *Lokmitra* (Chhindwara), 26 Aug. 1922, *RIN*, 1922: *Karmaveer*, 17 June 1922, *RIN*, 1922; Also *RIN*, 1921, p. 407.
119. *Young India*, 8 June 1921, M.K. Gandhi, *Communal Unity*, Ahmedabad, 1949, p. 12.
120. *RIN*, 1922, p. 354.
121. *Pranaveer*, 23 Oct. 1924, *RIN*, 1924.
122. *CPLC*, Aug. 1921, vol. II, p. 822.
123. Ibid., p. 823.
124. Chapter IV.
125. *CPLC*, Aug. 1925, p. 447, Shukla became the Congress Premier of the province in 1938–9.
126. SP 280076, File 93 I of 1927.
127. *CPLC*, Jan. 1923, vol. I, p. 245. Muhammad Yusuf Shariff, Muslim legislator (1930–7) and a Minister twice and a Leaguer, while keen on promoting Muslim political interests, was against exclusive schools for the Muslims. He viewed such schools as 'vicious' which had kept 'the communal rancour and prejudices going strong'. He wanted such schools to be abolished for improving inter-communal relations. *Indian Franchise Committee*, vol. III, *Calcutta, 1932*, p. 282, *Memorandum by the C.P. Provincial Franchise Committee*.
128. Such was the opinion of Malak too when Muslim notables wanted the projected Nagpur University to be of a residential type while the local Hindu gentry favoured an affiliating university. *Hitavada*, 23 Aug. 1913. The University came into being in August 1923.
129. *CPLC*, 31 Aug. 1931, p. 294.
130. Ibid., Jan. 1923, vol. I, pp. 236–50.
131. Ibid., Aug. 1921, vol. II, pp. 374–8; Aug. 1923, pp. 394–7.
132. Ibid.
133. The Moplahs of Malabar, Muslim peasants, rose against their oppressive Hindu zamindars. The zamindars, receiving the Government's protection, the outbreak assumed the character of both a revolt against the British authorities and a jehad (religious war) against the Hindu *kafirs* (non-believers).
134. Reforms Special, no. 66 of 1927, Notes: 'Communal Disorders', p. 19. The government knew that the Non-Cooperation Movement had bolstered up the 'spurious Hindu-Muslim Unity'. See also *Review of the Administration of the Central Provinces and Berar, 1923–4*, p. xix.
135. 'Communal Disorders', p. 14.

136. HP File 64, May 1918, FR, 1st half of April 1918.
137. Ibid., FR, 2nd half of Aug. 1922.
138. Ibid., FR, 1st half of May 1922.
139. Ibid., FR, 1st half of June 1922, 2nd half of August 1922.
140. Ibid., FR, 1st half of Feb. 1922.
141. Ibid., FR, 1st half of Oct. 1923. See Chapter IV.
142. *CPLC*, 13 Nov. 1916, pp. 360, 387–9, 390–1; Ibid, 8 March 1917, p. 91. Punitive police had to be imposed at Burhanpur. HP FR, 1st and 2nd half of Oct. 1923. *RACPB*, 1916–17, p. ix. Home (Police) Dept., Oct. 1918, no. 201: *Annual Report of Police Administration in the CP and Berar for 1917*.
143. HP FR, 2nd half of Nov. 1923.
144. *Maharashtra* (Nagpur), 23 Aug. 1922, *Pranaveer*, 17 Oct. 1922, *RIN*, 1922. *Prani Rakshak*, 5 Aug. 1922, *RIN*, 1922.
145. Ibid., FR, 1st half of July 1922.
146. Ibid., FR, 2nd half of Nov. 1923.
147. Ibid., FR, 1st half of Dec. 1923.
148. Ibid., FR, 2nd half of Aug. 1922.
149. The *Lokamitra* (Chhindwara), 19 Jan. 1924, condemned the Pact as 'not a compromise, but an ingenious desire for converting the Hindus to Muhammadanism'. The paper criticized Das for having 'not the least respect for Hinduism' because he was brought up and trained by English missionaries. *RIN*, 1924, p. 207. Under the Pact, Muslims would have 55 per cent of Government jobs; music before mosques would be banned and the Muslim right to kill cows during Bakr-Id would not be interfered with.
150. *Karmaveer*, 6 Jan. 1923, *Pranaveer*, 30 Sept. 1923, *RIN*, 1923. Raja of Mahmudabad, a prominent League leader, said that the Khilafat Movement was 'predominantly religious in character, though the politicians ran it'. 'Some Memoirs', C.H. Philips and M.D. Wainwright, eds., *The Partition of India, Policies and Perspectives, 1935–47* (London, 1970), p. 389.
151. *Pranaveer*, 22 Nov. 1923, *RIN*, 1923.

    At the Nagpur Congress (1920), Swami Shraddhanand, the Arya Samajist leader, had told Mahadev Desai, Gandhi's Secretary, that the Ali brothers had been misinterpreting Gandhi's views. Shraddhanand had also warned Gandhi that the call of *jihad* given by the *maulanas* at the Nagpur Khilafat Conference was subversive of the Gandhian idea of non-violence. Swami Shraddhanand, *Inside Congress* (Bombay, 1946), p. 122. Gandhi himself referred to have been warned about the Ali brothers. *Young India*, 29 May 1924, Gandhi, *Communal Unity*, p. 54.
152. HP FR, 2nd half of Aug. 1922.
153. The satyagraha began at Jabalpur in April 1923 and soon spread to Nagpur following the Government's ban on processions carrying the Congress flag through the civil lines. National leaders, Jawaharlal Nehru, Rajendra Prasad, Sarojini Naidu and Vallabhbhai Patel, came to Nagpur

to protest against the police repression of peaceful processionists. The Government ultimately withdrew the ban in August 1923. Patel played a great role in the event. Mojumdar, 'Nagpur, 1920–3', pp. 89–94. Subhas Chandra Bose, *The Indian Struggle*, Calcutta, 1948, pp. 127–8. *RIN*, 1923, pp. 179–80, 188–9, 208–10, 236–8, 252–8, 273–7, 289–94, 308–12, 371–4, 425–30, 450–2.

154. MAPM, File 11 of 1923, HP FR, 2nd half of April 1923.
155. *CPLC*, Aug. 1923, pp. 108, 124, 196.
156. HP FR, 1st half of July 1923. Muhammad Ali Fazl Ali, Abdul Majid Leader, Muhammad Ibrahim Khan Fana were also jailed for taking part in the satyagraha. Abdul Karim and Abdul Rafiq were injured. Maulana Abdul Natiq was also involved in the movement. M.Y. Quddusi, 'Some Freedom Fighters of Vidarbha', *Hitavada*, 20 Aug. 1976. Sahil, *Nagpur Ka Muslim*, pp. 175, 176. *RIN*, 1923, pp. 135, 145–6, 240. SP 280053, File July 1923.

    Maulana Tajuddin of Jabalpur, Bhai Abdul Gani of Sagar and a Muslim retired tahsildar also joined the satyagraha. Biswambarnath Pandey, 'Freedom Struggle in Madhya Pradesh', in *Samarpit Ardha-sati: Pandit Dwaraka Prasad Mishra Abhinandan Granth* (New Delhi, 1970), pp. 43, 44–6.
157. *CPLC*, Aug. 1923, p. 196.
158. HP, FR, 1st half of July 1923.
159. Ibid. Majumdar, 'Muslim Factor', p. 110.
160. *Pranaveer*, 22 Mar. 1923, *RIN*, 1923.
161. HP FR, 2nd half of July 1923.
162. HP File 66 Keep With, I/1924, FR, 2nd half of Nov. 1924.
163. HP File 5 of 1924, FR, 1st half of Nov. 1924.
164. *RIN*, 1924, pp. 139, 151.

CHAPTER III

Muslims in Provincial Politics

The Montford Reforms introduced electoral politics in the CP and Berar and the communal electoral system for the representation of the Muslims in the provincial legislative Council. This had a great bearing on Hindu-Muslim relations at the level of political leadership, the Hindus resenting it as the government's calculated scheme of creating a majority-minority syndrome in provincial politics, but Muslims welcoming it as an essential safeguard for their interests. The course of Hindu-Muslim elite conflict on the issue was both accelerated and intensified by the local impact of Congress-Muslim League differences on this and other issues at the national level.

After 1920, the Muslims became an in-group in the provincial political process from the out-group they were till then. The Muslim political elite acquired through their representation in the provincial legislature a role in the decision-making set up in the local administration and, in consequence, emerged as a factor for consideration when political alignments were formed and dissolved. For the government, Muslim leaders were politically useful, deserving closer attachment through patronage. The government appointed them on several committees for constitutional and administrative reforms which, besides being a recognition of the men's political ability, helped to articulate Muslim opinion on regional and national issues, particularly those concerning their community.

Between 1920 and 1937 four elections to the provincial legislature were held when at places and on occasions Muslim voters' turnout was more than Hindu voters',[1] indicating better mobilization of the voters by Muslim leaders and stronger feeling of community solidarity among Muslim voters.

Generally speaking, until 1937, though elected from exclusive Muslim constituencies, the Muslim legislators—in all seven—did not always function as a solid communal bloc in the Council. They belonged to no one party exclusively Muslim either in leadership or membership. There were moderates and liberals among them besides Independents, and all were led by the Hindu political elite. In the first Council (December 1920–October 1923), there were six moderate Muslims, three elected on Swarajist party tickets. In the second Council (January 1924–Septemper 1926) there were four Independents, two Liberals and one Swarajist Muslim MLC. Of the Muslim legislators in the third (January 1927–August 1930) and fourth Councils (December 1930–March 1937), some belonged to the Nationalist and Democratic parties and some others were Independents.[2] Some MLCs were retired government employees who held landed estates besides titles like Khan Saheb and Khan Bahadur. Sometimes they took opposite sides when they debated matters concerning their own community. During the Khilafat and Non-Cooperation Movements the Muslim and Hindu elites worked hand in hand, not at cross purposes.[3]

Hindu Swarajists in the provincial legislature valued Muslim MLCs' support and expressed some concern over the Muslims distancing themselves from the Swarajist party when it broke over the issue of office acceptance.[4] Like some Muslims of other provinces at the time, Samiullah Khan, a local Swarajist leader was closely associated with the Muslim League too, being a member of the Muslim Activities Committee set up by the party at its annual session at Lahore in May 1924.[5]

The Muslim elites of the province were divided by personal rivalries and political differences, but in course of time they tended to get united on five issues involving their interests as a community vis-a-vis the Hindus: resistance to the playing of music before mosques, freedom to kill cows to assert the Muslim religious right, promotion of Urdu to preserve the cultural identity of the community, demand for a larger share in public services, and a further extension of the communal electoral system to protect Muslim political interests. The first two issues agitating the Hindu and Muslim masses caused riots between them which ended in competitive shedding of blood;[6] the other three led to conflicts between the Hindu and Muslim elites groups.

Muslim leaders, particularly the MLCs, took a common stand against what they grudged as inadequate opportunities for Muslim education and Muslim employment in public services. But the stand was a propaganda ploy to rally the Muslims for a common cause and a political image building exercise for power seekers rather than a reflection of the real situation. Its object was to wring further concessions from the government on the plea that the Muslim minority suffered at the hands of Hindu ministers and Hindu bureaucracy who had made the most of the majority rule provided by the Montford reforms and dyarchical administration. This also justified the consistent Muslim pressure on the government to expand the communal electoral system to enable larger Muslim representation on the Legislative council and local bodies and a greater share in decision making at all levels of the provincial administration. And no issue caused a deeper division between the Hindu and the Muslim elite at the regional level than the communal electoral system.

The system had, in fact, been rather thrust upon the province by the government of India when the provincial government itself, besides the local moderate and pro-government Hindu and Christian leadership, had opposed it as impracticable and being against the spirit of representative government based on a party system operating in an elected legislature. The Chief Commissioner, Sir Benjamin Robertson, himself considered it 'next to impossible' to create separate constituencies for Muslims, so small in number and so scattered in habitation.[7] A committee of European officers examining the matter held a stronger view: communal constituencies were 'a fatal obstacle to the adoption of territorial representation' in legislatures; the idea of a Minister primarily amenable to a 'religious or racial minority' was the very 'negation of a responsible government'—the ultimate object of constitutional reforms.[8]

Such too was the opinion of the foremost loyalist and liberal leader of the province, Sir Bipin Krishna Bose, to whom the representation of minorities in legislatures through proportional representation seemed a better alternative.[9] Even the foremost and loyalist Parsi leader of the province, Sir M.B. Dadabhoy considered the communal electoral system as 'radically unsound' which 'deserved immediate abolition' wherever it had been introduced.[10] British officers of the province, however, felt that since it was then impossible to withdraw the concession to the minorities, it could better be restricted to only the upper chambers of legislatures[11]—and the CP and Berar had no upper chamber of the Council.

Muslims on the other hand welcomed the introduction of the communal electoral system as a fulfilment of their long-felt need which the Muslim League had expressed in the best articulated way in its Nagpur session in 1910.[12] Interestingly enough, at the session Jinnah was criticized for having opposed the communal electoral system though he himself was elected from a Muslim reserved constituency.[13] The provincial Hindu and Muslim press took an opposite stand on the issue,[14] the moderate *Hitavada* later condemning it as 'a disastrous blunder of the first magnitude'.[15]

The Congress-League scheme, better known as the Lucknow Pact, 1916, not only approved of the communal electoral system but provided for as much as 15 per cent of the elected seats in the provincial Council of the CP and Berar to the Muslims. It raised the Muslim expectations high. That such a percentage of seats to the Muslims was 'wholly disproportionate to the strength and standing of the community' in the province was stressed by the Chief Commissioner Robertson himself[16] who was well known for his sympathy and consideration for the community. Both the Southborough Committee (1919) and the Franchise Committee (1918–19) accepted the Lucknow Pact, the latter however, admitting that Muslim representation in the CP and Berar Council under the Pact was, indeed, 'far in excess of its population ratio in the province[17]—3.6 per cent'. The Government of India Act, 1919 gave 12.7 per cent of the elected seats in the provincial Council to the Muslims—7 out of 53, and 9.58 per cent of the total seats—7 out of 73. Even then, Muslims kept grumbling that their representation was inadequate; Hindus resented the concession as being utterly unjustified and politically motivated.

Hindu-Muslim differences on the communal electorate issue kept pace with attempts at further constitutional reforms. N.K. Kelkar, an MLC for nine years and once a Minister,[18] while giving evidence before the Reforms Enquiry Commission, 1924 (Muddiman Commission), firmly opposed communal electorates of any kind, for it stimulated inter-community ill-feelings. A point which he urged the government to take into account was that Muslims kept winning municipal elections at Balaghat and Jabalpur against Hindu candidates although no separate Muslim constituencies existed for local body elections[19]. In Nagpur municipal elections too Muslims won from predominantly Hindu wards.[20]

In later years, however, the division in the Muslim national leadership on the communal electorate issue was reflected among the Muslims in the CP and Berar too, a section opposing it and another appearing as 'completely reticient', having reposed their trust in Dr Ansari, 'the most patriotic and level headed Muslim leader in India',[21] then President of the Congress; Ansari had recently resigned from the Central Khilafat Committee and the Muslim League, branding both as communal organizations.[22] Ansari and Moreshwar Vyankatesh Abhyankar,[23] the leader of the Swarajist party in the CP (Marathi districts) and soon to become the most important Congress leader in the province. strongly supported the Nehru Report (1928) rejecting the communal electoral system. At a public meeting in Nagpur, Abhyankar hailed Ansari as 'an embodiment of Hindu-Muslim unity', and pointed out that the Nehru Report stressed that unity as well. Urging the Hindus and Muslims to stop quarrelling on cow slaughter and music before mosques, Abhyankar warned that riots caused by the two issues were the 'greatest catastrophe in the life of India today which will lead it to sure ruin'.

The Berar All Parties Conference, meeting at Akola under the chairmanship of Madhav Srihari Aney,[24] also supported the Nehru Report. The provincial liberal press sought to dispel the Muslim fear that their interests would be 'trampled upon' by the Hindus, while exhorting the All Parties Conference to sympathetically view the Muslim misgivings about the Nehru Report.[26]

The difference between the Hindu and Muslim viewpoints on the communal electorate issue came out more glaringly when leaders of the two communities deposed before the Provincial Franchise Committee and the Indian Statutory Commission, better known as the Simon Commission. N.K. Kelkar opposed reserved constituencies for the Muslims on the ground that they were 'humiliating and demoralising' for the Muslims themselves marking the whole community with 'the stamp of perpetual inferiority' vis-a-vis the Hindus. If the system could not be abolished forthwith Kelkar would retain it for at most five years as a 'necessary and regrettable evil'.[27]

Barrister Ramrao Deshmukh, a Berar leader,[28] saw no justification for separate Muslim constituencies on the mistaken supposition that they deserved special constitutional provisions for the protection of their interests. In his memorandum to the Franchise Committee he observed:

> . . . the whole Muslim community, with minor exceptions, is the one dominant community of India. It has greater solidarity and community of interests, greater striking power and power of concentration, and it is more

educationally and materially advanced and is capable of taking care of its own interests, in proportion to its population, in comparison to the various scattered and disjointed communities of India.[29]

Deshmukh stressed the point made by others as well: the community faced no difficulties in getting its men elected to local bodies in proportion to their number in the local population in spite of contesting from general constituencies for such elections. In Akola, for example, half the municipal members were Muslims although their ratio to the Hindus was one to four as voters for the elections and one to twenty five as municipality tax payers.[30]

However, since some time past the Muslims seemed to have developed a tendency to 'avoid the worry of an election and to pin their faith in nomination' by the government; they held quite a few posts in the higher bodies of municipalities and district councils which they 'used in a manner especially favourable to them'. Deshmukh would not agree that if the Muslims lost some elections, they could justifiably attribute it only to their being a minority community.[31]

Deshmukh was worried that if the Muslims continued to 'maintain a separate house within a house' and a 'separate nation within a nation' mentality, other minorities could also develop such an attitude in near future, and then any resistance to their demand for special concessions would 'inevitably lead to further conflicts and serious deadlocks' in constitutional settlements. Deshmukh had the Hindu depressed classes in mind, who in Berar formed one-seventh and together with other backward classes, one-fifth of the local population.[32] And by then, in Berar, particularly, political awakening of the backward classes and non-Brahmins, and their common hostility to the Hindu upper class leadership had become as apparent as some Muslims supporting them.

Sir Hari Singh Gaur, a prominent liberal leader of the province and a distinguished jurist, besides a member of the Indian Central Committee (Sankaran Nair Committee), also opposed the communal electoral system, agreeing with the majority of the members of the Committee that it be abolished in favour of a joint electoral system.[33] He wanted the Muslims to 'grow up' by 'abandoning the chimera of communalism' which would 'soon atrophy their mental vision and paralyse their national development.[34]

Even the Christian opinion in the province was in agreement with the Hindu opposition to special constituencies for the Muslims.

Barrister B.G. Kane pointed out that education having progressed 'very fast' among the Muslims, all round developments had taken place among them, thus they no longer deserved any special treatment as before. He deplored that the communal electoral system and weightage for the Muslims had been 'imposed on the local government' by the government of India, resulting in the existing disproportionately large Muslim representation in the provincial legislature. In the contemplated new constitution, Kane would have joint electorates for the Muslims whom he would give no more than 10 seats in a 100-member council—6 for the CP and 4 for Berar.[35]

The Muslim elite took an entirely different stand. Their spokesmen at the Indian Franchise Committee, Abdur Rahman Khan and Muhammad Yusuf Shariff, both MLCs, wanted not only the retention of the separate constituencies for the Muslims for Council elections but such constituencies for elections to local bodies also; the 'deep rooted prejudice against the Muslims' persisting among the Hindus justified the measure. Shariff rejected the suggestion of proportional representation of the Muslims in the upper house of the central and provincial legislatures through the system of single transferable vote. He pressed for as many as 17 Muslim reserved seats in the contemplated 100-member provincial legislature, one Muslim seat in the upper house of the central legislature and two in its lower house, one each for the CP and Berar.

Abdur Rahman and Shariff wanted voters to possess some educational qualifications—primary, *madrasa,* and for Muslim women particularly, even some home education. But they also demanded the total abolition of the existing property qualification for Muslim voters, arguing that about half the Muslim population living in towns did not have the annual income required for franchise, although their level of education was far higher than that of their economically better off rural brethren. It was this economic factor which accounted for the want of proportionate relationship between the Muslim population in some areas and the number of Muslim voters in them. Thus, while Wardha and Chanda with a Muslim population of 34,000 had 4,700 Muslim voters, in Yeotmal district, of the 52,000 local Muslims, only 2,500 were voters. Shariff's contention was that the government's declared intention of enfranchising 10 per cent of all people in the projected constitutional reforms could be realised only if property qualifications for franchise were either abolished for the Muslims or considerably reduced for them so that 10 per cent of them could qualify as voters.[37] It was known to the Muslims that years ago Ganesh Khaprade too had suggested lowering the qualifications for Berar Muslim voters, considering their backwardness in higher education and their 'not being blessed with worldly means'.[38]

Rahman and Shariff also suggested some special arrangements for Muslim voters such as covered polling booths staffed by women for the convenience of *pardanashin* Muslim women voters. They also pleaded for separate constituencies for Depressed Class Hindus contesting for Legislative Council seats.[39]

In the memorandum submitted to the Indian statutory Commission, the Muslim elite's opposition to the Hindu leadership came out more forcefully. The memorandum drawn up by Tajuddin, earlier a staunch Khilafatist and helpful to the Congress, and at this time a zealous League leader, was a scathing indictment of the 'Hinduised' transferred departments of the provincial administration, which under Hindu Ministers had gravely harmed Muslim interests in every respect. The memorandum listed the grievances of the Muslim community and urged the government to redress them by constitutional changes, of which the most imperative was increased Muslim representation in both central and provincial legislatures.[40]

Thus, in the lower house of the central legislature, the Muslims demanded 7 seats out of the total of 28 allotted to the province—that is no less than one-fourth; and in the upper house of the central legislature, three out of nine, that is one-third.[41] In the contemplated 200-member provincial legislature, Muslims to be elected from reserved constituencies were around fifty.[42] The Muslim population in the province then was less than 4 per cent. In case the Governor's executive council was to be expanded to have five or six members in it, at least two of them were to be Muslims who, among other subjects, would be given charge of Muslim education and Islamic culture besides the responsibility of protecting Muslim interests in public services, local bodies and the provincial judicial administration.

The Muslims in the executive council were to have direct access to the Governor in respect of matters concerning Muslim interests, their tenure and salary being matters to be decided not by the legislature as such but only by the Muslim members in it. Muslim constituencies needed to be made smaller if universal adult suffrage was to replace the existing limited franchise.[43] Muslims demanded a constitutional guarantee that if a bill concerning the interests of a community was opposed by three-fourths of its representatives in any legislature, central or provincial, it should be dropped.[44]

Tajuddin's memorandum embodied the general Muslim fear of Hindu domination in public services growing in proportion to the progressive Indianization of the administration; and hence the Muslim demand that they be assured of 25 per cent of posts in both the provincial services and in those under local bodies. Muslims wanted a definite ratio in terms of posts in every department of the provincial administration as had already been declared by the governments of Bengal, Madras, and UP, apart from the government of India itself.[45] The ratio of Muslim posts in the local administration needed to be incorporated into a Parliamentary statute to ensure its inviolability.[46]

Muslim leaders quoted figures to establish the overwhelming Hindu preponderance in all the departments of the administration, Hindu officers allegedly using 'their religious fervour to obscure their judgement and prejudice their conduct'; and even popularly elected Hindu Ministers allegedly drew their staff from the Hindu community alone. The recurrent communal riots for some years[47] had shaken the Muslim community's confidence in the 'Hinduised' provincial administration, the Muslim staff having allegedly disgraced by Hindu Ministers, Executive Councillors, and officers.[48]

The Muslims demanded the immediate stoppage of recruitment of Hindus in all departments in which they had already managed to secure a virtual monopoly, and the allotment of 75 per cent of posts to Muslims till their ratio of 25 per cent was reached in every department of the administration. An European officer, to be assisted by a Muslim Advisory Board, could be appointed to ensure adequate Muslim recruitment in public services.[49]

The Muslims also complained that non-existence of special and reserved constituencies for them for municipal and other local bodies elections accounted for their inadequate representation on them; and that inspite of the fact that, unlike the Hindus, Muslims were mainly an urban community,[50] constituting between 20 and 50 per cent of the population of as many as thirty four towns of the province. In 1925–8, no Muslim could win elections for municipal committees at Warora, Sagar, and Damoh where the local Muslim population was not inconsiderable. In 1925–6, out of about fifty municipal committees in the province, only one had a Muslim Chairman, and in 1928 only three. Of the one hundred Vice-Chairmen elected in

1925–6, only twelve were Muslims while in 1925, fifteen out of eighty five were Muslims. Consequently, Muslims had been reduced to such a 'position of utter dependence and subordination' to the Hindus in the local bodies 'as almost to eliminate their representation on them'.[51] Communal riots in the province then had indeed much to do with Hindu resentment against Muslims in local body elections.

To the Muslims the local bodies seemed functioning to the sole advantage of the Hindus and detriment to the Muslims. The want of Urdu schools maintained by the local bodies, non-employment of Muslims in them, denial of sanitary arrangements in Muslim areas, and restriction on cow slaughter hurting Muslim traders in hide and butchers were some of the grievances listed in the Muslim memorandum. Separate electorates for Muslims for local body elections could remedy the situation by ensuring adequate Muslim members on the local bodies. The Muslims demanded that their 'past historical and present political importance' should determine their representation on the local bodies, not their number in the local population.[52]

The Muslim memorialists also charged the provincial government with non-implementation of the successive directives of the government of India to promote Muslim education, the situation worsening further since Hindu Ministers took charge of education, a transferred subject. The 'Hinduised' education department was allegedly bent on 'de-Islamising Muslim students' by discouraging instructions in Urdu and forcing down their throats Hindi in Nagari script.[53]

Even Nagpur University came in for vitriolic Muslim attacks; it had become 'more or less a Hindu university' with no Muslims on its numerous bodies and no Muslims among the senior teaching staff in colleges affiliated to it. The university was functioning for the benefit of the Hindu community alone; Hindu teachers being 'generally unsympathetic to Muslim students' who were badly treated and their religion were 'despised'.[54]

Muslim interests in higher education could be safeguarded only by the provision of 25 per cent Muslim representation on every body of the university and on all its teaching departments. Other measures demanded were reservation of 25 per cent of seats for Muslims in institutions offering vocational courses, establishment of Chairs in Islamic history, Islamic philosophy, Arabic, Persian, and Urdu, and the formation of a Muslim Advisory Board for education as suggested by the Sadler Commission.[55]

More Urdu schools, more Urdu teachers, more freeships and scholarships for Muslim students, it was stressed, were urgently needed. A special Inspector of Muslim education, assisted by a Provincial Education Committee, should monitor the educational progress of the Muslims; the management of Muslim schools in districts should be entrusted to local Muslim committees. The Muslims demanded that their number among the urban population—16 per cent—not their ratio in the total population—less than 4 per cent—should determine their share in the government's financial allotment for secondary and collegiate education.[56]

The unity of the Muslim elite in so far as their community interests were concerned was clearly indicated by the support Tajuddin's memorandum received. Five thousand representative Muslims of all political shades and affiliations signed a manifesto in support of the memorandum. An all parties Muslim Conference, meeting in Jabalpur on 26–7 January 1929, appointed a 17-men committee to present the Muslim case to the Simon Commission. The committee, besides reiterating the demands made in Tajuddin's memorandum, made it clear to the Commission that law and order had better be the charge of the British, not Indians, and that the Muslims would never agree to full provincial autonomy unless they were securely represented on the provincial ministry and their interests adequately safeguarded by fool-proof constitutional provisions.[57]

However, the Commission clearly saw that the Muslim grievances and their litany of charges against Hindu ministers were unfounded. Figures which the provincial government itself submitted to the Commission disproved the Muslim grievance that they were being progressively 'eliminated' from public services since the reformed constitution had come into operation, and that under the 'Hinduised' administration, they had been systematically deprived of their due share in it.[58]

In fact, except for some little variations in a few departments, the overall Muslim share in the services taken together had remained about the same between 1919 and 1929—the figures being 10.6 per cent and 10.4 per cent respectively. The Muslims forming less than 4 per cent of the population held 12.6 per cent of the elected seats in the provincial legislature, 19.1 per cent of the posts of tahsildars and naib-tahsildars, 6.5 per cent of posts in the judicial service and 26 per cent of posts in the police service in 1929. In subordinate services, their proportion in 1919 was 24.7 per cent and a decade later 23.3 per cent—by no means a great diminution.[59]

Curiously enough, the Simon Commission's visit to the province brought out in clear relief the difference between Viceroy Lord Irwin and Governor Montagu Butler over placating the local minorities to get the government's purpose served. The visit, in fact, took place when Irwin's insistence prevailed over Butler's reluctance. Irwin wanted to use the Muslims, Depressed Class Hindus, and the business community in general to break the Congress-led boycott movement against the Commission. Butler, for himself, saw no need for it, not even for using the visit as a means to gauge the reaction of the minorities to the movement, if for nothing else, as insisted upon by the Viceroy.[60]

Butler had strong arguments: local Muslims were but a 'negligible quantity numerically'; the Depressed Class Hindus, though numerically large—18 per cent in the population—were 'so backward socially and educationally as scarcely to be vocal'; as for the non-Brahmins, their revolt against the Brahmins had yet 'not gone far enough as in Madras to produce a division among caste Hindus'.[61]

Butler did not share Irwin's hope that Muslims seen as not boycotting the Commission 'would be bound to affect the decision of the Hindus'.[62] Rather, if the visit were thrust upon the 'Hindu province',[63] which the CP and Berar indeed was, it would only consolidate the entire Hindu opinion against the Commission when it still was somewhat divided. In fact, no matter what the Congress activists proclaimed and actually did, the Governor knew that most Council members, Maharashtrians, especially, 'in their hearts' 'disbelieved in the boycott',[64] and Moropant Joshi, the ever loyal and highly respected liberal leader[65] and the first Home Member in the Governor's Executive Council, was, 'in fact, ashamed of having boycotted the Commission' though hesitant to come out openly against the boycott movement.[66]

As it turned out, the Commission, while in the province, did not receive any 'effective support' of the Muslim community[67] as Irwin had fondly hoped for; and this did not disappoint Butler, for, as the Chief Secretary, E. Gordon, made clear, the Commission had really no chance of any great Muslim support.[68] Even the pro-government Muslim MLCs had joined others in boycotting the Commission unlike Muslim MLCs in the UP who had dispatched effusive messages of welcome to it.[69] 'The Muslim elites' support to Tajuddin's memorandum indicated more their solidarity as a community against the Hindus than any overwhelming support for the Commission. Berar Muslims had attended the All-Parties Conference at Akola in 1929 and had not opposed the boycott resolution passed there, though they did not actively take part in the boycott movement itself.[70]

However, the Commission's report left the Muslims grumbling that they had not been given enough, although they were aware of not having done much to deserve any special favour from the government.[71]

More significantly, Butler was rather sore finding that throughout the report the Commission showed a tendency to treat him as though he existed specially to protect the interests of the minorities and European members of the services and 'to ignore the fact that the majority also have rights which it is the Governor's duty to enforce'.[72]

Butler knew that the Muslims blamed him for being rather pro-Hindu, as reflected in his appointing S.B. Tambe, a Hindu Unity activist, as the Home Member in his council and for passing the Akola Order, which for the Muslims was a bitter drought to swallow.[73] In their memorandum to the Commission, the Muslims had, in fact, projected the Governor as being keen to placate the Hindus so that he could 'pass his term of office comfortably and with ease'.[74] The supposed influence on him of his Hindu Ministers, Hindu Executive Councillors and legislators made him indifferent to the accumulating injustice to the Muslims in the province.

Making no bones of his sympathy for Indian nationalism, Butler deplored what appeared to him as the government having 'departed from its traditional policy of impartiality between the Hindus and Muhammadans'[75] and was setting them against one another. He even sounded a note of warning:

> The alliance of the Government with the Muhammadans first to pass its current legislations and subsequently to obtain support for the Statutory Commission has welded the Hindus into an opposition which it is the fashion to deride or to ignore but which will have sooner or later, I am sure, to be met.[76]

The Round Table Conference in London gave the communal electorate issue a still sharper focus. At the Minorities Committee,

Dr Muhammad Shafi, representing the Muslims, quoted extensively from Moonje's speeches at Hindu Mahasabha meetings condemning the communal electoral system.[77] Moonje did not hide it himself, reiterating his preference instead for a system of suitable weightages to Muslims and other minorities under a joint electoral system. He fully supported the Nehru Committee's (1928) contention that separate communal electorates, impeding the growth of national spirit, needed to be discarded completely 'as a condition precedent to any rational system of representation'.[78] Moonje would not 'placate' any community whatsoever by giving it a larger representation than warranted by its ratio in the local population. He disclosed having always supported the Parsi, Dadabhoi's elections to the Central Assembly,[79] ignoring the claims of Hindus who included at times even his own relatives. He also declared having merely acquiesced in—not approved—the Congress acceptance of the communal electoral system at Lucknow in 1916 in deference to the advice of senior leaders there, Tilak, in particular.[80]

Muslims of the CP and Berar resented Gandhi's statements on communal electorate issue as being hostile to Muslim interests.[81] The Hindu press rebutted it by welcoming the Congress Working Committee's scheme for the adjustment of conflicting communal claims of the minorities; the press also condemned the Muslim League for rejecting the Congress scheme.[82] Shaukat Ali, by then a thorough Leaguer, was sharply criticized in the Hindu press for his fulminations against the Hindus and his 'mischievous propaganda' against the Congress.[83] The press found no justification for 'undue representation of communalist and reactionary Muslims' in the Round Table Conference, resulting in the 'neglect of nationalist Muslims'.[84] It attributed the failure of the Minority Committee of the Round Table Conference to resolve the communal tangle to the 'selfish obstinacy of the Muslims and other minorities' represented there.[85]

II

Governors of the province made use of the Muslim political elite, particularly the MLCs, in forging a pro-government bloc to contend with the most troublesome and truculent section of the Hindu leadership—the Maharashtrian Brahmins, who dominated the provincial political life. Besides the Muslims, the bloc included non-

Brahmins, mostly Marathas, and men of the depressed Hindu classes, all hostile to the Brahmins and all eager for the government's patronage.[86]

In 1924, when troubled by the Swarajists[87] and having no love lost for the Khilafatists, Governor Sly made Hifazat Ali a Minister, although the 32-year old Independent MLC believed to be a liberal and opposed to the Swarajists, was once a staunch Khilafatist; he was really 'an almost unknown Muhammadan pleader' in Khandwa, as Sly himself admitted to the Viceroy Lord Reading.[88] The Hindu press criticized the appointment of the 'raw recruit' who had neither any administrative experience nor political influence.[89] It warned the government against what appeared as a 'suicidal policy of giving communal representation' to the Muslims in the administration.[90] Hifazat Ali's term lasted for just ten months before the Swarajists, the dominant party in the Council, pulled down the ministry—thus giving a handle to the Muslim detractors of the Hindu leadership of the province.[91] No Muslim could again make it to a ministry till about a decade later[92]—further disheartening the Muslim political elite. Some Hindu newspapers dubbed the Muslim MLCs as being 'totally possessed by communal bias 'and thus unfit to be considered as ministerial material by the Responsivist party led by Moonje in 1926.[93] The 1926 Council elections were held on communal lines, the atmosphere being surcharged with the riot at Akola and Muslims inflamed over the Akola Order.[94] Bitterness between the Congress and the Hindu Mahasabha for winning elections—the latter playing the communal card—further strained Hindu-Muslim relations.

Sly welcomed the non-Brahmin movement because these men, though educationally backward, were 'likely to support the Government'.[95] He was also happy 'seeing a great advance among the depressed classes, an advance, to my mind greater than has been made by any other community within the same period'.[96] Muslims attended the non-Brahmin conference at Amravati in December 1925 which at the time, however, reflected more their hostility towards the Brahmins than their solidarity with the non-Brahmins. Some prominent non-Brahmins in fact stayed away from the conference resenting 'Muhammadan intrusion'.[97]

The non-Brahmins led by Rai Bahadur K.S. Naidu of Wardha claimed membership among the Muslims and Depressed Classes whom he sought to rally against the Brahmins who dominated the services besides the local politics.[98] Deposing before the Simon Commission, Naidu strongly supported communal representation not only in legislatures and local bodies but demanded its extension to public services for all non-Brahmins and Depressed Classes according to their strength in population; as for the Muslims, a weak community in Naidu's consideration, they deserved representation in excess of their ratio in the population.[99] This non-Brahmin leader, Naidu however, had no hesitation in teaming up with B.G. Khaparde, a blue-blooded Brahmin, later an ardent Hindu-Mahasabhite and all along a Muslim baiter, to form a ministry in 1934–6.[100]

All the Governors of the province after Sly engaged E. Raghavendra Rao as an instrument to build up a pro-government front in local politics.[101] Rao, belonging to Bilaspur, had a strong clout among the Muslims, non-Brahmins, and depressed classes besides the Hindi speaking leaders of the province who had no love lost for their Marathi speaking collagues.[102] In the parties Rao joined—the Nationalist and later the Democratic[103]—Muslims figured prominently; with their support he twice became a Minister in 1927–8. Next year, when he and his erstwhile colleague, Ramrao Deshmukh, staked rival claims to form a ministry,[104] Muslim MLCs assumed something like a bargaining position, offering support to whoever of the two would give them a ministerial berth.[105]

For a while five of the seven Muslims in Rao's Democratic party went over to Deshmukh's Nationalist Party,[106] some hoping to make it to a ministry. They knew that Deshmukh, though a non-Brahmin, was 'guided a good deal by the experienced Brahmins of Berar.[107] 'Soon hereafter, Deshmukh went to London with the Hindu Mahasabha delegation to appear before the Joint Select Committee.[108] However, neither Rao nor Deshmukh could risk striking an open deal with the Muslims for fear of certain opposition by their Hindu partymen equally eager for ministerships.[109]

However, on becoming the Home Member in 1930 and later the Acting Governor, and in both capacities wielding considerable influence at all levels of the administration,[110] Rao was able to patronize his Muslim supporters with government jobs and greater educational opportunities. Besides, in 1930, Muzaffar Hussain of Rao's Democratic party was elected the Deputy Chairman of the fourth legislative Council, defeating a Hindu, M.P. Kolhe of Deshmukh's Nationalist party. Soon thereafter, another Rao protege, S.W.A. Rizvi of Raipur, was elected President of the Council defeating another Hindu. Rizvi's election was hailed by some Hindu MLCs, mostly Rao supporters, as suggesting Hindu-Muslim unity at a time when on several political issues Hindu-Muslim elite conflict had increased in the rest of the country.[111] Rao helped yet another of his Muslim supporters, Muhammad Yusuf Shariff, in becoming a Minister in 1933–4. On himself becoming a Minister for the third time, in 1937, Rao took Rizvi as his colleague. Rao's influence among the Muslims raised his stock with the Governors also eager to win the Muslims over.[112]

Rao helped the Governors to forge an anti-Congress front as well. Muslims taking no part in the Congress celebration of 26 January as the Independence Day was for the government a 'satisfactory feature' of the political developments of the time.[113] More important was the virtual non-participation of the Muslims in the Civil Disobedience Movement in the province; of the 2,670 persons clamped in jail during the movement, barely 20 were Muslims.[114] Muslims remained unmoved—all their shops staying open—when even Gandhi and Ansari were put behind the bars;[115] they rather vented their anger by rioting—as in Berar—when Congress volunteers picketed Muslim shops demanding their closure and subjecting the Muslims at places to social and economic boycott.[116] There was no Muslim reaction to the complete hartal in the Amravati town to condole the death of Jatindra Nath Das at the Lahore jail in September 1929.[117]

The government was both tough and tactful in dealing with the very few Muslims who either actively joined the Civil Disobedience Movement or supported it by attending meetings held by the Congress. The few Muslim teachers who took part in the movement suffered either summary dismissal from service or penal transfer to unwelcome places.[118] The government ignored the few Bohra merchants attending a 'non-Congress and cosmopolitan meeting of the citizens of Nagpur' where they supported a resolution condemning the government's repression of Congress activists. The government chose to dismiss them as those who 'would like to run with the hare and hunt with the hound', their business dealings with the Hindus, the government alleged, obliged them to make what was but a show of support to the Congress movement[119] which by then raised passions of the Hindus all over the province. At Betul, Muslims were exempted from the payment of a punitive tax imposed on the local people for involvement in the Civil Disobedience Movement.[120]

At the time the Hindu-Muslim rift had become so clear that the Congress attempt to mobilize the local Muslims through propaganda by Muslim Congress leaders like Abdul Bari of Patna yielded result[121] no more than the efforts of Muslim Communists like Yusuf Meher Ali of Bombay did to inspire the Muslim youth to work hand in hand with Hindu youngmen to bring about a revolution in the country.[122] Sundarlal Sharma who authored the well known book, *Bharat me Angrez Raj,* urged the Muslim weavers of Nagpur to join the Hindus in the anti-British agitation only to invite a caustic remark by some Muslims that they would prefer being slaves of the British to those of the Hindus if the British made India free.[123]

Rather Shaukat Ali's propaganda that the Congress movement would promote the cause of the Hindu *raj*—not *swaraj*[124]—made a far greater impact on the Muslims than Abhyankar's call for their support to the Congress for the promotion of the nationalist cause; and Abhyankar had so long stood high in the estimation of the local Muslims.[125] The Congress support to the general Hindu opposition to Berar's apprehended return to the Nizam[126] was also a factor to prejudice the Muslims against the Congress, all Muslims wanting Berar's retrocession to the Nizam. In such circumstances the government had no fear of the local Congress agitators being able either to 'entice' or 'inflame' the Muslims.[127]

Only the news of the involvement of the Muslim Red Shirt volunteers of the North West Frontier Province in the Civil Disobedience Movement could work the Muslims up.[128] But it was taken care of by the non-Brahmin and anti-Congress ministry in the province;[129] in the Council too Rao's Democratic party had a clear edge over the Congress. Rao, now the Home Member, kept his 'riot schemes' ready to deal with any threat to law and order anywhere in the province.[130]

The Communal Award (1932) worsened the Hindu-Muslim relations. It increased the Muslim representation in the Council which appeared to the Hindus as an unjustified concession to the community. Led by Moonje and Tambe, the former Home Member, the Hindus condemned the Award as a 'deliberate and anti-democratic attempt' to perpetuate inter-community rivalry among the Indians for the sake of British imperialism; Mrs Tambe decried the Award as 'a cup of poison'.[132] Muslims gave the Award a 'qualified approval', covering their satisfaction by only a 'show of protest' against what they gave out as still inadequate representation of the community in the council.[133] They showed no great enthusiasm either in an agreement which a local 'consultative committee' drew up with some Hindu, Muslim and, Depressed Classes, all favouring joint electorates instead of communal ones.[134]

In fact, the Muslim signatories to the agreement carried no weight with their community.[135] The government also knew that Moonje had failed in driving a wedge between the Muslims and Mahars by insinuating that the government favoured the former, a small community, and ignored the rightful claim of the latter, a far larger and more backward community.[136] The Hindu Mahasabha meanwhile had tried in vain to unite the mahars and other untouchable Hindus against the followers of Dr B.R. Ambedkar who favoured the conversion of the Depressed Class Hindus to Islam.[137] The local government was happy seeing the Muslims giving a rousing reception to Irwin when the latter visited Nagpur and other places in the province.[138]

Meanwhile, the Congress party in the province received a jolt; Aney left it in protest against the party's ambivalence regarding the Communal Award, allegedly inspired by its fear of losing Muslim support.[139] Aney, an old Tilakite and ever an activist for the Hindu cause, condemned the Award as anti-national; in many a meeting held at that time he spoke in the same vein as the Hindu Mahasabha leaders,[140] further denting the Congress image among the Muslims.

It would appear from the Muslim elite's reaction to events and issues in provincial politics in 1920–36 that their grievances and demands for their redressal were inspired more by their increasing spite against the dominant high born Hindu leadership than by any genuine fear of insecurity caused by a 'Hinduized administration'. Under the dyarchical government the Governors had the last word in the local administration, and they often called the shots when many groups, miscalled parties fought among themselves, and no party emerged strong enough to challenge the powers of the Governors and the bureaucracy. Even the Swarajists' challenge was ably met by the Governors, the party's woes being in no small account due to in-fighting. The political elite, irrespective of party affiliations, were eager for the favours of the Governors which enabled them to influence the elite groups. As far as the Muslims were concerned, the Governors and the bureaucracy were determined to protect their interests rather than let them suffer at the hands of the Hindus.

However, there was one important result of the Muslim elite rather exaggerating the community's sense of insecurity: they drove home to the government that the Muslims of the province shared the feelings of their brethren elsewhere in the country—majority rule and minority insecurity had a directly proportional relationship; and that allaying the Muslim minority's sense of insecurity was as much the British government's responsibility as was the establishment of majority rule as the right of the Hindus under the new dispensation of the Government of India Act, 1935.

NOTES

1. In the Council election in November 1926, 50 to 60 per cent Muslims of Berar voted while only 20 per cent local non-Muslims, mostly Hindus, exercised their franchize. HP FR, 1st half of Nov. 1926. In the 1930 elections, the percentage of votes cast in Muslim constituencies was 63, while that in general constituencies was 59. *CLPC*, vol. IX, 26 Jan. 1935. p. 280.
2. *The Central Provinces and Berar: A Review of the Administration of the Province*, vol. II (Nagpur, 1933), p. 12. *CLPC*, 8 Nov. 1939, p. 482.

   The Nationalist Party was a coalition of the Responsivists, Independent Congressmen, non-Brahmins, Muslims, and Liberals, which Moonje set up in 1926. The Responsivists were old Tilakites and closely allied with the Hindu Mahasabha. The Nationalist Party soon split with one faction forming the new Democratic Party.
3. Chapter II.
4. The CP and Berar Swarajists, led by Moonje, were in favour of responsive cooperation as the only viable alternative to Gandhian policy of non-cooperation. The Berar Swarajist leader and President of the provincial Council, Sripad Balwant Tambe, accepted the Home Membership in the Governor's Executive Council which was strongly resented by the national leadership of the Swarajist party led by Motilal Nehru. In the 1926 election no Muslim Swarajist was returned to either the Provincial Council or the Central Assembly, unlike in the earlier elections when in both the legislatures Muslim Swarajists got elected. David Page, *Prelude to Partition: The Indian Muslims and the Imperial System of Control, 1920–1932*, pp. 137–8. D.P. Mishra, *Living an Era*, pp. 78-82.
5. H.N. Mitra, ed., *Indian Quarterly Register, April-June 1924*. Samiullah Khan was elected a member of the Central Assembly in 1923. He did not stand for election to the Assembly in the 1926 election. Page, *Prelude to Partition*, p. 138.
6. Chapter IV.
7. *Constitutional Reforms*, vol. IV: *Opinions of Governments on Montagu-*

Chelmsford Report, pp. 4, 8, CC's Note, 30 Oct. 1918.
After the Montford reforms were implemented, the CP government, in fact, disfavoured further advance in the direction of responsible government in the province. *Report on the Reforms Enquiry Committee, 1924* (Muddiman Committee), Calcutta, 1929, p. 14.

8. *Constitutional Reforms*, vol. IV, Note recorded by a committee of officers serving in the CP and Berar.
9. Ibid; Note by Sir B.K. Bose, 7 Sept. 1918.
10. Ibid; A Note on Reforms Scheme by Sir M.B. Dadabhoy. Dadabhoy was elected to the Central Assembly in Aug. 1914 by members of the newly set up Provincial Council. *Hitavada*, 17 Aug. 1914.
11. *Constitutional Reforms*, vol. IV, Note recorded by officers.
12. Pirzada, *Foundations of Pakistan*, p. 217.
13. Ibid.
14. *Marwari*, 12 July 1911, *Subodh Sindhu*, 12 July 1911, *Maswara*, Feb. 1911, *RIN*, 1911.
15. *Hitavada*, 27 June 1926.
16. Reforms, Notes (1917-29), no. 9: Communal representation on the legislatures and local bodies, 1917, p. 31.
17. *ISC*, vol. I, *Survey*, Calcutta, 1930, pp. 138, 146–7. B.R. Ambedkar, *Pakistan or Partition of India*, Bombay, 1945, pp. 244–6.
18. Kelkar was Minister of Education in 1920-3.
19. Reforms, Notes, 1917-1929, no. 9, pp. 68-9. Appendix no. 6 to the *Report of the Reforms Enquiry Committee, 1924: Oral Evidence*, vol. I, pp. 68–9. 97, 121.
20. Chapter II.
21. SP File 280057/1928.
22. *Swatantra Hindustan* (Amraoti), 24 July 1926, *RIN*, 1926.
23. Abhyankar (1886-1935) began his political career as an ardent Tilakite. He won the election to the Central Assembly in 1934, defeating Moonje. But he died shortly thereafter. Abhyankar Nana, *Vasistechi Pani Arthat Narkesari Barrister Moreshwar Vasudev Abhyankar Yanche Charitra* (Life of Abhyankar, in Marathi, Nagpur, 1965). K.S. Kshirsagar and N.G.S. Kini, 'Neo-Tilakite Narkesari Bar. M.V. Abhyankar, 1886–1935', P.L. Joshi, ed., *Political Ideas*, pp. 105–20.
24. *Hitavada*, 1 Nov. 1928. SP File 280057/1928. Abhyankar wondered why Hindus objected to cow slaughter by the Muslims, and not by the Europeans. DIG, CID Intelligence and Special Wing, Bombay, Police Diaries: Abstract of Intelligence, CP, vol. XLII, 1927.
25. Aney (1880–1968), a Tilakite, joined the Swaraj Party in 1925. He became an MLC in 1924. In 1930, as a staunch Gandhian he led the 'jungle satyagraha'. He left the Congress in 1932 over the Communal Award issue and formed the Democratic National Party. He later returned to the Congress. He was a member of the Viceroy's Executive Council in 1941–2, but resigned when Gandhi was arrested during the Quit India Movement.

He was Governor of Bihar from 1948 to 1952. V.M. Peshwe, 'A Synthesis of Tilak and Gandhi: Loknayak M.S. alias Bapuji Aney (1880–1968),' in P.L. Joshi, ed., *Political Ideas*, pp. 156-66.

26. *The Hitavada* (1 Nov. 1928) appealed to the minorities (Muslims, Depressed Classes, and non-Brahmins) to place their views before the Simon Commission in a helpful manner so as to foster inter-communal unity in the country, so essential to its progress. SP 280037/1928.
27. *IFC*, vol. V, *Selections from Memoranda and Oral Evidence*, Calcutta, 1932, p. 286.
28. Ramrao Deshmukh headed the Democratic Swaraj Party formed by old Tilakites in October 1933 to oppose the Communal Award. He was Minister twice (1927–28, 1929–30), He had strong links with the Hindu Mahasabha, and like many Mahasabhites, he too was once a Responsivist. He 'infiltrated into Congress' like M.S. Aney, another Responsivist, and became a Minister in the first Congress ministry in the province headed by Dr N.B. Khare. D.P. Mishra, *Living an Era*, pp. 96, 252.
29. *IFC*, vol. V, p. 307, Memorandum by R.M. Deshmukh.
30. *Prajapaksha* (Akola), 26 July 1925, *RIN*, 1925. The paper warned the electors to be careful about the Muslim preponderance in local municipal committees—the result, allegedly, of manipulation 'dexterously made' by some Muslim members. Ibid.
31. *IFC*, vol. V, p. 311. Muslims were 28 per cent in the population of the Sagar town. In 1931, 13 Muslims were elected to the municipal committee of the town. In the earlier two elections no Muslim could be elected. *CLPC*, 27 Feb. 1931, p. 248.
32. *IFC*, vol. V, p. 308.
33. Gaur said that communal electorates provided for local bodies in other provinces, though not in the CP and Berar, had converted them into 'cockpits of communal conflicts rather than instruments for disposal of public issues resulting in their paralysis and which threatens to be permanent'. *Report of the Indian Central Committee*, Calcutta, 1929 pp. 268–9.
34. K.B. Krishna, *The Problem of Minorities or Communal Representation*, pp. 198–9. *Report of the ICC*, p. 41.
35. Ibid., pp. 323–4.
36. In the CP and Berar Franchise Committee, majority of members recommended 5 seats to the Muslims in a 100-member provincial legislature and 2 seats to them out of the 12 seats provided for the province in the lower house of the central legislature. Yusuf Shariff, a member of the Committee, appended a note of dissent.

    The CP and Berar government recommended 10 seats for the Muslims in a 100-member provincial legislature, 1 Muslim seat out of a total of 7 allotted to the province for the upper chamber of the central legislature, and 2 Muslim seats out of 12 allotted to the province for the lower chamber of the central legislature. The government wanted to enfranchise 10 per cent of the people as against the 1.1 per cent provided for by the Montford reforms. Reforms Department File 38/32–R, 1932: Notes on Discussions between the Central Franchise Committee and the Provincial Franchise Committee; Note on the Replies to the Questionnaire of the Indian Franchise Committee by the Government of the Central Provinces and the CP Provincial Franchise Committee. *IFC*, vol. III, *Memorandum submitted by the local Governments* (Calcutta, 1932), Letter from Officer-On-Special Duty, Reforms, CP to Joint Secretary, Indian Franchise Committee, 26 Feb. 1932, pp. 240–8. *IFC*, vol. V, pp. 266–82; Ibid., vol. III, pp. 264, 281.

37. *IFC*, vol. V, pp. 269–82.
38. MA Khaparde Papers, Bundle no. 19, Political Work—'Memorandum on Franchise in Berar' (undated).
39. *IFC*, vol. V, p. 267, Statement of Rahman and Shariff.
40. *ISC*, vol. XVII, *Selections from Memoranda and Oral Evidence by Non-Officials*, pt. II, London, 1930, pp. 467-501.
41. Ibid., pp. 467, 501.
42. Ibid., pp. 467.
43. Under the Montford scheme only 1.1 per cent of the population had been enfranchised. The provincial government proposed to the Indian Delimitation Committee, headed by Sir Laurie Hammond, to reduce the size of the average Muslim constituency from the existing 16,655 sq. miles to 8,326 sq. miles as well as the population of the average Muslim constituency from the existing 1,13,783 adults to 50,100 adults. *IDC*, vol. I, *Report*, Delhi, 1936, p. 72.
44. *ISC*, vol. XVII, pt. II, *Tajuddin's Memorandum*, p. 467.
    In its 42nd session (Madras) in December 1927, the Congress had passed such a resolution. Maurice Gwyer and A. Appadorai, *Speeches and Documents on the Indian Constitution, 1921–47*, vol. I (London, 1957), p. 242.
45. The Bengal government in 1925 decided to fill 45 per cent of vacancies in public services by directly recruiting Muslims alone. In Bengal Secretariat staff 33 per cent of all vacancies were reserved for the Muslims. The Bombay government decided to recruit a 'fair proportion' of Muslims in all services in the presidency proper and 50 per cent in Sindh. The Madras government's decision was to recruit 20 per cent Muslims in the public services. In 1920 the UP government decided that of the six vacancies to be filled in the Provincial Executive Service, two shall go to the Muslims. In 1923 the Government of India laid down its policy 'to prevent the preponderance of any community, caste and creed in the services under its control'. *ISC*, vol. XVII, *Tajuddin's Memorandum*, p. 468.
46. Ibid., p. 469.
47. Chapter IV.
48. *Tajuddin's Memorandum*, pp. 469–73.
49. Ibid., p. 473.
50. Ibid. 414 Muslims per mile lived in towns as against only 86 Hindus.
51. *ISC*, vol. XVII, pt. II, pp. 473–9.
52. *Tajuddin's Memorandum*, p. 480.

53. Ibid., pp. 491–2.

S.B. Tambe, Home Member and also in charge of the Education Department, in 1926 was alleged to have suggested to the government the stoppage of all government grants to the Muslim high school at Amravati on the ground that its management was communal. *CPLC*, vol. I, Jan.-March 1930, p. 864.

Earlier, Kelkar, the Education Minister, had turned down a Muslim MLC's demand for special representation of the Muslims on the bodies of the projected Nagpur University. *CPLC*, vol. III, Nov. 1922, pp. 261–77. However, another Muslim MLC had opposed such representation. See Chapter II.

Some Muslim MLCs and a section of the Muslim press expressed soreness over what appeared to them as Kelkar's promoting Hindi and Marathi at the cost of Urdu. *CPLC*, vol. I, Jan. 1923, pp. 90-2. *Al Burhan* (Burhanpur), *RIN*, 1926, p. 62, *Al Haq*, 20 Dec. 1925, *RIN*, 1925.

S.M. Chitnavis succeeded Kelkar as Minister for Education.

54. *Tajuddin's Memorandum*, pp. 481-4.
55. The Calcutta University Commission, headed by Sir Michael Sadler, was appointed in 1917.
56. *ISC*, vol. XVII, pp. 484–5, 492–3.
57. Ibid., pp. 499–502.
58. Ibid., pp. 501–3.
59. Ibid., pp. 503–4. In 1931, Muslims filled 16 per cent of posts in the Provincial Subordinate Service and 38 per cent of posts in the Forest Department. Their average in all departments was 15–16 per cent. In the Revenue Department there were 13 per cent Muslims. By the 1931 census, the Muslim were just 3.92 per cent of the population. *CPLC*, 31 Aug. 1931, pp. 330–1.
60. Barl of Birkenhead, Frederick Edwin Earl of Birkenhead, *The Last Phase*, vol. II (London, 1935), Birkenhead to Irwin, 19 Jan. 1928, pp. 254–5.
61. *Views of Local Governments on the Recommendations of the Indian Statutory Commission, 1930* (Calcutta, 1930), pp. 365–6, E. Gordon, CSCPB to Jt. Secy., Reforms Office, 12 Aug. 1930.

The growth of the non-Brahmin movement in the province could be dated to the years immediately after the first world war. It was referred to in the 1921 Census Report (p. 329).

Maharaja Shahu of Kolhapur, who led the non-Brahmin movement in western Maharashtra, encouraged the depressed class leader in Vidarbha, G.A. Gavai, in the latter's work for the uplift of depressed classes. Shahu invited Gavai to Kolhapur. At meetings of the depressed classes in Amravati, and Yeotmal in 1919, resolutions were passed praising Shahu's work for the depressed class men. B.D. Khane, 'Shahu's Crusade against Untouchability', P.B. Salunkhe, ed., *Chhatrapati Shahu, the Pillar of Social Democracy*, Bombay, 1994, pp. 162–3.

Shahu presided over the All India Depressed Classes Conference in Nagpur in 1920, urging all to support Dr Ambedkar and other leaders of the Depressed Classes. Shahu took dinner with Ambedkar and other leaders. Gale Omvedt, 'Shahu Maharaj: Descendant of Shivaji, Protector of Non-Brahmins', Ibid., p. 61. See also, C.U. Diwan, 'The Bahujan Samaj Movement in Vidarbha', P.L. Joshi, ed., *Political Ideas,* pp. 230–51.

62. Halifax Collection, Reel no. 3900, Irwin (Halifax) to Butler, 15 June 1927. However, during Butler's absence from the province on leave, the Acting Governor, J.T. Marten, assured Irwin that, barring a few Muslims in the Congress, most others of the community would cooperate with the Commission. Ibid., Marten to Irwin, 28 Nov. 1927.
63. Ibid., Butler to Irwin, 29 July 1928.
64. Ibid. In the 73 member Council, only 18 were Congressmen. Ibid., 25 Jan. 1928.
65. Joshi was a leading member of the Bar before being made the Home Member in the Governor's Executive Council in December 1920 and served as such for five years. He 'took a strong line' in dealing with the Non-Cooperation Movement. A moderate in politics, he acquired a 'wide reputation for exceptional ability and strength of character', proving himself 'a tower of strength to the Government'. Frank Sly, the first Governor of the province, regarded him as 'by far the most competent non-official in the province 'deserving all support of the Government. Reading Papers, Reel no. 3358, Sly to Reading, 20 Feb, 22 July 1923: Reel no. 3359, Sly to Reading, 19 Nov. 1924.

    Butler, Sly's successor, found Joshi 'a splendid colleague, clear-headed, frank and reasonable', whom he wanted to offer some appointment after he retired as the Home Member in 1925. Halifax Papers, Reel no. 3899, Butler to Cunningham, 31 Dec. 1926. Joshi became the Chairman, All India Liberal Federation in 1927.
66. Ibid., Butler to Irwin, 25 Jan., 1 Nov. 1928.
67. *Views of Local Governments on the Recommendations of the Indian Statutory Commission,* Gordon to Jt. Secy., Reforms, 12 Aug. 1930, p. 366. Ibid.
68. Indian Muslim leadership was divided on the issue of the Simon Commission's visit. A section, led by Muhammad Shafi, favoured cooperation with the Commission; another section, led by Jinnah, favoured non-cooperation.
69. SP 280057/1928. The Muslim deputation which gave evidence before the Commission consisted of Hafiz Wilayatullah, Retired DC. M.Y. Shariff, Barrister, Abdul Rahim Khan, mining proprietor, Abdul Raza Khan, pleader in High Court, Tajuddin, merchant, Mahfazul Kabir, pleader, Qazi Muhammad Khan, landholder, and Abdul Hadi, Municipal Commissioner. *ISC,* vol. XVII, p. 501. Excepting CP and Berar, all Provincial Councils in the country extended cooperation to the Commission, due mainly to the Muslim support to the Commission in the Councils. The CP and Berar Council passed a resolution against cooperation with the Commission. Page, Prelude to Partition, pp. 177-8.
70. SP 280057, File 45/1928, quoting *Udaya* (Amravati), 30 Nov. 1928.

However, no Muslim attended another All parties conference in Nagpur on 9 Dec. 1928 called by Moonje to arrange for the boycott of the Commission. HD FR, 1st half of Jan. 1929. Muslim shops stayed open when Hindus observed *hartal* to register their protest against the Commission's visit. Bombay Govt., Abstract of Intelligence CP, vol. XLII, 1928.

71. *Views of Local Governments on the Recommendations of the ISC*, Gordon to Jt. Secy., Reforms, 12 Aug. 1930
72. Ibid.
73. *Al Haq* (20 Dec. 1925) criticized the appointment of Tambe but asked the Muslims to cooperate with the Government because 'their salvation lies in the stability of the British government'. After a riot at Akola in 1926, when Tambe was the Home Member, the Government passed the Akola Order to deal with communal riots. The Order appeared to the Muslims as biased against them. See Chapter IV.
74. *Tajuddin's Memorandum*, p. 470
75. Halifax Papers, Reel no. 3901, Butler to Irwin, 17 Sept. 1928.
    'The support of the Muslims had secured certain temporary advantages, but it raised their hopes unduly, consolidated the Hindus against us and made suspect our impartiality.' Templewood Papers, 65: Extracts from Governors' letters on the communal problem, quoted in Page, *Prelude to Partition*, p. 255.
76. Halifax Papers, Reel no. 3901, Butler to Irwin, 17 Sept. 1928.
    Butler also disapproved Irwin's idea of making a direct appeal to Hindu and Muslim religious leaders in the country regarding communal riots, for fear that it would stoke communal jealousy further. Ibid., Reel no. 3900. Butler to Irwin, 27 June 1927.
77. Presiding over a Hindu Mahasabha meeting in Calcutta on 25 July 1926, Moonje regretted 'that the Hindus were living under two dominations: the political domination of the English based on its trading and machine guns, and the domination of the Muhammadans based on their aggressive mentality'. Quoted by Muhammad Shafi at the Minorities Committee meeting, *Indian Round Table Conference*, vol. III (Calcutta, 1931), p. 61.
78. *IRTC*, 12 Nov. 1931–19 Jan. 1931, *Proceedings of Sub-Committees*, vol. III, *Sub-Committee no. 3 (Minorities)*, Calcutta, 1931, p. 69.
79. Dadabhoy was a member of the Central Assembly for twelve years, 1914–26.
80. *IRTC*, vol. III *(Minorities)*, pp. 101–7. Moonje said 'Leave the Mussalmans alone for some time and they will themselves see the futility and evil of separate electorates.' Ibid., p. 101.
    Moonje exerted pressure on M.R. Jayakar and Gandhi at the Round Table Conference so much so that Jayakar viewed Moonje as 'a tactless and unpopular man whom nearly everybody dislikes'. M.R. Jayakar, *Years of Destiny,* quoted in R.J. Moore, *The Crisis of Indian Unity*, Delhi, 1974, p. 122. See also Moonje Papers, Diary, p. 263, 17 May 1931.
81. HP FR, 1st half of April 1931. Gandhi opposed separate electorates at the RT Conference.

82. HP FR, 2nd half of July 1931.
83. Ibid.
84. Ibid., FR, 1st half of Aug. 1931.
85. Ibid., FR, 1st and 2nd half of Oct. 1931. The Muslims at the Minorities Committee of the RTC demanded 15 Muslim seats in the CP and Berar legislature as agreed upon by the Lucknow Pact, 1916. *IRTC, Second Session, Proceedings of the Minority Committee,* Appendix III.
86. In no ministry between 1923 and 1934 was there a Maharashtrian Brahmin. The ministries were composed of non-brahmins and Muslims. In 1934, BG. Khaparde, a Maharashtrian Brahimn, was appointed a Minister because he was pro-government and strongly anti-Congress.
87. In the second Council (1923-6), the Swarajists held 41 out of 54 elected seats. Throwing out the budget was a part of their political tactics to bring the government to a stalemate. SP 280056, File 931 of 1927. *Reports on the Working of the Reformed Constitution* (Calcutta, 1928), *Note on the working of the second Reform Council during 1924–26 in CP and Berar.* B.B. Mishra, *The Indian Political Parties* (Delhi, 1976), p. 221. D.P. Mishra, *Living an Era,* p. 67.
88. Reading Papers, Reel no. 3359. Sly to Reading, 19 Sept. 1924. HP FR, 1st half of Jan. 1924.
89. *Pranavir,* 10 Jan. 1924, *Udaya,* 15 Jan. 1924, *RIN,* 1924. Hifazat Ali had served for some years as Chairman of the Khandwa Municipality.
90. *Manwatar* (Yeotmal), *RIN*, 1924, p. 29. Sly was then keen on breaking the newly formed Congress-Swarajist-Khilafat Party.
91. *Al Burhan, RIN,* 1926, p. 62.
92. Muhammad Yusuf Shariff became a Minister in 1933.
93. *Prajapaksha*, 12 Dec. 1926, *RIN,* 1926, p. 404. *Swatantra Hindustan* Amravati (26 Dec. 1925) accused the Muslims and non-Brahmins of being afflicted by 'Brahmophobia' and causing harm to the freedom struggle led by the Brahmins. *RIN,* 1925, p. 729. Responsivists favoured Council entry which was opposed by the Congress. Both the Responsivists and the Hindu Mahasabhites in the province were dominated by the Brahmins and other high caste men.
94. HP FR, 1st and 2nd half of Oct. 1926. See Chapter IV. The Muslim press stressed the need for a new political party to unite the community, the League having acquired as yet no influence worth the name. *RIN,* 1926, p. 70. Communal riots of the time increased the urgency of Muslim unity as a measure of security.
95. Reading papers, Reel no. 3358, Sly to Reading, 20 Feb. 1923. The non-Brahmins were anti-Swarajists and were welcome to the Governor's scheme of meeting the Swarajist challenge in the Council. *A Review of the Administration of the CP and Berar, 1923–4,* p. vi.
96. *Report of the Reforms Enquiry Committee, 1924,* p. 147.
97. HP FR, 2nd half of Nov., 2nd half of Dec. 1925. A Joint Secy. of the Congress, a Muslim, attended the conference, Ibid.

    In January 1929, at a meeting of the depressed classes in Nagpur resolutions were passed for cooperation with the Muslims and welcoming the Simon Commission to the province. HP FR, 1st half of Jan. 1929. Interestingly enough, the loyalist, Morepant Joshi, 'though a Brahmin of the Brahmins' openly supported the non-brahmin movement with a view to weakening the Berar Responsivists. Halifax papers, Reel no. 3899, Butler to Cunningham, 31 Dec. 1926. Joshi had then retired as Home Member, and not being financially very well off needed Butler's favour; Butler was willing to help him in some way. Ibid.

98. Brahmins, 2.9 per cent of the population, held roughly 31 per cent of the seats in the third Council (1927–30) and 20 per cent of the seats in the fourth Council (1930–7). Out of 106 officers in the Provincial Executive Service, there were 36 brahmins; of 138 in Provincial Judicial Service, 95 were Brahmins; in the police service, out of a total of 19 officers, 6 were Brahmins. *ISC*, vol. XVII, pp. 514, 516, *Memorandum submitted by the President, CP and Berar Non-Brahmin Political Association.* The President, Naidu, charged that brahmin Home Members (Moropant Joshi and Shripad Tambe) encouraged brahmin recruitment in the services. Ibid., p. 514. See also *ISC*, vol. XV, *Excerpts from official oral evidence*, London, 1930, p. 520, Hyde Gowan, CSCPB'S statement.

    Later, Gowan, as Revenue Member in the Governor's Executive Council, informed that of the men recruited in the provincial services in 1925–9, 45 were Maharashtrian Brahmins, 25 other Brahmins, 43 other caste Hindus, 14 Muslims and 17 Christians, *CPLC*, 31 March 1931, p. 328.

99. *ISC*, vol. XVII, p. 514. Also *CPLC*, vol. I, Aug.-Sept. 1931, pp. 317–18, 328, 336–7.

100. B.G. Khaparde was the son of Ganesh Khaparde and his biographer.

101. Rao's political career began as an elected member of the Bilaspur municipal committee and the Bilaspur district council in 1915. Later he joined Annie Besant's Home Rule League. He became an ardent Gandhian in 1920–2, participated in the Non-Cooperation Movement and became the President of the CP Provincial Congress (Hindi) committee. When the Swarajya party was formed, Rao became its President and made his mark in the Provincial Council as an effective leader who played an important role in making the ministry unworkable.

    In 1925, Rao, supporting office acceptance, veered close to Butler, the Governor. In 1926 he formed the Independent Congress party and joined Moonje's Nationalist coalition, emerging soon after as the rallying point of pro-Government and anti-Congress groups in provincial politics. Till his death in 1942, Rao functioned as the Man Friday of successive Governors.

102. Conflict between Marathi and Hindi speaking leaders was an important element in the politics of the Central Provinces and Berar. For details see Baker, *Changing Political Leadership*.

103. The Responsivist party of Moonje, formed of old Tilakites in 1926, entered into a coalition with the Independent Congress party of Rao, both

opposed to the Congress on the issue of office acceptance. Muslims, non-Brahmins and depressed class leaders also joined the coalition to form in Dec. 1926 the Nationalist Party. The coalition lasted for only two years. In 1928 it broke, Rao forming the Democratic Party, and R.M. Deshmukh, the non-Brahmin leader of Berar, leading the rump Nationalist Party. In Rao's new party, of the 27 members, 7 were Muslims. Halifax Papers, Reel no. 3901. Butler to Irwin, 29 July 1928. Bombay Govt. Police Diaries, Abstract of Intelligence, CP, vol. XLVII, 1927. D.P. Mishra, Living An Era, p. 96.

104. Both Rao and Deshmukh, members of the Nationalist coalition, were colleagues in a ministry in 1927–8. They fell out over distribution of portfolios breaking the party and the ministry. Baker, *Changing Political Leadership*, p. 162. Halifax Papers, Reel no. 3901, Butler to Irwin, 22 Aug. 1928.
105. Ibid.
106. Ibid., Reel no. 3903, Butler to Irwin, 26 Jan. 1929.
107. Ibid., Reel no. 3901, Butler to Irwin, 29 July 1928. Deshmukh was disliked as a 'Brahmanized non-Brahmin' by the non-Brahmins. D.P. Mishra, *Living An Era*, p. 97.
108. HP FR,. 1st half of June 1933.
109. Halifax Papers, Reel no. 3901, Butler to Irwin, 22 Aug., 25 Aug. 1928. Ultimately, Rao formed a ministry with T.J. Kedar, a non-Brahmin leader, in Sept. 1928, only to be ousted by Deshmukh after three and a half months. Deshmukh again became a Minister taking P.C. Bose as a colleague and held office for about a year. Ibid., Butler to Irwin, 4 Sept. 1928. *Hitavada*, 30 Aug. 1928. *CPLC*, vol. III, 17 Aug. 1928. pp. 176–7. *ARCPB, 1928-9*, p. 1.
110. Rao was Home Member from 1930 to 1936. He became Acting Governor in 1936, then an Advisor to the Secretary of State in 1939 and finally a member of the Viceroy's Executive Council in 1941. He died in June 1942. D.P. Mishra, op. cit., p. 259. Bakar, Changing Political Leadership, pp. 163–8.
111. *CPLC*, vol. II, Aug.-Sept. 1931, pp. 132–4. *ARCPB*, 1929–30, p. 5.
112. Some Hindu papers blamed the government as being pro-Muslim; it allegedly 'pampered the Muslims and danced to their tune'. *Prajapaksha*, *18*, 28 Oct. 1925, *RIN*, 1925, pp. 589, 600.
113. HP FR, 2nd half of Jan. 1930; 2nd half of Jan. 1932.
114. B.B. Mishra, *Indian Political Parties*, Delhi, 1976, p. 321. Syed Ahmed was 'Dictator', Hindi CP during the Civil Disobedience Movement. He was sentenced to 18 months rigorous imprisonment and a fine of Rs. 750. *CPLC*, vol. 1, Dec. 1930 to March 1931, p. 79. Insan Ali, the captain of the Congress volunteers at Kurhadi village in Gondia tahsil, was suspected of having incited a surprise attack on a police party leading to firing. SP 280064, Compilation for CD Movement, 1931, File 324/CDM/1931.
115. SP 280086, File 31/CDM/1932.
116. HP File 18 Sept. 1930, FR, 1st half of Aug. 1930; HP FR, 1st half of Jan. 1931, 1st half of March 1932.

117. Das was a Bengali revolutionary who undertook a prolonged fast which cost him his life. HP FR, 2nd half of Sept. 1929. Some Muslim shops were forcibly closed.
118. Jaora Khan, Head Master, Asonda School, was dismissed, and Umriar Beg, teacher in a school at Baloda Bazar, was transferred.
119. SP 280088, File nos. 75 to 131/CDM/1932; SP 280092, File no. 165/CDM/1932; Abhyankar addressed a meeting at Chitnis Park, Nagpur which was attended by two to three hundred Muslims. SP 280086, File nos. 31 to 59/CDM/1932.
120. *CPLC*, 26 Feb. 1931, p. 467. At Betul, where the forest satyagraha led by Aney was successful, Muslims suffered from Hindu boycott. HP File 18, Sept. 1930, FR, 1st half of Aug. 1930. S.M. Rahman, MLC, decried the movement as 'a negation of all stable governments', the 'principle' motivating it being 'a very hazardous and dangerous one'. *CPLC*, 3 March 1931, pp. 40–1.
121. HP FR, 1st half of June 1932, 1st half of Sept. 1931. Bari declared *swadeshi* as a means of helping the impoverished Muslim weavers rather than winning *swaraj* for the country. HP File 18 Oct. 1932, FR, 1st half of July 1932.
122. HP FR, 2nd half of Oct. 1931.
123. HP FR, 1st half of Dec. 1931.
124. *Young India*, 12 Mar. 1930, Gandhi, *Communal Unity*, pp. 160–3.
125. Addressing several meetings, Abhyankar urged for Hindu-Muslim unity while condemning the Responsivists, led by Moonje, his political rival, for communal troubles. DIG, CID Intelligence and Special Wing, Bombay, Police Diaries, Abstract of Intelligence, CP, vol. XLII, 1927. Also HP FR, 1st half of March 1924.
126. HP FR, 2nd half of Oct. 1931; HP File, 18 Nov. 1931, FR, 2nd half of Nov. 1931. Most Hindus, moderates including, opposed Berar's retrocession to the Nizam. Ibid. *Lokmat* (Yeotmal) expressed happiness over Viceroy Reading's firm rejection of the Nizam's claim to Berar, 9 April 1926. The Muslim paper, *Al Haq*, deplored Reading's decision, saying that the British government treated the princes as ordinary zamindars, and that it would unsettle British relations with them, 11 Apr. 1926, *RIN*, 1926, pp. 153–4. See also *RIN*, 1924, pp. 96–7, 106–8, 167, 509–10. For the Berar issue, see Chapter VI.
127. HP FR, 1st and 2nd half of May 1930; FR, 1st half of Jan. 1932. However, the DC Akola thought of keeping the Muslims away from the Civil Disobedience Movement by playing on their communal feelings. He wrote to the Berar Commissioner on 4 Mar. 1930: 'We shall have to fall back mainly on communalists who would naturally expect some reward as recognition for their services. This puts us sometimes in a rather awkward position.' MAPM File 10 of 1928.
128. SP 280089 File no. 137/CDM/1932, Secy. HD, GOI to H. Gowan, CSCPB, 16 Jan. 1932. The Govt. of India wanted the CP government to make the local Muslims aware of the fact that the Red Shirt movement was 'essentially a Congress movement', and that it was viewed by the

Government as a subversive movement. The CP government was asked not to interfere with the local Muslims protesting against the Government's repression of the Red Shirt activists till they created a law and order problem. SP 280088 File no. 97/CDM/1932.

129. The ministry was composed of Punjabrao Deshmukh and G.P. Jayaswal, which lasted for three years (1930–3).
130. MAPM, File 20/1931–2, H.C. Gowan, CS to all DCs, 21 Apr. 1931.
131. It recommended 14 Muslim seats in a house of 112.
132. HP File 18 Nov. 1932, FR, 2nd half of Aug. 1932. N. Mitra, ed., *Indian Annual Register*, 1935, vol. I, p. 235.
133. HP File 18 Nov. 1932, FR, 2nd half of Aug. 1932.
134. HP File 18 Dec. 1932, FR, 2nd half of Sept. 1932.
135. HP FR, 1st half of Sept. 1932.
136. Moonje pointed out that the CP government and the Franchise Committee proposed to give only 10 seats in the provincial legislature to the depressed classes and 15 to the Muslims, although the former, according to the 1931 census, formed 26 per cent of the population while the latter were only 3.92 per cent of the population. HP FR, 2nd half of Mar. 1932. Moonje also said that on the strength of their number in the population, Muslims deserved no more than only 5 seats in the legislature and the depressed classes no less than 20. HP FR, 2nd half of Dec. 1931.

    According to the 1921 census, Muslims were 3.64 per cent of the population but given 7 out of 73 seats by the Montford reforms while the Backward Classes, being 19 per cent of the population, had only 4 seats. *Indian Central Committee* (Sankaran Nair Committee), *Report*, Calcutta, 1929, p. 86.
137. HP File 18 Mar. 1936, FR, 2nd half of March 1936. Conversion of some Mahars and *Mehtars* (scavengers) to Islam for their social uplift was referred to in the 1921 census, *Report*, p. 131.
138. HP FR, 1st half of Dec. 1932.
139. The Congress Working Committee passed a resolution on 17–18 June 1934 saying that in view of the divided opinion among the party men on the Communal Award, the party, officially, could 'neither accept nor reject' it. But the AICC in the party's election manifesto (Aug. 1936) condemned the Communal Award as 'unacceptable as being inconsistent with independence and the principle of democracy. . . a barrier to national progress', and that it 'strikes at the root of Indian unity'. Quested in K.B. Krishna, pp. 334, 338.

    The Independent (Nagpur) accused the Congress of pro-Muslim sympathies, 18 April 1936.
140. HP File 18 Aug. 1934, FR, 2nd half of Aug. 1934; Ibid., File 18 Sept. 1934, FR, 1st half of Sept. 1934. Aney formed the Congress Nationalist Party to oppose the Communal Award. DIG, CID, Intelligence and Special Wing, Bombay, Police Diaries, Abstract of Intelligence, CP, vol. XLVII, 1934.

CHAPTER IV

Raging Riots

Communal Riots in the CP and Berar were caused by ruffled religious feelings when Hindus played music before mosques, and Muslims, in vengeful retaliation, slaughtered cows in public. Riots were both an indicator and aggravator of the worsening societal and political relations between the two communities.

Socio-political changes among the Hindus and Muslims leading to consciousness and assertion of communal identity by them and inter-communal ill-feelings culminating in riots were two closely and causally related developments. Both local disturbances and troubles elsewhere received wide—and at times distorted—publicity through press and public platforms, further inflaming communal passion. To compound the problem was the fact that local issues were often viewed in the backdrop of national politics in which communalism, a factor at first, grew fast into a force, determining the course of politics.

Hindu identity assertion, manifested in hostility towards the Muslims, was the result of a Hindu *sangathana* (unity) movement in the province. Originally a socio-religious reform process, the movement acquired a political character in the context of the pan-Islamic movement and the rash of communal riots in the province and elsewhere in the 1920s, creating in the Hindu mind the spectre of Muslim aggressiveness encouraged by Hindu weakness. Besides, 'the democratisation of the lower ranks of Hinduism',[1] indicated by the assertion of the Backward Classes, and the non-Brahmin challenge to the existing Brahmanical predominance in society and politics were two other factors to influence the course and character of the Hindu unity movement, which initially was Brahmin-led.

The rejection of the caste system, a declared object of the movement, was inspired as much by the idea of human brotherhood as by the Brahmin concern over the influence of Islam and Christianity on Depressed Class Hindus. Leaders of the movement held Hinduism as a 'social and national system' embracing all Indians rather than as 'an exclusive body of religious beliefs'.[2] In the 1920s, in the more advanced tracts of the province, Hinduism seemed to pass through a 'fifth renaissance',[3] suggested alike by liberal ideas on marriage, rejection of the *pardah* for women and a general relaxation of religious orthodoxy.

Moonje spearheaded the Hindu *Sangathana* Movement in the province, setting up Hindu *sabhas* for the purpose. The growth of the movement was accelerated by the Muslim atrocities on the Hindus beginning with the Moplah outbreak in Malabar.[4] Moonje organized the second session of the Maharashtra Hindu Dharma Parishad at Nagpur in December 1921, returning from his on-the-spot study of the situation in Malabar and his report on the Hindu sufferings submitted to the Shankaracharya of Kamakoti. He went round the province raising funds for the Hindu victims of the Moplah outrage. In November 1923, he set up the Nagpur branch of the Hindu Mahasabha to unite and organize the Hindus and protect their socio-religious interests.[5] Moonje and his organization grew increasingly anti-Muslim when riots became the local manifestation of communalism hardening into a factor in national politics. Hindu *sabhas* were involved in the reconversion of 'Hindus' from Islam and Christianity, removal of untouchability, attempts at the welfare of Depressed Class Hindus, and resolution of the Brahmin-non-Brahmin controversy.[6]

Moonje established himself in provincial and later national politics as the strongest and most vocal defender of Hindu interests. In 1927, while a member of the Central Legislative Assembly, he suggested the setting up of a tribunal by the government to settle issues like cow slaughter by the Muslims and music playing before mosques by the Hindus.[7] He attended the Round Table Conference in London 'to prove that the Muslim demands were against Indian national interests.' He vehemently opposed communal electorates for the Muslims and separate electorates for the Backward Class Hindus. He worked to rally Hindu opinion against the Communal Award (1932).[8]

Physically strengthening the Hindus for their own self defence was an important programme of the Hindu unity movement; and so came up a number of gymnasia, rifle clubs and *akhadas* whose members took on the Muslims during riots. *Akhadas*, which earlier were 'little more than wrestling exhibitions of the lower order of society', were now patronized by the elites of the Hindu society.[9] In 1935, Moonje set up the Central Hindu Military Education Society, and two years later the Bhonsle Military School at Nasik which received the government's recognition, the Governor himself inaugurating it.[10]

Many prominent Hindus of the province were associated with the Hindu *Sangathana* Movement—pro-government notables, liberals and extremists, retired and serving government employees, professionals and publicmen, businessmen and landholders,[11] all sharing a common concern over Muslim atrocities on the Hindus and all realizing alike the need for Hindu unity to defend the community. And defending the Hindu community involved taking on the Muslims.

Moonje made the Hindu unity movement in the province a part of the wider programme of the All India Hindu Mahasabha, of which he remained the President for six years—1927–33. He made the Mahasabha a force in provincial politics, organizing its annual sessions and setting up its local branches in districts and *taluks*. The Hindu Mahasabha arranged inter-caste marriages and encouraged the Hinduization of the animist aboriginals.[12]

The Hindu Mahasabha in the CP and Berar was for long mostly Brahmin in leadership, and its cadres were drawn largely from high born Hindus. This was an important reason why it was initially opposed by the non-Brahmins, depressed class Hindus and always by the Muslims. At first its members were mostly Tilakites who differed from Gandhi, his political techniques and programmes. Even a section of the Hindu press for a time condemned the Hindu unity movement for having harmed the poor people, victims of riots and economic boycott of the Muslims by the Mahasabhites.[13]

The Rashtriya Swayamsevak Sangh (RSS) was another organization committed to defend the Hindu interests when threatened by what appeared as Muslim bellicosity. Set up in 1925 in the backdrop of communal riots in Nagpur, its founder, Dr Keshav Baliram Hedgewar, was once a Congress worker, involved particularly, in the Non-Cooperation Movement, and later a close associate of Moonje.[14] For long the RSS functioned as the strong arm of the Hindu Mahasabha, particularly during election campaigns and communal riots. The Sangh's aim was to infuse among the Hindus a spirit of self-less work for the nation; to it *Rashtriyata* (nationalism) and *Hindutva* were synonymous.[15]

The RSS first displayed its organizational strength in the 1927 riot in Nagpur which took a toll of many lives. From the CP and Berar it spread to many other parts of India. It avoided open involvement in politics but allowed its cadres, in their individual capacity, to take part in some political movements. Like the Hindu Mahasabha, initially overwhelmingly Brahmin in membership, the RSS in later years drew to its fold all classes of Hindus, seven-eighths of its cadre in 1934 being non-Brahmins.[16] Most prominent members of the Hindu community in the province were ardent admirers of the RSS, though not all were its active workers.

Nationalism and the Hindu unity movement developed in the province simultaneously as an inter-related phenomenon. For the local dominant Maharashtrian Brahmin leadership under Tilak's influence, the promotion of national interests and the protection of Hindu religious cause were the two objects of a single political programme.[17] The community celebration of the Ganapati worship and Shivaji festival, besides the observation of the Tilak and Baji Rao Peshwa days were means of political education and mass mobilization of the Hindus. In fact, all Tilakites and Mahasabhites, most Hindu Swarajists and even some Hindu Congressmen carried their religious conviction through their political activities. The reaction of the Muslims of the province to all these Hindu political activities was at first one of unease and later avowed hostility.

Early in the twentieth century, the Muslim community in the province too underwent some socio-political changes, particularly due to education. Besides the provincial body of the Muslim League, another political organization—Majlis-i-Islam was set up at Elichpur in Amravati district. Several *anjumans* (associations) had already come up, being mainly socio-cultural organizations though 'liable to political activities' as well.[18] The Berar Anjuman Islam invested money for earning interest—an act of rejection of the Islamic injunctions against such investment.[19] Many Muslims shaved off their beard,[20] as though to flaunt their freedom from tradition. A number of Urdu schools started functioning, some set up and kept going by private individuals and government officers.[21] Urdu books, some in Devanagari script and a few Urdu newspapers made their appearance to form and focus Muslim opinion on matters concerning the community.[22]

An important feature of this Muslim awakening was the developing ties between the local Muslim elite and prominent Muslims outside the province and the involvement of the Nizam's government in Muslim political and educational activities in the province, several institutions receiving the Nizam's patronage. Such patronage to Muslim education was also extended by some high ranking British officers. Frank Sly, when Commissioner of Berar, sent a personal donation to Muslim Educational Conference at Akola in 1911; Robertson, the Chief Commissioner, took an equally avid interest in the Muslim educational progress.[23]

A strong feeling of solidarity grew among the Muslims in the context of the Hindu *Sangathana* Movement. Muslim *akhadas* were set up for popularising physical culture among the Muslim youth; branches of the Jamait-ul-Musalman appeared as a reaction to Hindu *sabhas* [24] while *Tabligh* was the Muslim answer to the Hindu *Shuddhi* Movement, which the Sankaracharya of Kamakoti, among others, strongly supported.[25] As a spokesman of the Hindu unity movement he made anti-Muslim speeches at places in Berar; he also reportedly said privately that he preferred India being under the British rule for another hundred years to being free with Muslim assistance.[26] When some north Indian Muslims went to Chanda to convert local Hindus, Hindu newspapers appealed to the Hindu *sabha* at Nagpur to send volunteers to Chanda to prevent Hindu conversion to Islam.[27]

Hindu and Muslim press tended to get polarized on issues concerning interests of the two communities. The Muslim elite, irrespective of their political views, later made the most of this growing communal solidarity to further their own political objectives.

Local British authorities contributed not a little to the growing inter-community bitterness. Chief Commissioner Craddock, for example, filled public services—the police department in particular-with Muslims to tackle militant nationalism led by Maharashtrian Brahmins, the *bete noire* of the British government.[28] Except during the Khilafat and Non-Cooperation Movements, the Muslim elite stayed loyal to the government while the upper class Hindu political elite became progressively alienated from the government after 1920 when the Gandhian era of Indian nationalism began. Till the British rule ended in the province, Muslims retained their over-representation in the public services,[29] suggesting the government's pro-Muslim policy. Unlike many Hindu papers, the local Muslim press was never openly anti-government.

However, proselytization had no direct bearing on communal riots in the province. Unlike some other provinces, the CP and Berar during the British rule had no record of any organized preselytization drive before the 1920s, when the forcible conversion of Hindus by Moplah Muslims worked up the Arya Samajists. They reconverted a few Malakhamba Rajputs whose ancestors had forcibly been Islamized centuries ago. In retaliation, Muslims also converted a few low class Hindu women who had been ostracized for moral lapses or rendered destitute by widowhood.[31] To local authorities the 'Hindu missionary effort' appeared far better organized than Muslim activities in this regard, although the number of people converted and reconverted to the two faiths was inconsiderable.[32]

Generally speaking, local Hindus took no notice of such stray cases of conversion until the Arya Samaj and the Hindu Mahasabha from the 1920s launched a definite programme of reconversion of apostates and assimilation with the Hindu fold of adherents of other faiths, thus giving Hinduism a new proselytizing character. With *shuddhi* now held indispensable for Hindu *sangathana*, reconversion was made a public affair reported through the press and even cinematic films.[33]

In Berar, too, *shuddhi* had, before the 1920s, made no public impact whatsoever. In fact, but for some politicians' involvement in them, the very few cases of Muslims and Christians of Elichpur and Amravati reconverted to Hinduism by local Arya Samjists would have gone wholly unnoticed by most people.[34]

In such circumstances, local authorities had no reason to ban proselytization, for although it could create some inter-communal ill-feelings for a time, it really caused no actual communal riots ever. The Deputy Commissioner of Jabalpur, where later communal troubles became endemic, viewed the *Shuddhi* Movement being carried on in an 'informal and unorganised manner' as but a means of unifying different Hindu sects, not as a calculated scheme of large scale conversion of non-Hindus.[35] Similar was the reaction of the local authorities at Sagar where in 1923–4, both Hindus and Muslims conducted a 'fair amount of proselytization.'[36]

II

Not until the 1920s did the CP and Berar government have any grave and persistent problem of communal riots, although earlier, in the 1890s, some Hindu-Muslim fracas had occurred at Jabalpur and

Burhanpur during Ganapati festival and Muharram.[37] The vigilant British Residents reported no Hindu-Muslim riots in the Nagpur state ruled by the Bhonsles where Muslims led a life of security. Muslim soldiers in Hindu dress were a common sight as was the presence of the Bhonsles in marriages celebrated by the Nizams in Berar and Hyderabad. Respect for religious feelings typified Hindu-Muslim societal relations; Muharram, Holi and Diwali which were later to become occasions for riots, were till the 1920s jointly celebrated by the two communities.[38] The Hindu gentry's proficiency in Persian, the court language, brought them closer to Muslim grandees.

However, between 1920 and 1930 as many as 25 communal riots broke out in the province as against about nine Hindu-Muslim fights between 1905 and 1920 and just one affray between them in the years 1889–1905.[39] Contemporary official reports suggested that the communal problem in the province after 1920 was coeval, correlated, and coextensive with the introduction of electoral politics by the Montford reforms and the constitutional changes that followed, setting off a competition for power and position between the Hindu and Muslim political elite groups,[40] the one established and the other emerging. The clashing political ambitions of the two groups influenced the inter-communal relations at the mass level when religion was made a handmaid of politics and fanaticism gained increasing political justification.

Each fresh delegation of authority to the Indians under the reformed constitution caused not only the demand for more but fresh frictions and rivalry between Hindu and Muslim aspirants for power, the latter refusing to concede that the Hindus, being the majority community, besides being more politically advanced and better articulated, deserved a larger share of the delegated authority and power. The Muslim demand that in every department of the administration in the country they should be represented on a fixed scale, amounted to crying for 'an eye for an eye and a tooth for a tooth'.[41] They grudged that the Hindus, once their 'down-trodden' subjects, had 'too much their own way under the reformed system of Government', thereby threatening legitimate interests of the Muslims.[42] Official records referred to an obsessive fear of Hindu political domination gripping the mind of the Muslim elite. The Hindu leadership viewed the Muslim assertion of their rights as aggressiveness which needed countering by the new militancy advocated by the Hindu Mahasabha and the RSS. Communal tension in the province was also related to the adverse economic situation caused by crop failure at places and heavy floods at others.[43]

Hindus playing music before mosques and Muslims slaughtering cows in public were the two most immediate and persistent causes of communal riots which in the 1920s were almost of annual occurrence in many parts of the province. Hindu and Muslim leaders at both the provincial and national levels could not resolve the two issues any more than the government could. Sir Frank Sly, the first Governor of the province, while reporting to the Governor-General, Lord Reading, about political developments in the province, deplored that in his long public life he had not seen so much ill-feelings between the two communities as prevailing in the early 1920s.[44] The Muslims, he added, though being an 'insignificant fraction'[45] of the population, had asserted themselves, encouraged by the activities of their correligionists in other provinces.[46]

In September 1923, the police having prevented a Hindu music-playing procession from going past a mosque at Ganeshpeth in Nagpur, the protesting Hindus staged a month-long satyagraha. A serious riot was somehow staved off by a committee of community leaders who referred the matter to the Provincial Khilafat Committee which had both Muslim and Hindu members.[47] While Shaukat Ali, then a leading Khilafatist and an admirer of Gandhi, condemned the bellicosity of Nagpur Muslims,[48] Muhammad Yusuf Shariff, Maulana Abdul Natiq, Professor Moafizul Kabir and Mirza, Muslim leaders of Nagpur, pleaded with the Hindus to show deference to Muslim religious sentiments.[49]

Sly appointed a three-member committee to enquire into the causes of communal riots and to suggest measures for their prevention,[50] but other than bringing to the fore the conflicting opinions of its members, the committee could do nothing.[51]

In 1924, incidences of communal riots in Calcutta, Lahore, Delhi, Bhagalpur, Sambalpur, Moradabad, Gulbarga, Allahabad and Kohat,[52] all reported in the press in Nagpur and Jabalpur, caused riots at the two places. The Hindu press blamed Gandhi's softness for the Muslims as responsible for the latter's 'highhandedness and turbulence'.[53] Gandhi was condemned for committing 'the blunder of blending religion with politics' during the Khilafat and Non-Cooperation Movements,[54] and for having 'laid the axe at the root of Hindu-Muslim solidarity which was an achievement of the late Lokamanya Tilak'.[55]

The Ali brothers' public declaration that they were 'Muslims first and everything else afterwards'[56] and their dissociation with Gandhi was not lost on the Hindu mind which, through the press, expressed its worry over 'manifest religious intolerance and pan-Islamic aims of its extreme Muslim supporters'.[57]

Local Khilafat committees failed to compose the growing Hindu-Muslim differences, and the resolution of the Delhi Unity Conference[58] had no effect either.[59] A meeting held in Nagpur to restore Hindu-Muslim amity had to be abandoned for lack of public attendance.[60] However, in another meeting prominent leaders of the two communities passed a resolution to settle all local disputes on music before mosques in accordance with the decision of the Delhi Unity Conference and in consonance with prevalent local customs and practices.[61] Moafizul Kabir, a Swarajist, called upon all the Muslims and Hindus 'to remember God, purify their minds of prejudice and solemnly and truthfully declare' what the local customs regarding music playing actually were.[62] But, it turned out to be a cry in the wilderness.

In 1925, following another riot in Nagpur, the Congress deputed Motilal Nehru, Maulana Azad, and Dr Syed Mahmud (as Gandhi's personal emissary) to resolve the 'music before mosque' issue.[63] Suggestively, although Moonje and other Hindu leaders of Nagpur had made prior arrangements for Mahmud's stay with Sir Gangadharrao Chitnavis, the most respected and pro-government liberal leader of the province,[64] and then the Chairman of the Provincial Legislative Council, Mahmud preferred staying with Yusuf Shariff, then a young Muslim barrister; Mahmud's declaration that he wished to hear the Muslim grievances first and then those of the Hindus[65] did not endear him to the latter.

Fortunately, local Hindu and Muslim leaders managed to pull off a settlement, the latter agreeing to 'sacrifice' the Muslim rights for the sake of the country's interests in general and inter-communal amity in particular. They left the matter to the 'good sense of the Hindus' who undertook to stop playing music before five local mosques during prayer hours between 1-30 and 2 p.m. and between 5 and 5-30 p.m.; the mosques were listed in the agreement signed by the leaders of the two communities. Nehru and Azad in a press communique extolled the Muslim gesture and its reciprocation by the Hindus, their leader, Moonje, making a public pledge to honour the settlement.[66]

The government, however, kept its fingers crossed; the settlement, appearing to be 'an almost complete climb down on the part of the Muhammadans',[67] provided no guarantee whatsoever against its rejection by the 'more ignorant and fanatical section of the community.[68] It really was not an unduly pessimistic prognosis. Only a week after the Nagpur 'peace Pact' was signed, a fresh fracas occurred at Arvi in Wardha district, and two years later, two serious riots rocked Akola and Nagpur—and all due to one reason: music before mosque. An all party conclave to address the issue yielded no result.[69] Moonje proposed a conciliation board of six members—three Hindus and three Muslims—to tour the province and bring about an agreement between the two communities in accordance with the resolution of the Delhi Unity Conference; but he would not agree to a general ban on music before all mosques at all times, as insisted upon by M.A. Siddiqui, a prominent Muslim leader of Nagpur.[70] Ironically enough, Moonje and Siddiqui were members of the same Swarajist party which was all for Hindu-Muslim unity. Thus the matter returned to square one, Hindu and Muslim leaders blaming one another for bad faith.

III

Meanwhile, communal riots having become a serious problem in the country at large, the government of India had, in October 1924, asked the CP and Berar government to report on the local communal problem besides itself suggesting measures to lessen its frequency and intensity, if not prevent its recurrence altogether.[71] The suggested measures included the constitution of conciliation boards with local community leaders as members and government officers as advisers, prevention of communal propaganda through press and public platforms and improvement of the government's intelligence gathering machinery.[72]

The local government was also asked to frame regulations regarding the Hindus playing music before mosques, Muslims killing cows during religious festivals and the routes taken by religious processions. In framing the regulations, the provincial government was required to take into consideration the prevalent customs, conventions, and practices at places prone to communal violence.[73] Administrative measures to be effective required willing public cooperation for communal peace was not an object of the government alone but a social need of the people in general.

Drawn on local officers' own experiences, the CP and Berar government's comprehensive report on the communal problem made some important points: the acute ill-feelings between the Hindus and Muslims were a recent development; that the ill-feelings between them had intensified in proportion to competition for power and position between the political elite of the two communities; that the competition was directly related to electoral politics and the increasing Indianization of the administration; that the competing elite groups used the mass religious frenzy for their own political ends; and that the administrative changes after 1920 had weakened the erstwhile authority of local official peace-keepers besides damaging their accustomed apolitical and impartial image.[74] Local officers' problems had grown in direct proportion to the government's general need to balance its own administrative compulsion with the Indian elites' soaring and often clashing political ambitions. In such circumstances communal riots were no longer just a local law and order problem; it had grown into a complicated political issue which required addressing at a much higher level than purely local or even provincial.

The provincial government was particularly sore over the fact that constitutional changes and administrative reforms which underlay the communal problem had rather been thrust on the province; Sir George Lloyd and Sir George Clarke had 'actually carried on a vendetta' against the implementation of the Montford reforms—but in vain.[75] Sly had also stressed the political immaturity of the provincial elite which made the reforms difficult to implement.[76]

None of the steps suggested by the government of India to tackle the communal problem impressed the provincial officers; some were viewed as impractical while others were dismissed as counter-productive. Conciliation boards, for example, were not easy to constitute and were likely to fail to realize their intended object if constituted; few community leaders would accept membership of the boards and risk becoming 'easy targets of misrepresentation and abuse' by their own followers.[77] Some of them could at best show only 'lip sympathy with the efforts of conciliation' while actually seeking to 'foment trouble in their own following by direct or indirect incitement'.[78] Educated leaders had no mass following worth the name; none among the Muslims, particularly, was able to speak for the entire community. Perceived as being more intolerant and volatile than the Hindus, the Muslim commoners were seen as prone to reject any settlement made by their leaders, blaming them for having wilted under the pressure of Hindu leaders, politically more experienced, abler and more resourceful.[79]

In the existing communally surcharged atmosphere, even a standing provincial conciliation committee would be 'little better than a farce' and a 'highly ridiculous body'; its members, sharply polarized on communal lines, would rather turn it into a 'religious debating society' than use it as a trouble-shooting mechanism. During actual riots conciliation boards would be particularly useless, their members unlikely to function cohesively against a variety of sudden situations which called for 'resource, authority and happy improvisation'.[80] They could at best patch up troubles for the moment, not prevent their recurrence.

Should such boards be set up at all, British officers disfavoured any direct involvement in them. This was also because Indians were wont to blame them for 'magnifying differences of opinion'[81] between Hindus and Muslims in order to further the colonial government's ulterior political object—divide and rule. British officers wanted the Indians to solve their communal problem themselves, considering particularly their clamour for an even larger share in the provincial administration.

Local officers wanted no sharing of power and responsibility for the maintenance of law and order with either private arbitration committees or officially sponsored conciliation boards, for both would suggest weakness in the local administration and aggravate the problem. The officers at Berar opined that these may even become advertisements of the communal problem rather than a means to solve it.[82] In fact, the public at large still had the fullest confidence in European officers, whose *lathi* order, even if imposed '*zabardasti se*' was more acceptable to both the fighting Muslim and Hindu ruffians than a settlement made by their own community leaders in conciliation boards.[84] The officers also pointed out that the formation of local peace committees at troubled places had for long been an established, though informal, practice of the local administration involving no explicit delegation of power or, sharing of any responsibility with local community leaders. The Deputy Commissioners strongly held that the existing rules and regulations were indeed good enough to deal with the problem of peace-keeping created by communal riots.

The officers were not too enthusiastic either about the government of India's suggestion that fiery speeches in public be curbed as also incendiary writings in the press, because riots could break out all too suddenly and for no graver reason than just the 'throwing of a rotten egg or a child blowing a penny whistle'.[85]

One contemporary development having an immediate bearing on the communal problem everywhere was the dogged defence of their religious rights by both the Hindus and Muslims. The rights, being prone to divergent and conflicting interpretations by both the communities, and reflected as such in the local press, intensified the mass religious frenzy besides polarizing the political elite on communal lines. This development stemmed directly from electoral politics in which mass mobilization measured the merit of political power seekers and their standing as community leaders.

The religious rights bitterly fought over by the two communities were based on local customs, conventions and practices regarding playing music before mosques, killing cows in public, and the routes taken by religious processions. Before the 1920s at most places neither the Muslims nor the Hindus had ever made much of these rights and the places had so long been free from communal troubles. There were places where such conventions and practices did not exist at all. Wherever they did, there were many local variations, irrespective of the Hindu-Muslim ratio in the local population. At places, before the 1920s, music playing Hindu processions, in consideration of Muslim sentiments, either avoided the routes flanked by mosques or stopped the music before the mosques, especially during prayer hours. And there were also places where local Muslims had never objected to Hindu marriage processions playing music went by mosques. At Bhandara local custom allowed only soft music before mosques while at Balaghat town local convention disallowed Hindu and Muslim religious processions traversing the same route at the same time. At Jabalpur Hindus before the 1920s adhered to the Lucknow Pact (1916) in refraining from playing music before mosques.[86]

At Wardha there were no 'ascertainable customs' whatsoever, and local Muslims were too few in number 'to have been ever excited themselves to establish many customary rights'. There were places like the Mandla town where the 'standing annual trouble' was due not to any Hindu-Muslim riot but due to clashes between Muslim groups over *tazia* processions taken out during Muharram. Such troubles took place between Muslims of the Chanda town too.[87]

At some places communal bitterness had more apparent economic than religious reasons. At Nandura and Islampur in the Buldana district, for example, tensions followed the looting of Hindu cotton stores by the Muslims while at Sagar Muslim butchers angrily reacted to the closure of slaughter houses following Hindu agitation against cow killing. In contrast, there were places like Chhindwara with no history of communal troubles ever and having no local factor either to cause such troubles; there the local Hindus and Muslims had well-entrenched and inter-dependent economic interests as an insurance against any outbreak of communal riots.[88] In Nagpur, men engaged in the same profession but belonging to two religious communities often came to blows—for example, the Hindu *koshtis* and the Muslim *momins*, both weavers.[89]

Then there were places where large scale communal disturbances had till then been averted by agreements made by local Hindus and Muslims themselves to maintain peace, both actuated by a spirit of mutual accommodation and compromise. For example, at Khandwa, in 1915, Muslims had agreed to a ban on music only at a specified distance from mosques, not along the entire stretch of the roads where they stood.[90] Hindu-Muslim agreements at Lonar and Deolgarh Raja at the same time had the specific object of averting any fracas when religious celebrations of the two communities coincided.[91] Hindus of Khamgaon had, in 1922, undertaken to stop music before only a few specific mosques, not all, and that too during only specific hours.[92] In 1915, at Darwa too, the two communities had made such an agreement.[93] All these agreements had so long been upheld by local authorities and held good for years.

In Berar too communal problem had been a recent phenomenon, the result of the 'rude awakening' of the Muslims in general caused by the Moplah outbreak and the failure of the Khilafat Movement 'which made the Indian Muslims look silly' in the eyes of their coreligionists outside India.[94] Muslims supporting the Nizam's claim on Berar and the Hindus opposing it was also a factor to generate ill-feelings between the two communities.[95] Muslims refused to suffer subordination to the Hindu majority rule, the inevitable outcome of the on-going process of constitutional changes.[96]

As for the Muslim right to slaughter cow in public, official enquiries established that it was more a retaliatory step recently adopted by the Muslims against the Hindus playing music before mosques than a traditionally observed and an essential religious rite of the Muslims, as was now claimed by them. Historically speaking too the Muslims had a weak case. Thus, in the Nagpur state under the Bhonsles, public cow slaughter was strictly banned though winked at when performed in the privacy of Muslim homes. In respect to British soldiers' camps and cantonments, however, the ban was neither rigidly enforced nor officially suspended, the Bhonsles and the British Residents sharing a 'common delicacy' in making the matter an issue between the two governments.[97]

More importantly, the cow protection movement in the province that grew from the late 1880s had initially no political motivation let alone any anti-Muslim overtone.[98] British officers testified to the fact that most Hindus supporting the movement did so 'without any political bias' whatsoever.[99] The Hindu press even appealed at times to the Muslims to save cows for the sake of agricultural interests, also stressing the fact that some Muslim leaders like Malak of Nagpur, Murtiza Khan of Seoni and Liaquat Hussain of Calcutta, too had supported the movement.[100] In fact, before the 1920s, public cow slaughter, never widely performed in the province, had caused at worst some occasional communal ill-feelings, no large scale communal riots ever. The Hindu press also drew attention to the fact that during the Khilafat Movement Gandhi and the Ali brothers had together pleaded for Muslim desistance from beef eating to foster Hindu-Muslim unity.[101]

Not even during Bakr-Id did the Muslims kill cows in public as a religious rite. Even in Jabalpur, having no pubic stall for the sale of beef till the 1920s, the Muslims, partly in deference to Hindu sentiments and partly in obedience to a forty-year old ban on public cow slaughter,[102] killed cows 'with the utmost secrecy within the precincts of their own house'; many Muslims of the town, living in predominantly Hindu localities, slaughtered goats and sheep during Bakr-Id instead of cows.[103]

All this, however, changed after the Khilafat and the Non-Cooperation Movements ended. The CP Slaughter of Animals Act created Hindu-Muslim ill-feelings, the Hindu press supporting it while the Muslim papers condemning it.[104] Even local officers of the time hesitated to take measures to restrict cow killing fearing that it would provoke the Muslims to kill more cows than before; the men 'in order to show their independence would also thrash anyone preventing the hawking of beef in public'.[105]

Local officers were indeed hard put to determine the historicity, object and currency of what the two communities held as their religious rights, for 'aided by large scale deception, which is bedfellow of ignorance', both the Hindus and Muslims claimed as their ancient rights what in fact were new practices and customs.[106] Then there were places with no history of communal troubles, and so there were no official records of local customs and conventions which officers could refer to while settling disputes now occurring at the places.

Local British officers were remarkably free from prejudice while blaming either the Hindus or Muslims for communal troubles. D.A. Smyth, the Chief of Nagpur police, found the Hindu leaders, especially those associated with the Hindu *sabhas*, revelling in communal riots to thrash the Muslims and show off the Hindu might;[107] they would not abide by the Delhi Unity Conference resolution restricting music playing processions to specified routes; instead, at Nagpur, in 1924, they took Ganapati processions through altogether new routes, playing loud music before the Jama Masjid—an unprecedented event and a patently provocative act.[108]

But C.A. Cartie, Commissioner of Nagpur, blamed the Muslims more for causing communal troubles, if not for aggravating them, though conceding that both the communities were 'really the victims of circumstances'. To him the Muslims appeared 'the more ignorant and uneducated, the more bigoted fellow to start with', the bigotry having intensified with the spread of pan-Islamism and the Muslim awakening in the world in general.[109]

Besides, 'never able to see much' beyond their immediate religious interests and 'now even less able than ever', to do so, the Muslims refused to accept any long term communal settlement with the Hindus. Any such settlement could be made with a 'spirit of compromise' alone, the spirit itself being 'the fruit of education and enlightenment'; the spirit was yet to grow 'in such a soil of ignorance and fanaticism' as still persisting among members of both the communities.[110]

One more reason why the communal problem tended to become graver from the 1920s was that local authorities could no longer deal summarily with it as they were accustomed to do before the Montford reforms brought changes in the administration. Peacekeeping now became more difficult because public men condemned the accustomed discretionary powers of local executive and police officers as wanton arbitrariness and gross misuse of authority. And hence the officers' reluctance to adopt the hitherto well-tried rough and ready measures to deal with rowdies in the society lest such measures set off critical comments in the press, public platforms and legislatures where elected leaders were often swayed by the common man's communal outlook with which to berate the strict government officers. To worsen the situation, unlike earlier, public men now doubted government officers' impartiality during riots, though not their efficiency.[111]

And this the Nagpur Divisional Commissioner himself admitted when referring particularly to Indian officers. An Indian officer, so Cartie held, laboured under the suspicion of being hostile to the community not his own; he also had to 'fight against the additional impression that he must feel for his community'; consequently, with a view to displaying his impartiality, he at times tended to 'please both sides too openly', thereby compromising his own 'ever conscious sense of right or wrong',[112] and hence ending up being unfair to the really wronged party.

All in all, the official view seemed to be one of resignation—what cannot be cured must be endured. Cartie made it amply clear:

> If therefore it is recognised that the cause of the disunion (between the two communities) are to be found in the disputes over delegated authority, in the fostering of religious and social antagonism, and the immobility of the mass below, it must be conceded . . . that they have become organic in the body politic and must develop with its growth. Against organic sickness no standard or uniform treatment can prevail.

The situation had indeed been 'the unavoidable consequence of events which no statesmanship can change'.[113]

Unlike earlier, Hindus and Muslims would no longer ungrudgingly obey the old executive orders regarding music before mosques, for example, because the very self-respect of the two fighting communities seemed now hinged on one's ability to play the music and the other's success in preventing it; and this self-respect was asserted by the national leadership of both the communities.

The acuteness of the communal problem came to the fore during the Akola riot in 1926.[114] It was now that the government realized that banning music before mosques was too complicated a matter to be left any longer at the disposal of local peace-keepers. The provincial administration at the highest level needed to decide if the ban should cover all mosques or only the old and important ones; whether the ban would hold good for the whole day or for the prayer hours only; if the latter, who to determine the hours; whether all forms of music should come under the ban or an exception be made in respect to light music; and how far from the mosques should the music stop.

All this was a part of a bigger issue: whether or not the government should restrict the civil right of one community to use public thoroughfares for the sake of the religious sentiments of another, and whether or not any executive order enforcing such restriction could hold good for years later when the local situation earlier necessitating the restriction had changed considerably.

Naturally, therefore, the Governor, Montagu Butler, who took over from Sly in 1925, was wary while framing a new regulation regarding music before mosques; he was aware of the conflicting assertions of Hindu and Muslim leaders who had met him.[115] Butler also knew that in Berar, particularly, which for long had been under Muslim rule,[116] music playing Ganesh processions were a recent introduction which the Hindu Mahasabha had been popularizing disregarding the long-held local tradition of respecting Muslim religious sentiments.[117] The tradition had a strong foundation in an order issued by a Hindu Prime Minister of the Hyderabad state, Raja Chandu Lal, in 1836, forbidding any music before mosques.[118] Later executive orders issued by local British officers and agreements between local Hindus and Muslims had confirmed the ban.

However, it was unlikely that the local government was unaware of what the leading liberal newspaper of the province, *Hitavada* had reported: even in Ottoman Turkey, ruled by the Caliphs, military processions playing martial tune on military bands passed by local mosques; also, Christians in Jerusalem held celebrations playing loud music before local mosques; such practices had not been banned there ever.[119] The *Hitavada* also brought to public notice another fact: in recent years Muslims had been acquiring places for ordinary purposes in predominantly Hindu areas where mosques soon came up and then they demanded total ban on any music around that place which left the local Hindus intensely and justly irritated.[120] Thus grew communal problems at places for long free from them.

The Hindus of Akola, who had till then obeyed the executive orders and inter-communal agreements, now condemned them as showing the government's pro-Muslim bias—an impression deepened by the arrest of some Mahasabha leaders, who, as Butler strongly suspected, sought to incite Hindu communalism for electoral gains.[121] R.V. Mahajani, President, Hindu Sabha, Akola, had, in fact, written to Moropant Joshi, the erstwhile Home Member, about the arrests, warning that the government's partiality towards the Muslims would provoke a strong Hindu reaction.[122]

In such a situation, Butler struck what looked like a deft compromise. His Akola Order permitted the Hindus to play music before all mosques situated on public streets on all occasions except during prayer hours. The new principle laid down was: '. . . in a general way no civil restriction on the use of a thoroughfare arises from the existence beside it of any place of worship'.[123]

The Muslim contention that long-standing conventions existed at many places against music playing before mosques was rejected until such ban was upheld by fresh judicial pronouncements. But all Ganapati processions were now required to obtain prior licences; no *lathi*-wielding ruffians could mingle with the crowd of devotees; no public killing of cows was allowed on the routes of religious processions nor any assembly of five or more Muslims permitted on the routes taken by Hindu religious processions.[124]

Muslims condemned the Akola Order as patently pro-Hindu, grudging particularly the abrogation of even earlier executive orders banning music before mosques and thus preserving local peace. As though to vent their anger over the new Order, Muslims at Jabalpur killed cows 'with unnecessary ostentation'.[125]

To complicate the situation further came up the difference of opinion between local British officers themselves. C. Brown, the D.C. Akola, claiming to give 'an equal and impartial feeling of consideration' to both the Hindus and Muslims, held that the 'danger of violence is no justification for the limitation of civil rights' of any community. But the Commissioner of Berar, F.C. Turner, while dismissing the Hindu allegation that earlier executive orders restricting music before mosque were pro-Muslim in effect, and at the same time deprecating the Muslim opposition to the recent Akola Order, favoured a compromise: stopping music before all old mosques and allowing it before all new ones, Hindus being required to re-route their processions whenever possible to avoid clashing with the Muslims.[126]

Butler's decision was really an outcome of his own political compulsion: the Governor needed to keep the Swarajists, mostly old Tilakites, in good humour to avoid the problem they had created for

Sly, Butler's predecessor.[127] Hence, Butler had only recently made Sripad Balwant Tambe, a prominent Swarajist, the Home Member in his executive council, thereby creating a breach in the Swarajist Party.[128] And it was Tambe who did most in finalizing the Akola Order after an on-the-spot enquiry into the riot there. His contention officially noted was:

> A community building a place of worship in a locality mostly inhabited by people of any other community has no equitable claim to interference with the observance of religious rites and social functions by the other community according to its religion and custom.[129]

Tambe strongly recommended the withdrawal of the old executive order at Akola banning music before mosques as an 'unnecessary restriction' on the right of people to use public thoroughfares. To Tambe, who was closely associated with the Hindu unity movement, it was also unreasonable to stop music playing in Hindu burning *ghats* just because of their proximity to some Muslim burial grounds where music playing was forbidden.[130]

Henceforth the Akola Order prevailed over all earlier executive orders and local Hindu-Muslim agreements dealing with the music-before-mosque issue. It also served as a point of reference for officers of other provinces dealing with the same issue.[131] A judgement of the Allahabad High Court in 1931 set the seal of finality on Butler's Akola Order.[132]

But European officers continued to express reservations on the Order. When the Order was implemented to deal with a riot at Wasim in 1928, local British authorities regarded the step as being rather soft towards the Hindus and unduly unfair on the Muslims.[133] Hence, hereafter the government's policy was to avoid 'any general probing' into religious customs, for fear that it would 'stir up the very trouble which it is desired to escape'.[134]

The Akola Order secured but an uneasy peace. It was put to test in the very next year when Nagpur was rocked by perhaps the gravest ever communal riot. Military police had to be called in to restore order after nineteen men had been killed, a hundred and twenty four injured and more than six hundred Muslims needed to be evacuated from Hindu localities.[135] The RSS was involved in this riot, as if determined to avenge Hindu killings in earlier riots. Butler acted on the suggestion of the veteran Gangadharrao Chitnavis when forming a citizen's committee to act in close concert with local officers to restore peace.[136]

IV

The communal problem persisted through the 1930s, though in its first half riots were fewer in number and less fierce than before; this was in no small measure due to the able handling of the problem by the new Home Member, E. Raghavendra Rao, Tambe's successor and political rival. Rao, who till 1926 was a Swarajist, later fell out with the Marathi leadership of the party; he reached high in provincial politics with government support and higher still in the government itself—all along willingly playing the role assigned to him by successive Governors: a foil to the anti-government front sedulously forged by Indian nationalists.

Rao was popular with the Muslims whose support he garnered for his own political rise; when in power as Home Member he rewarded them with government jobs and greater educational opportunities. Held in high esteem for his administrative acumen, by government officiers,[137] high and low, Rao relied on local officers' tact and firmness to tackle the festering communal problem. He gave a free hand to the officers who imposed punitive police action exclusively on either the Hindus or Muslims after establishing who of them were really guilty.[138]

A young Indian civilian, R.K. Nehru, effected a Hindu-Muslim settlement at Lonar in Buldana district after satisfying himself that the playing of music before mosques by the Hindus was 'quite obviously an innovation 'and violative of an earlier agreement they had made with the Muslims.[139] But Nehru also marked a new trend which in later years became quite a common practice which kept the communal pot boiling: Hindus, flaunting their right to use public thoroughfares, insisted on taking their music playing processions through altogether new routes, where old mosques stood; the Muslims, retaliating, set up altogether new mosques on old streets only to assert their right to stop Hindu processions passing through them.[140]

The government drew up 'riot schemes' for places prone to communal violence such as Nagpur, Jabalpur, Amravati, Akola, Sagar, and Raipur besides forming local peace committees of community leaders. Activities of all important public men and political parties were closely monitored and the press warned against any provocative reporting of news and views.[141]

In the 1930s both the Hindu Mahasabha and the RSS stepped up their activities, the former's anti-Congress posture being pronounced, besides. The Akola Order proved a shot in the arm for the Mahasabha. It invited Sir Sankaran Nair, a liberal leader, who later headed the Central Committee, to address the All India Hindu Mahasabha meeting at Nagpur in August 1927, where before a gathering of some 25,000 men (of whom 15,000 were *lathi* wielding) twelve anti-Muslim resolutions were passed, condemning the murder of Swami Shraddhanand by a Muslim and asserting the Hindu right to play music before mosques.[142] The Ganapati festival at Nagpur in 1928 was 'the grandest ever', its new feature being men dressed as tigers dancing on streets; this was a signal to the Hindus not to take any part in Muharram when, going by tradition, both Hindus and Muslims performed the tiger dance to entertain the public.[143]

The Mahasabha, besides converting some Christians to Hinduism,[144] stoked anti-Muslim feelings in Berar to increase its membership; it also was a diversionary tactics against the growing non-Brahmin movement.[145] The Mahasabha urging economic boycott of the Muslims drove them closer to the non-Brahmin movement which soon the Mahars too were to join.[146] The Nagpur Muslim Association encouraged the conversion of the Depressed Class Hindus to Islam, the *Tabligh* committee gearing itself up for the purpose. Muslims attended Mahar meetings as well, prompting the Mahasabha activists to work among a section of the Mahars with a view to uniting them against the section led by Dr Bhimrao Ramji Ambedkar who favoured Mahar conversion to Islam.[147] This non-Brahmin-Muslim-Mahar combine formed in the background of communal troubles was later used by the provincial government as a counter-weight to the long-entrenched Brahmin leadership in regional politics.[148]

The RSS also grew strong in the 1930s. It became involved in district council election politics apparently with a view to utilizing for propaganda work the teachers appointed by local bodies.[149] By December 1934, when Gandhi visited its annual camp at Wardha,[150] the RSS had set up 125 branches all over India having some 12,000 members.[151] Its 'definite communal bias' and 'actively anti Muslim character' were reported by the police attending the meetings addressed by Moonje, Hedgewar, and Ganesh Savarkar, brother of the Mahasabha President; in RSS meetings the slogan 'India for the Hindus' rent the air.[152]

The government was convinced of the RSS being anti-government as well; its clear proof lay in RSS cadres found involved in the Civil

Disobedience Movement despite the organization claiming to be a non-political body.[153]

Raghavendra Rao struck hard; the government banned its employees' association with the RSS in any form[154] whatsoever despite strong protests from even two former Home Members, Moropant Joshi and Sripàd Tambe, both keen on defending Hindu interests.[155] In the Provincial Council too the government's action was condemned, some members asserting that the RSS was a nationalist organization, not a communal outfit.[156]

In the 1934 election to the Central Legislative Assembly, the RSS was found 'unusually active' in Nagpur, Wardha, and Chanda, Moonje contesting the election as the Democratic Nationalist Party[157] candidate against Abhyankar, the Congress leader. Moonje, backed by the Hindu Mahasabha, made use of RSS volunteers to disrupt Abhyankar's election meetings.[158] Abhyankar, who was popular with the Muslims, bitterly condemned Moonje and other Hindu *sangathana* leaders for intensifying communalism in the province.[159]

During municipal elections also communal feelings ran high;[160] the local press spewed fire and brimstone when commenting on communal riots in other provinces, the activities of Jinnah, and the growing differences between the Muslim League and the Congress on constitutional reforms. The Communal Award, 1932 further intensified the communal bitterness.

Communalism had by the 1930s become an important element in the public life of the province, but the Muslims had not yet become a politically united group to effectively influence the provincial politics. Though now strongly identity conscious and determined to defend their community rights, the Muslims were still without a party to mobilize them for a common political purpose under a strong and determined leadership. This political want of the Muslims was met by the Muslim League which sprang into renewed life after the 1937 elections, giving a new turn to the communal problem in the province.

NOTES

1. W.H. Shoobert *Census, 1931, CP and Berar, Report*, pp. 329–30.
2. Ibid.

3. Ibid. The Maharashtra Hindu Dharma Parishad at Yeotmal resolved that no untouchability would be practised at public places barring temples, tanks and wells. *Prajapaksha*, 25 Feb. 1923, *RIN*, 1923.
4. Chapter III.
5. Vina Balasastry Hardas, *Life of B.S. Moonje* (in Marathi), vol. II, Pune, 1966, pp. 49–64, 121. In June 1933, explaining why he joined the Hindu Mahasabha, Moonje said: 'the Mopla riots in 1921 and the Presidential speech of Muhammad Ali at the Kakinada Congress in 1923, in which he expressed the view of distributing the untouchables equally between Hindus and Muslims and thus solving the problem of untouchability, gave me a new insight and I was attracted towards the work of Hindu Mahasabha', quoted by S.V. Bhalerao, 'A Militant Hindu Nationalist: Dharmaveer Dr B.S. Moonje (1872–1948)', P.L. Joshi, *Political Ideas*, p. 55.
6. *Census, CP and Berar, 1931*, pp. 327–8. The Census Report made a pointed reference to the growing assertion of the non-Brahmins and Depressed Classes against the Brahmins. Ibid., p. 329. The Hindu *sabhas* were mostly Brahmin-led. In the 1921 census, 2,847 Hindus returned 'caste nil'. Ibid., p. 330.
7. Vina Hardas, *Life of Moonje*, pp. 237–8.
8. Chapter III.
9. SP 280134, File 113/1924, D.A. Smyth, DSP, Nagpur, to IGP, CPB, 12 Oct. 1924.
10. V. Deshpande, 'Militant Nationalism in Maharashtra, 1925–51', unpublished Ph.D. thesis, University of Jammu, Jammu, 1989, p. 60.
11. Moonje set up the Hindu Mahasabha branch in Nagpur in March 1923. Its important office bearers were Raja Raghuji and Laxmanrao Bhonsle (scions of the old Bhonsle family of Nagpur), Sir Visheswardas Daga, Gangadharrao Chitnavis, and his brother Shankarrao Chitnavis, Sir Moropant Joshi, then Home Member in the Governor's Executive Council, Rai Bahadur Kinkhede, Rai Bahadur Banait, Rai Bahadur Kelkar, Madhavrao Deshpande, Daji Saheb and Keshavrao Buty and Bhau Saheb Talatule. Sir B.K. Bose was the President of the Legal Advisory Committee of the Mahasabha, Sir Hari Singh Gaur was its Vice-President, Barrister Ramrao Deshmukh its Secretary. Other members of the new body were M.V. Abhyankar, Dr K.B. Hedgewar, Dr N.B. Khare and Dr L.V. Paranjpe. Vina Hardas, *Life of Moonje*, pp. 121–2. Thus, all prominent Hindus, some Government officers, businessmen, public men and professionals were associated with the new body.
12. *Census, CPB, 1931*, p. 27.
13. *Samalochak* (Sagar), 7 Oct. 1925, *RIN*, 1925.
14. Hedgewar was jailed for one year for participation in the Non-Cooperation Movement. He was in charge of the volunteer corps at the Congress session at Nagpur in Dec. 1920. He was earlier a member of the militant Anushilan Samity of Bengal. He and Moonje set up the Rashtriya Utsav Mandal to celebrate functions like the Ganesh *utsav*, Ramdas *navami*, *sankrant*, etc....,

and to arrange lectures on Shivaji and other historical characters with a view to infuse nationalistic spirit among the Hindus.

15. SP 280072, Report on the RSS; 280076, File 250/1943, Report on Hindu Mahasabha and the RSS; 280077, File 93/1944, Note on Voluntary Organizations in CP.
16. So declared Moropant Joshi when addressing the annual RSS camp at Wardha in 1934. HP FR, 1st half of Dec. 1934.
17. In 1928, presiding over the Hindu Mahasabha session at Jabalpur, N.C. Kelkar said: 'Swaraj will not be worth having if we cannot purchase it with any price less than the loss of Hinduism itself.' Quoted in Deshpande, 'Militant Hinduism', p. 35. Kelkar, like other Tilakites, such as Bhopatkar, Moonje and D.V. Gokhale, was closely associated with the *Hindutva* movement.

    Moonje explained the object of the movement: '. . . to keep together all Hindus and to extend the Hindu religion so that India might be called Hindusthan, the land of the Hindus.' Quoted by Muhammad Shafi at the Minorities Committee meetings, *RTC*, vol. III, Calcutta, 1931, p. 61.
18. Marten, *Census, CPB, 1911*, p. 66. There were *anjumans* in Nagpur, Jabalpur and Narsingpur to promote Muslim education. *RACP, 1889–90*, p. 105. At this time Muslims had no 'purely political society'. Ibid., *1885–6*, p. 73.
19. Shoobert, *Census, CPB, 1931*, p. 332.
20. Ibid., p. 175.
21. Ibid. Russell, *Nagpur Dist. Gazetteer,* p. 70.

    Some rich and large hearted Muslims of Berar lent their homes for use as schools besides instituting scholarships for Muslim pupils. R. Nathan, *Progress of Education in India, 1897–98 to 1901–02, Fourth Quinquennial Review,* vol. II, Calcutta, 1904, p. 382; *Progress of Education in India, 1887–92*, p. 334. A.H.L. Fraser, Chief Commissioner, laid the foundation of the Muslim primary school set up by the Anjuman-Hami-e-Islam in Nagpur. Reginald Craddock, another Chief Commissioner made it a high school in 1908, M.S. Sahil, *Nagpur Ka Muslim* pp. 87–9.

    Also *Hind Kesari* (Nagpur), 5 Sept. 1908, *RNP*, 1908; *Hitavada*, 30 Aug. 1913, *RIN*, 1913.
22. In 1910, there were four Urdu papers, weeklies and monthlies. In 1926, there were five Urdu weeklies in the province. *RIN*, 1910, 1926. In 1931, the province had four Urdu weeklies. *Census, CPB, 1931*, p. 283. *RACPB* for the years 1909 to 1920, and 1923–4, 1926–7.
23. *Hitavada*, 30 Aug. 1913, 22 March 1919. *Kartavya* (Amravati), 22 April 1911, *RIN*, 1911.
24. HP FR, 1st half of June 1923, 1st half of Jan. 1924.
25. HP File 1-4/1928, FR, 1st half of April 1928.
26. HP FR, 1st half of Feb. 1925. Report on the Political situation in the CP and Berar for the 1st half of April 1928.
27. *Swatantra* (Nagpur), 27 March 1924, *RIN*, 1924, p. 167.

28. 'Bengalis and Maratha Brahmins are in the main seditious and revolutionary'. Maratha Brahmin movement was 'the only dangerous movement' so opined the Chief Commissioner of the province. SP 280132, Files for 1916 to 1918: Indian Territorial Army; File 18 of 1912, Note by CCCPB.

    Some European officers were strongly prejudiced against Brahmins. DC's office at Elichpur issued a circular inviting applications for employment except from Brahmins. *Subodh Sindhu*, 10 May 1905, *RIN*, 1905. Cleveland, the provincial police chief, was strongly opposed to Maharashtrian Brahmins, who were in leaque with Bengali militant nationalists. *Warhad Samachar* (Akola), 17 Sept. 1906, *RIN*, 1906.

29. In February 1947, the Muslims held 10 per cent of the executive jobs under the government; in the subordinate ministerial and executive services, they held 11 per cent and 18 per cent of the posts respectively. By 1941 census, Muslims were 4.6 per cent of the population. *CPLA*, 25 Feb. 1947, p. 23; 2 April 1947, p. 15. See also Chapter VI.
30. In Berar many Hindu *koshtis* (weavers) embraced Islam voluntarily in the nineteenth century.
31. *RIN*, 1923, pp. 120, 251.
32. *Census, CPB, 1931*, p. 328. Conversion to Islam and Christianity outnumbered conversion to Hinduism by at least 10 to 1. Ibid., p. 330.
33. SP 280134, File 113/1924, DC Sagar to Commr. Jabalpur, 23 Oct. 1924.
34. Ibid., Commr. Berar to A.E. Nelson, CSCPB, 18 Nov. 1924.
35. Ibid., Commr. Jabalpur to Nelson, 1 Nov. 1924.
36. Ibid., DC Sagar to Commr. Jabalpur, 23 Oct. 1924. Moonje was once opposed to the *shuddhi* movement, considering it both 'unnecessary and harmful'. Vina Hardas, *Life of Moonje*, p. 119.
37. HD Police, July 1893, nos. 206–8, Report on the Police Administration in CP, 1892; Ibid., 1894. Exemplary punishment to the miscreants at Jabalpur had a great effect.
38. *NRR*, vol. I, no. 17: H.T. Celebrook, Resident, to GG, 25 June 1799. T.E. Celebrook, *The Life of H.T. Celebrook*, London, 1873, pp. 152, 173. S. Landge, *Samsedhananjali* (Marathi), Nagpur, 1960, p. 33. P.L. Saswadkar, 'Nagpur at the end of the 18th century', *PIHC 1969*, pp. 399–415.

    Several Hindus used to instal and worship *tazias*. *Maharashtra*, 20 July 1924, *RIN*, 1924.

39. *ISC*, vol. XV, *Extracts from Official Oral Evidence*, London, 1930, p. 523. However, the Government informed the provincial legislature that between 1924 and 1930, 23 communal disturbances occurred, causing death to 31 people, and injury to 721. *CPLC*, vol. I, Jan.–Mar. 1930, p. 191.

    In its Memorandum to the India Office, the GOI stated that in the period 1923–7, 46 deaths and injury to 329 persons took place in communal riots. *ISC*, vol. IV (London, 1930), cited by Page, *Prelude to Partition*, p. 74.

    In another Government paper different figures occur. In the 31 years 1889–1920, only 10 riots of mostly petty character had taken place. But in the seven years after 1920–1, 33 riots took place (one each in 1921, 1922 and 1923; 9 in 1924; 10 in 1925; 4 in 1926; 6 in 1927 and 1 in 1928). Of the 33 riots, Berar accounted for 11, Nagpur for 7 and Jabalpur for 4. And all the riots originated in dispute over music before mosques issue. *Memorandum on the working of the Reformed Government in the Central Provinces and Berar,* vol. I, *Memorandum* (Nagpur, 1930), pp. 90–3, cited in Kamalesh Sharma, *Role of Muslims in Indian Politics, 1857–1947* (New Delhi, 1985), pp. 157–8.

Communal riots in the 1920s were discussed in the provincial legislature. *CPLC,* 10 March 1926, p. 303; 17 Jan. 1928, p. 43; 17 Jan. 1929, p. 7; 1 March 1929, p. 518; 22 Aug. 1929, pp. 37, 83; 22 Jan. 1930, pp. 183–4.

40. In 1924, the Reforms Enquiry Committee (Muddiman Committee) found a clear correlation between constitutional reforms and communal frictions. *Report*, Cmd. 2360, 1925, p. 51. In a later report, the Home Department of GOI stressed the inter-relation between 'the two problems of communal disagreement and political advance'. Reforms, Special, Notes, no. 66 of 1927: 'Communal Disorders', p. 28. See also *The Moral and Material Progress and Condition of India, 1926–27*, p. 19.

    However, H.C. Gowan, the CSCPB, hesitated to 'make a definite assertion' that the great increase in communal troubles at the time 'had any connection with the introduction of the Reforms'. *ISC*, vol. XV: *Extracts from Official Oral Evidence*, London, 1930, p. 523.
41. SP 280134, File 113/1924, H.C. Gowan, Commr., Nagpur, to Nelson, 19 Oct. 1924. This file, marked Confidential, contains letters and notings of most district officers of the province on the local communal problem.
42. Ibid., Commr. Jabalpur to Nelson, 1 Nov. 1924.
43. *Reports on the Police Administration of the CP and Berar for the years, 1926, 1927, 1928 and 1932.*
44. Reading Papers, Reel no. 3359, Sly to Reading, 19 Sept. 1924.
45. According to the 1921 census, Muslims were only 3.64 per cent of the population.
46. Reading Papers, Reel no. 3359, Sly to Reading, 19 Sept. 1924.
47. Hardas, *Life of Moonje*, p. 123. Nawab Niazuddin and Gangadharrao Chitnavis did a lot in easing the tension. *RIN*, 1923, pp. 355, 564.
    Chitnavis was the first representative of the CP to sit in the Central Legislative Assembly in 1893. He was also the first President of the Provincial Council from 1920 to 1925.
48. HP FR, 2nd half of Nov. 1923. Hardas, *Life of Moonje*, p. 127.
49. Ibid., p. 125.
50. The members of the committee were Baker, the Judicial Commissioner, Bapurao Kinkhede, the Addl. Judicial Commissioner, and Hafiz Muhammad Wilayatullah Khan, DC Durg. *Hitavada*, 9 Apr. 1924. MAGAD, File–1-22/1926.
51. Ibid., SP 280134, File 113/1924, Gowan to Nelson, 19 Oct. 1924.
52. HP File 88/1926. There were 70 riots in India in 1923–6. HP File 179–II/1926.
53. *Udaya*, 5 July 1924, *RIN*, 1924.

54. *Maharashtra*, 15 Oct. 1924, RIN, 1924; *RIN*, 1923, p. 479.
55. *Udaya*, 6 July, 1924, *RIN*, 1924.
56. Ibid., Reforms (Special), Notes, no. 66 of 1927: 'Communal Disorder', p. 11.
57. Ibid. Muhammad Ali, by then no more a Gandhi loyalist, declared in a public meeting at Lucknow: 'Yes, according to my religion and creed, I do hold an adulterous and a fallen Mussalman to be better than Mr Gandhi'. *Times of India* (Bombay), 21 Mar. 1924, cited in B.R. Ambedkar, *Pakistan or Partition of India* (Bombay, 1945), p. 296.
58. The Conference (Sept.–Oct. 1924) was attended by prominent Hindu and Muslim leaders of the country to resolve Hindu-Muslim ill-feelings erupting into communal riots.
59. 'Delhi Unity Conference has not produced any real change of heart'; '. . . the situation in Nagpur has not materially altered by the Delhi Unity Conference'. SP 280134, File 113/1924, Cartie to Nelson, 12 Oct. 1924.
60. Ibid.
61. Ibid.
62. Ibid.
63. MAGAD, File 1-22/1926.
64. See Note no. 47 above.
65. SP 280134, File 113/1924, Cartie to Nelson, 18 Oct. 1924.
66. MAGAD, File 1-22/1926. Hindu leaders who signed the pact were Moonje, M.V. Abhyankar, D.W. Kathalay, B.H. Shinde, G.D. Dalvi, K.P. Vaidya, Dr Hedgewar, G.R. Deshmukh, M.A. Desphande, Y.S. Doke, M.B. Neogi, Dr N.B. Khare and V. Gujar.

    Muslim leaders who signed the pact were Lal Muhammad, Yusuf Khan, Md. Kaseem Khan, Ahmad Khan, Muhammad Alim, M.A. Siddiqui, Nizamuddin Khan, Badruddin, Muhammad Hussain, Muhammad Akbar Hussain, Abdur Rashid, Hussain Khan, Sultan Beg, Sheikh Ibrahim, Munshi Muhammad Ali, Muhammad Amir, Ilahi Bux, Muhinuddin, Bismillah Khan, M.Y. Shariff, R. Khan and A. Khallique. Ibid. *Hitavada*, 25 Oct. 1925.
67. HP FR, 2nd half of Jan. 1925. However, police reports had it that some Hindu leaders were indeed very eager to see the communal tension relaxed and peace restored. While Shankarrao Chitnavis, the Minister, disliked being pressurised by the Hindus to take a pro-Hindu stand in the on-going dispute over music before mosques, Raja Raghuji Bhonsle, a scion of the former ruling family of Nagpur and a patron of the Hindu *Sangathana* Movement, expressed concern and despair over what he grudged as the people's growing inattention and even disrespect to him. He said: 'formerly, while he was passing through the city, everybody paid respect to him, whether high or low, Hindu or Mohammadan. Since the dispute has started, people have stopped saluting him and turn their faces away from him or look on him with dislike'. SP 280134, File 113/1924, Cartie to Nelson, 19 Oct. 1924, enclosure.

68. HP FR, 2nd half of Jan. 1925.
69. *Hitavada*, 25 Oct. 1925.
70. Ibid. Moonje appeared to Cartie as 'the most cunning figure on the stage', as also the 'most unrelenting on the Hindu-Muslim issue'. Cartie to Nelson, 19 Oct. 1924, SP 280134, File 113/1924.
71. Ibid., Telg. from GOI to CSCPB, 10 Oct. 1924.
72. Ibid.
73. Ibid.
74. Ibid., Nelson to Secy. HD, GOI, 19 Dec. 1924.
75. CPLC, 26 July, 1933, p. 201.
76. Sly wrote to Reading on 20 Feb. 1923: 'In this province there has been no real development of the party system and party leaders'. Reading Papers, Reel no. 3358. He also stressed 'the ignorance and irresponsibility of the electorate' and 'paucity of suitable material for membership of the Legislative Council.' Ibid., Sly to Reading, 27 Aug. 1924.
77. SP 280134, File 113/1924, IGP, CPB, to Nelson, 16 Oct. 1924.
78. Ibid.
79. Ibid., Gowan to Nelson, 19 Oct. 1924.

    G.A. Khan, Commr. of Berar, also said that even Muslim MLCs had little influence on the Muslim commoners and hence their ineffectiveness as arbitrators to resolve communal disputes. Khan to CSCPB, 12 Nov. 1925, MAGAD, File 1-22/1926.
80. SP 280134, File 113/1924, IGP, CPB to Nelson, 16 Oct. 1924, DC Sagar to Commr. Jabalpur, 25 Oct. 1924.
81. Ibid., Gowan to Nelson, 19 Oct. 1924.
82. Ibid., Commr. Amravati to Nelson, 18 Nov. 1924.
83. That is, forcibly.
84. D.A. Smyth, the Nagpur police chief, for example, created public confidence by his very presence at places of trouble. Even Moonje would go to him as a 'pacificator', saying to him 'Here I am, Mr Smyth, at your orders. What are your orders?' Ibid., Cartie to Nelson, 22 Oct. 1924.

    After the 1927 riot in Nagpur, Gangadharrao Chitnavis urged Governor Butler to appoint Smyth as a member of a committee of prominent citizens and officers to facilitate the restoration of peace in the troubled town. Chitnavis testified to both the efficiency and impartiality of the police chief. MAGAD, File 4-17/1927.
85. SP 280134, File 113/1924, DC Seoni to Commr. Jabalpur, 19 Oct. 1924.
86. Ibid., DC Sagar to Commr. Jabalpur, 23 Oct. 1924, DC Jabalpur to Commr. Jabalpur, 22 Oct. 1924, Gowan to Nelson, 19 Oct. 1924.
87. Ibid., DC Mandla to Commr. Jabalpur, 18 Oct. 1924.
88. Ibid., DC Chhindwara to Commr. Nimar, 24 Oct. 1924.
89. MAGAD, File 4-17/1927.
90. SP 280134, File 113/1924, IGP CPB to Nelson, 16 Oct. 1924.
91. MAGAD, File 24/1932.
92. Ibid., File 4-15/1927.
93. Ibid., File 4-4/1927.

94. SP 280134, File 113/1924, Commr. Berar to Nelson, 18 Nov. 1924.
95. HP FR, 2nd half of Nov. 1931, 2nd half of Dec. 1932. See also Chapter VI.
96. SP 280134, File 113/1924, Gowan to Nelson, 19 Oct. 1924, Commr. Jabalpur to Nelson, 1 Nov. 1924. HP File 25/1924 FR, 1st half of March 1924.
97. NRC (unprinted), Letters, 1827–34, F. Wilder, Resident, to Lt. Col. Pollock, Commanding the Nagpur Auxilliary Force, 27 July 1827, Wilder to Lt. Col. Farron, 11 Dec. 1830. *NRR*, vol. II, p. 121, Jonkins, Resident, to Col. B. Close, 4 Dec. 1809.
98. Chapter III. Seth Mojilal, an MLC, referred to the 'Chief Justice of the British court [being] the President of the All India Cow Conference'. *CPLC*, Aug. 1923, p. 223.
99. SP 280132 File 18/1912, CC's note, no date.

    In 1888 the Gorakshana Sabha was set up in Nagpur. Then there were 49 branches of the *sabha* all over India. Annual sessions of the *sabha* were held in Nagpur attended by delegates from all over India. One Fakruddin Muhammad of Calcutta attended the 1895 session. Following a Hindu-Muslim fracas in 1893–4, only 25 out of 125 branches of the *sabha* survived. In 1912 there were 35 *sabhas*. In 1896 the central office of the Bharat Gorakshana Sabha was set up of which Tilak and Madan Mohan Malaviya were members. A.M. Napier, the popular DC of Raipur, started an institution for cow protection in the interest of agriculture. It urged the mahars not to sell cows to butchers nor to purchase cows from butchers, and not to act as brokers for the butchers. Vithu Sant Mahar was deeply involved in the cow protection movement. *Gao Raksha* was a monthly newspaper published from Nagpur to popularise the movement.

    In 1906, the paper urged that the Cow Protection Movement be merged into the wider Indian national movement to strengthen itself. In 1902, the organizers of the Cow Protection Movement had sent a memorial to King Edward VII for his intervention to prevent cow slaughter. Charles Crosthwaite declared the movement seditious. *RIN*, 1903, 1904, 1906. *Desha Sewak*, Nov. 1902, *RIN*, 1902.
100. *Marwari*, 9 Nov. 1910, *Subodh Sindhu*, 28 Dec. 1910, RIN, 1910. *Desha Sewak* (Nagpur), 30 Jan. 1905, *RIN*, 1905, Hardas, *Life of Moonje*, p. 188.
101. Chapter III. Khalid Bin Sayeed, *Pakistan: The Formative Years*, Lahore, 1960, p. 52. *Gao Raksha*, 7 Sept., 5 Oct. 1904, and *Desha Sewak*, 30 April 1906, 7 Sept., 5 Oct. 1904, while reporting some communal tension over Hindus playing music before mosques, urged the Muslims to desist from beef eating for the sake of communal amity and agricultural prosperity. *RIN*, 1904, 1906.

    The Muslim League session in 1919 under Hakim Ajmal Khan's presidentship, carried a resolution favouring cow protection. The Ali brothers reportedly gave up beef eating at their home 'for the sake of their Hindu countrymen'. *Young India*, 8 June 1921, Gandhi, *Communal Unity*,

p. 12. Gandhi held 'cow slaughter and man slaughter are in my opinion the two sides of the same coin'. *Young India*, 29 Jan. 1925, Ibid. p. 25. Gandhi wanted Hindus to stop playing music before mosques, and Muslims to give up cow slaughter. Ibid., p. 16, *Young India*, 5 Jan. 1928.

102. The order was passed in 1887 following a Brahmin's representation against public cow slaughter. Rejecting Muslim protests, the DC maintained the restriction on sanitary ground. SP 280121 File 1/1926, compilation from personal files of DC, Jabalpur, DC Jabalpur to Commr. Jabalpur, 17 June 1926.
103. Ibid.
104. *Karmaveer*, 17 June 1922, *Nagpur Samachar*, 27 June 1922, *Pranaveer*, 15 Aug. 1922, *Pranirakshak* (Akola), 5 Aug. 1922, *Taj*, 16 June 1922, *RIN*, 1922.
105. SP 280134, File 113/1924, Commr. Nimar to Nelson, 31 Oct. 1924.
106. Ibid., Gowan to Nelson, 19 Oct. 1924.
107. Ibid., Gowan quoting Smyth's letter to him.
108. Ibid.
109. Ibid., Cartie to Nelson, 22 Oct. 1924.
110. Ibid., Gowan to Nelson, 19 Oct. 1924.
111. Report on Police Administration of the Central Provinces and Berar, 1927.
112. SP 280134, File 113/1924, Cartie to Nelson, 22 Oct. 1924.
113. Ibid.
114. Halifax Papers, Reel no. 3899, Butler to Irwin, 26 Apr. 1926, MAGAD, File 1-22/1926. The riot was caused by the local Hindus defying a magisterial order banning music playing Ganesh processions before mosques. Hindus led by Moonje staged a satyagraha, and the army was called to avert the situation getting worse. MA HD (Police), File 75/8/1928, Police Report for 1927.
115. MAGAD, File 1-22/1926. RIN, 1925, pp. 614–15, 649–51, 671–2.
116. Berar, once ruled by the Bhonsles, was given to the Nizam by the British in 1803, at the end of the second Anglo-Maratha War. It remained under the Nizam's authority till 1903 when the British obtained the tract from the Nizam on perpetual lease. Chapter VI.
117. The Muslim delegation informed Butler that the Ganapati processions in Berar were 'imported from Puna' around 1907, and they were taken out in 'an inoffensive manner' till 1923, when Swami Shraddhanand, the Arya Samajist leader, toured through Berar, 'inculcating his own cult' and insisting that the Hindus play music before mosques. MAGAD, File 1-22/1926, Muslim representation to the Governor, 9 Nov. 1925. The *Prajapaksha*, however, claimed (22 Nov. 1925) that Ganapati processions in Berar antedated Tilak's scheme of popularising them in Maharashtra in 1893. *RIN*, July 1925 to Jan. 1926, pp. 671–2. Halifax Papers, Reel no. 3899, vol. I, R.A. Wilson, CSCPB, to Commr. Berar, 25 Mar. 1926 as enclosure to Butler to Irwin, 26 Apr. 1926. See also Ibid, Butler to Irwin, 27 June, 1927.

118. MAGAD, File 1-22/1926, Dept. Notes, see also ibid., R.V. Mahajani to Moropant Joshi, 10 Oct. 1925.
119. *Hitavada*, 10 Apr. 1924. The paper received this information from a letter written to the Editor, *Kesari* (Poona) by Taraknath Das, a Bengali revolutionary settled in Washington DC. *Kesari* published it on 6 April 1924.
120. Ibid., 12 Nov. 1925.
121. *Samalochak* corroborated it. *RIN*, July 1925 to Jan. 1926, p. 652. Later, the government was informed that the 'music question is only a cover and that the communal feeling has been deliberately brought about by the Brahmin leaders in order to forward local politics and personal animosity'. H.M. Stewart, DSP Buldana, to DC Buldana, 27 Oct. 1926, MAGAD, File 4-13/1927.
122. MAGAD File 1-22/1926, Mahajani to Joshi, 30 Sept., 10 Oct. 1925.
123. Ibid., Dept. Notes.
124. Ibid., Wilson to Commr. Berar, 25 Mar. 1926.
125. *Hitavada*, 15 Apr. 1926; *Al Haq*, 10 Apr., 30 May 1926, *RIN*, 1926, MAGAD, File 1-22/1926, S.A. Rahman, MLC, to CSCPB, 16 June, 1926. Hindu and Muslim press took opposite sides regarding the Akola Order. *RIN*, 1926, pp. 159, 167, 208, 215. Muhammad Ali described Moonje as 'the Hero of Nagpur', warning him against teasing the 'Muslim tiger'. *Karmaveer*, 31 Oct. 1926. *RIN*, 1926.
126. MAGAD, File 1-22/1926, Correspondence between DC Akola, Commr. Berar and CSCPB.
127. In the second legislative Council which met in January 1924, the Swarajists held 41 out of 54 elected and the total of 73 seats; there were 4 Independents who generally supported the Swarajists. The Swarajists rejected the budget and caused the ministry's fall. Hifazat Ali was one of the two ministers. SP 280056, File 93 of 1927.
128. Tambe's appointment divided the Swarajists, weakening their hold on the Council besides attaching a section of the party to the Government. The appointment was a sort of a coup effected by the Governor. Baker, *Changing Political Leadership*, pp. 160–1.
129. Tambe said: 'No person has a right to obstruct others when making lawful use of a public street, and customs to the contrary founded on religious intolerance should not be recognised'. MAGAD, File 1-22/1926, Tambe's Note, 14 Feb. 1926.
130. Ibid.
131. Ibid., C.G. Adam, Secy. HD (Special), Bombay, to Wilson CSCPB, 21 Apt. 1926; Nelson to H.C. Haig, Secy. HD GOI, 19 May 1926; Nelson to G.B. Lambert, CSUP, 19 May 1926. Some officers, British and Indian, wanted old executive orders and local inter-communal agreements to be enforced, while some others wanted their replacement by new orders in view of changed circumstances. MAGAD, File 24/1932.
132. Ibid.
133. Ibid., File 19/1928.

134. MAPM, File 20/1931–2, H.C. Gowan, CSCPB, to all DCs, 21 April 1931.
135. Ibid., File 133/1927. The riot was caused by the Muslims inciting the mahars to thrash local Brahmins. MA HD (Police), File 75/8/1928, Police Report for 1928, p. 3. See also HP File 32/1927 FR, 1st half of Sept. 1927; MAGAD, File 4-13/1927. Muslims generally picked on Maharashtrian Brahmins for attack. Ibid., Commr. Nagpur to Gowan, 25 Aug. 1927.
136. Respectable Muslim leaders listed by Chitnavis were M.E.R. Malak, Abdul Bari, Nawab Niazuddin Khan, Muhammad Samiullah Khan, Muhammad Yusuf Shariff, Fida Hussain, Abdul Latif Khan, Abdul Natiq, and Abdul Razak Khan. Chitnavis to Governor, 12 Sept. 1927, MAGAD, File 4-17/1927. Chitnavis urged for a ban on inflammatory speeches made from mosques, temples and political platforms, Chitnavis wanted British officers like D.A. Smyth, DSP Nagpur to be included in the committee, stressing their proven ability and impartiality. Chitnavis to Private Secy. to Governor, 12 Sept. 1927.
137. Baker, *Changing Political Leadership* p. 165. Governor Gowan praised Rao as Home Member: '. . . his attitude towards questions of public security has been unexceptional and . . . his dealings with all branches of the police have been beyond criticism'. P.N. Chopra, ed., *Towards Freedom*, New Delhi, 1985, p. 723.
138. MA Police Dept. File 6-3/1931, 6-2/1935. Halifax Papers, Reel no. 3901, Butler to Irwin, 29 July 1928.
139. MAGAD, File 24/1932. An earlier agreement made in 1919 was broken necessitating a new agreement. Ibid.
140. Ibid., Nehru to Commr. Berar, 19 May 1932.
141. MAPM Files 20/1931–2, 472/1935.
142. HP FR, 1st half of Aug. 1927.
143. Ibid., I half of Oct. 1928. *Maharashtra*, the largest circulating Marathi paper in the province, had been urging the Hindus to avoid performing tiger dance during *muharram* which only brought 'disgrace to themselves as well as to their Hindu religion'. It asked Hindus to avoid participating in Muharram altogether. *Maharashtra* (Nagpur), 30 July 1924, *RNA*, 1924.
144. V. Deshpande, 'Militant Nationalism', p. 31.
145. 'Communal strife means unity among the Hindus and suspension of the anti-Brahmin feeling which is strong in this district.' H.M. Stewart, DSP Buldana, to DC Buldana, 27 Oct. 1926. MAGAD, File 4-13/1927. Non-Brahmins wee getting tired of communal strife and even Marwaris, often targeted by the Muslims for attack, and whose business had been affected by communal disturbances, demanded Rs, 5,000 as price for supporting communal troubles incited by the Brahmin leaders. Ibid. See also HP FR, 2nd half of Feb. 1925.
146. *Swatantra Hindusthan*, 26 Dec. 1925. *Al Haq*, 11 Oct. 1925, RIN, July 1925–Jan. 1926, pp. 8, 578. HP FR, 2nd half of Dec. 1925, Muslims incited the Mahars against the Brahmins, in particular. MAGAD, File 4-13/1927.

147. HP File 18–3/1936 FR, 2nd half of Mar. 1936; File 18-5/1936 FR, 1st half of May 1936. Muhammad Zakir was the General Secretary of the *Tabligh* committee with which was closely associated Maulavi Nazir Ahmad. Ibid., File 18-2/1936, FR, 2nd half of Feb. 1936.
148. *RIN*, no. 1, 1926, p. 12. HP FR, 1st half of Jan., 2nd half of March 1929. G.A. Gavai, an important depressed class leader, became a member of the Hindu Mahasabha. He opposed Ambedkar's views on the conversion of Depressed Class Hindus to other religions. G.M. Thawre was another Depressed Class Hindu leader closely associated with the Hindu Mahasabha. At the All India Hindu Mahasabha session in Nagpur in 1938, he was the Vice-President of the Reception Committee. In 1941, he became a member of the Executive Committee of the Mahasabha. However, in 1945 he joined Ambedkar's All India Scheduled Castes Federation. M.E. Bhagat, 'Dalit Ideas and Leadership in Vidarbha' (in Marathi), Joshi, ed. *Political Ideas*, pp. 302, 307.
149. HP File 18-10/1934, FR, 2nd half of Oct. 1934; File 18-12/1933, FR, 2nd half of Dec. 1933.
150. H.V. Sheshadri, ed. *RSS: A Vision in Action*, Bangalore, 1988, p. 10. N.H. Palkar, *Dr Hedgewar* (in Marathi) Pune, 1959 p. 23. Hedgewar tried to remove both the Government's and the Congress party's misgivings about the RSS. Jamnalal Bajaj of Wardha, a close confidant of Gandhi, sent a questionnaire to Hedgewar regarding the political ideology of the RSS. Hedgewar met Bajaj and explained that the RSS was a non-political body and that anybody of any party could join it. Palkar, *Dr. Hedgewar*, p. 23.
151. In October 1931, the RSS had 60 branches in the province and 6,000 members. The Government viewed it as 'radically communal'. HP File 18-10/1931; File 18-1/1934, FR, 1st half of Jan. 1934; File 18-5/1934, FR, 2nd half of May 1934. The Government found a clear link between communal temper running high at Khamgaon, Ballarshah, Burhanpur, Warud and Narsingpur and RSS activities at all those places which had a considerable number of Muslims. Ibid. File 18-10/1934. See also Ibid., File 18-12/1933, FR, 1st half of Oct. 1933.
152. HP File 18-11/1932, FR, 2nd half of Aug. 1932; File 18-10/1934, FR, 2nd half of Oct. 1934. In Chanda, close to the Hyderabad state, the RSS was reportedly 'actively anti-Muhammadan' in its activities. Ibid.
153. Hedgewar himself, in his individual capacity, participated in the movement, breaking the forest rules at Dhamangaon in Yeotnal district. He was arrested. See also Deshpande, 'Militant Nationalism', p. 92. HP File 18-10/1932. FR, 2nd half of July 1932; File 18-7/1934, FR, 2nd half of July 1934; File 18-10/1934, FR, 2nd half of Oct. 1934.
154. HP File 88/1933, Note on RSS by the CPB government. HP File 18-12/1933, FR, 1st half of Dec. 1932; File 18-1/1933, FR, 1st half of Jan. 1933.
155. Moropant Joshi took salute at the annual camp of the RSS at Wardha in 1934 where he asserted that the RSS was a non-political body. HP 18-12/1934, FR, 1st half of Dec. 1934. For the RSS activities see also HP File

18-10/1934, FR, 2nd half of Oct. 1934; File 18-1/1933, FR, 1st half of Jan. 1933; File 18-12/1933, FR, 1st half of Oct. 1933; File 18-4/1933, FR, 2nd half of April 1933.

156. *CPLC*, vol. II, 18 Jan. to 9 March 1934, p. 709, vol. VII, pp. 188, 970. SP 280C59, File 107/1934. Hedgewar, the RSS chief, who had withdrawn himself from the Congress party, congratulated it in 1929 on its Independence resolution. Deshpande, 'Militant Nationalism', p. 90.
157. The party was led by Aney, who had left the Congress for not rejecting the Communal Award (1932). Both Moonje and Aney were 'allied in thoughts', particularly in respect of Hindu interests. Linlithgow Papers, Reel no. 2197, Heny Twynum, Governor CPB, to Linlithgow, GG, 23 Oct. 1940; Reel no. 2198, Twynum to Linlithgow, 10 June 1941.
158. HP File 18-10/1934, FR, 2nd half of Oct. 1934; File 18-11/1934, FR, 2nd half of Nov. 1934.
159. Abhyankar won the election, avenging his earlier defeat (1927) by Moonje. In the 1927 election, Moonje had freely used RSS volunteers to distrupt Abhyankar's meetings. Attacking Moonje became, 'almost an obsession with Abhyankar'. HP FR, 1st half of April 1928. However, shortly after he won the 1934 election, Abhyankar died. Then the Congress mantle fell on his close associate, Dr N.B. Khare.
160. HP File 18-7/1934, FR, 1st half of July 1934.

    Muslims began organizing themselves to fight local body elections in a big way from the end of 1934 when the RSS and the Hindu Mahasabha also became closely involved in them. In December 1934 elections to the Nagpur municipal committee, of the 165 men elected the 'Muslim party' returned 7. HP File 18-1/935, FR, 2nd half of Jan. 1935; File 18-9/1935, FR, 2nd half of Sept. 1935.

    Earlier, in the July 1934 elections to 17 municipalities and 2 Notified Area Committees, neither the Hindu Mahasabha nor the Muslim League contested. The Congress won 43 seats, while the Responsivists, of whom some later went over to the Mahasabha and some others to the Congress, won 40 seats. HP FR, 1st half of July 1934.

CHAPTER V

The Congress Ministry, 1937–1939

Communalism in the CP and Berar intensified in the two-year Congress rule, its trend and character influenced by such factors as the aggravated conflict on constitutional issues between the Congress and the Muslim League at the national level, the League propaganda against the Congress, and the stepped up activities of Hindu and Muslim communal organizations.

Elections in 1937 and the developments that followed turned communalism from an intense religious feeling into a festering political factor, with the Hindu Mahasabha and the Muslim League sniping at one another and both flinging their barbs at the Congress. Provincial Muslim leaders' insistence that they were Muslims first and Indians next served as grist to the Mahasabha's propaganda mill.[1] The Mahasabha and the RSS, both determined to defend faith with force, triggered Hindu-Muslim tension at even nondescript places which raised alarms and terrors of riots. The Mahasabha condemned the Congress for appeasing the Muslims at the cost of Hindu interests; Muslims were taken in by the League propaganda that the Congress was a Hindu communal party bent on harming the Muslims.[2]

The Government of India Act, 1935 enlarged the provincial electorate from 1.1 per cent to 12.5 per cent of the population;[3] it also increased the membership of the provincial legislature from 73 to 112, and the Muslim representation in it from 7 to 14. The Muslims, elected from reserved constituencies, would now hold 12.5 per cent of the total seats instead of 9.5 per cent as before.[4] This, however, reflected no large increase in their number in the local population,[5] but indicated the importance Muslims acquired in the government's political calculations. Governors of the province,[6] none with any love lost for the Congress, reared an anti-Congress front in provincial politics with Muslims as one of its constituents. This too had a bearing on the communal politics of the province.

The Muslims went to the polls self-divided, the division exposed most in the provincial organization of the Muslim League itself. The League so long somnolent,[7] had been reorganized by Shaukat Ali in October 1936, when a 42-member provincial parliamentary board was set up for the forthcoming election. Muhammad Yusuf Shariff, a well-known Muslim political figure and earlier a Minister, headed the revamped provincial League as well as the parliamentary board. However, Shariff filling the board with his favourites and intending to give the League tickets to them only split the party itself. Defying Shariff's leadership, Abdur Rauf Shah of Yeotmal and S.W.A. Rizvi of Raipur formed a rival board, packing it with their own men as prospective candidates for the election. This led to Jinnah's intercession and then both Shariff's and Rauf Shah's grumbling acquiescence in a pact to bury the hatchet for the sake of Muslim unity.[8] The two settled for an angry peace for a while.

However, the pact was almost immediately broken when a fuming Jinnah rushed to Nagpur and then left it in a huff, failing to compose the 'fundamental' differences between Shariff and Samiullah Khan, an ally of Rauf Shah, over who to contest the prized Nagpur-Ramtek seat as the League candidate. Jinnah refused to recognise either of the two fighting factions of the party till the elections were over.[9]

The Rauf Shah group and the Yusuf Shariff group, calling themselves, respectively, the Muslim Parliamentary Board and the Muslim League Parliamentary Board—but both fully accepting Jinnah's leaderships of the party—set up rival candidates for all the fourteen Muslim reserved constituencies. Several other Muslims also stood as Independents, drawing on the support of Raghavendra Rao, the Governor's man.[10] The Congress fielded only two Muslim candidates,[11] thereby, in effect, admitting its want of influence among the Muslims. It did not set up any Muslim candidate from any general constituency.

The presence of as many as forty-one Muslim candidates, divided into four groups,[12] fighting for fourteen seats was a clear enough pointer to their personal ambitions getting the better of the spirit of communal solidarity which Jinnah was then working hard to build up. Through the Muslim press which the Shariff group—claiming to be the real Muslim League in the province—controlled, rival Muslim candidates competed rather in mutual vituperation than clarifying their political programmes to the electorate. In Berar, particularly, the contest between the Muslim candidates was expected to be 'purely on personalities rather than on principles', based on party lines.[13].

The communal problem during the elections and after had much to do with the Congress inability to draw the Muslims to its fold; and hence the League's success in impressing on the Muslims that the Congress was a purely Hindu party. In fact, except during the Khilafat and Non-Cooperation Movements, the provincial Congress party could claim little following among the Muslims, the least so in the Marathi-speaking areas of the province.[14] Riots in the 1920s which bedevilled Hindu-Muslim relations at the mass level also affected the general Muslim attitude to the Congress party despite its denunciation of communalism of any kind.

Muslim political elite preferred supporting the pro-government groups like the Responsivists, non-Brahmins, harijans, and liberals, particularly after Raghavendra Rao rallied these groups as an anti-Congress front in the provincial politics. Muslims winning elections as Rao's partymen and getting rewarded with government favours[15] further affected whatever lingering influence the Congress still had among the Muslims. This notwithstanding some ambitious Muslims obtained Congress support to realise their personal political objectives.[16]

By the 1930s there were only a few Muslims in the provincial Congress organization such as Samiullah Khan of Nagpur and Syed Ahmad of Sohagpur. But these men had so long confined their activities mostly to municipal committees and local units of the provincial Congress party organization.[17] In municipal elections they received constant support from Hindu wards. Only a very few like Siddiqui and Masud Khan had made it to the provincial legislature as Congress Swarajists for a short while.[18]

Muslim leaders really could hope for no further political advancement as Congressmen when the Muslim League widened its mass appeal among the Muslims all over the country. The Muslim elite in the provincial Congress realized that they were the right men in the wrong party. By 1937 Samiullah Khan, Abul Hasan, Abdul Majid Leader, Tajuddin, Abdul Natiq, and Muzaffar Hussain, all old Khilafatists, and some also active participants in the Congress-led Non-Cooperation Movement and the Flag satyagraha, had gone over to the League. Some of these men held positions in the national committee of the League[19] though doing nothing to promote the party's cause at the grass roots' level; the result was that the League remained a virtual non-starter in the provincial politics till the 1937 elections.

The Congress becoming increasingly anti-government and its deepening differences with the League in national politics further affected its dwindling influence among the local Muslims, who knew that many Maharashtrian Congressmen, mostly highborn Hindus, had close links with the Hindu Mahasabha and the RSS. This the League made much of during electioneering.

As Gandhi's name worked like a 'magic' among the Hindus, making it easy for Congressmen to win elections, his image among the Muslims kept getting blighted, Jinnah's anti-Gandhi propaganda accelerating the process. Gandhi's unifying absolutism in Congress affairs appeared to the Muslims as the main reason for a change in the very character of the party. Muslim legislators made feeling references to Tilak, C.R. Das and Srinivas Iyengar, old Congress leaders[20] who had drawn Muslims to the party and who still lived in their fond memory.

Communal feelings ran high during election campaigns, particularly at Jabalpur. A serious riot broke out in the town immediately before the elections when 'intentional playing of music near mosques' by the Hindus was retaliated by 'purificatory cow slaughter' by the Muslims.[21] Provocative music playing persisted at Jabalpur at the instance of the President of the district Congress unit himself, when Muslims refused to fall in line with the party.[22] Denied of Congress tickets due to their criminal record, some history sheeters contested the election as Hindu Mahasabhites, threatening to use 'their shoes on Congress speakers'—Dwaraka Prasad Mishra and Seth Govind Das, in particular—and expose their 'immoral lives'. [23] The Mahasabha—controlled press, while praising Jawaharlal Nehru, the Congress President, for 'ridding the Congress of the influence of Gandhism' blamed the party for placating the Muslims and, in consequence, alienating the Hindus.

The Hindu press, dubbing the Muslims as 'communalists first and nationalists afterwards' lambasted Jinnah's fourteen points as being the greatest impediment to Hindu-Muslim unity.[24] Going by the propaganda campaign, the elections were expected to be a real fight between the Congress and the Mahasabha, which prompted Nehru to 'invade' the province for countering the Mahasabha propaganda.[25]

The Congress did well enough, capturing seventy of the hundred and twelve Assembly seats; but its two Muslim candidates failed dismally. The Mahasabha, contesting the Congress in all constituencies, managed to win just one seat, its anti-Congress and anti-Muslim fulminations having served no purpose whatsoever. Of the fourteen Muslim winners, five belonged to Shariff's group, six to Rauf Shah's and three Independents, of whom two promptly joined Rauf Shah's faction.[26] Shariff won the Nagpur-Ramtek seat, the voters, 70 per cent of the women—many *burqa*-free, and 60 per cent of the men, rejecting his rival Samiullah Khan till lately a Congressman and so fit to be dismissed as pro-Hindu.[27]

Politically, an uncertain interlude supervened between the end of the elections and the beginning of the Congress rule in the province. Rather surprised[28]—perhaps even sore—over the sweeping success of the Congress, the Governor, Sir Hyde Gowan, could stave off a Congress ministry for a little over three months by political manoeuvrings in which Raghavendra Rao and the Muslim MLAs were his willing accomplices. Gowan encouraged Rao to form a minority ministry with his newly formed United Independent Party of 25 MLAs, of whom almost half were Muslims, many eager to be ministers.[29] Rao, becoming Premier, picked Rizvi, his tried protege, as one of his colleagues,[30] leaving Rauf Shah fidgetty for being passed over and Shariff green with envy—particularly after his group eroded with desertions to Rizvi's ranks.[31]

Desperate, Shariff now made overtures to the Congress party, pledging it Muslim support provided he was made a Minister. His close associate, Tajuddin of Jabalpur, even thought of appealing to the Governor to secure Muslim representation in the Congress cabinet, whenever formed.[32] To Dr Narayan Bhaskar Khare,[33] the leader of the Congress party in the Assembly and the Premier in waiting, obliging Shariff appeared as a sound political investment. Besides beating Rao and Rizvi in their own game of winning over Muslim MLAs, and foiling the Governor's scheme of using the latter as political cat's paws, it would challenge the League propaganda that the Congress was a Hindu party.

Rao's minority ministry soon fell, seventy three out of a hundred and twelve MLAs passing a vote of no-confidence against it; but of the fourteen Muslim MLAs, none but Shariff and Abdul Razak Khan, an Independent, favoured Rao's ouster.[34] Khare assumed power as the Premier on 14 July 1937 and took, on Maulana Azad's prior approval,[35] Shariff in the cabinet as the new Congress Minister of Law.

For Shariff, still President of the provincial Muslim League, walking over to the 'Congress parlour' was indeed a political somersault.[36] To the Muslim community, going by the salvo of press attacks on him, deserting one party for the sake of a salaried job in another was not just political apostasy but a 'political crime'. Even the moderate *Hitavada* condemned Shariff for betraying his constituency, if not his own conscience; it urged him to contest afresh and win as a Congress candidate to justify his climb to power as a Minister. Both Jinnah and Shaukat Ali led the chorus of attack against Shariff before turning him out of the party, Jinnah rejecting his plea that some other prominent Leaguers in the country too had worked for the Congress and that the League's constitution did not ban such action. Shariff, now a Minister again, reached the zenith of his political career, though not realising it himself that he had really reached the top of a greasy poll. Curiously enough, Gandhi did not view Shariff's act as politically iniquitous; maybe he thought that the realities of the situation required some mitigation of the moral code of conduct as applied to his party. This further smudged his image among the Muslims.

II

It was not long before the Congress ministers realized the wisdom of the old adage: 'uneasy lies the head that wears the crown'. They became the butt of attacks by Muslims and all other non-Congress groups—a development which left the Governors the least unhappy. Unlike ever before, Muslim MLAs now functioned as a solid communal bloc at the urgings of the Muslim League's national leadership.

Matters concerning the local Muslims were now bloated into issues affecting the interests of the entire Muslim community in the country. Muslim MLAs played the League game of pilloring the Congress government to validate Jinnah's contention that minority Muslim interests were unsafe under majority Hindu rule, which the Congress government represented. The MLAs trotted many evidences of Muslim rights being systematically 'trampled upon' and many 'wrongs and atrocities on the minorities' committed—all inspired by the 'Gandhi Cult'. The Congress ministry was condemned for the continuing communal riots for which Muslims alone were victimized, for the declaration of the idolatrous and anti-Islamic *Vande Mataram* as the national song, for the calculated policy of discrimination against the Muslims in appointment to posts under local bodies and the government, and for the imposition of such an educational programme on the Muslims as intended to 'de-culturalize' them.

The first issue to excite the Muslims after the elections was the new Congress ministry's mass contact movement among them. It really served the provincial Congress little purpose; it rather strengthened the provincial Muslim League, now under Rauf Shah's stewardship. Syed Ahmad, the defeated Muslim Congress candidate in the election, took the initiative in enrolling Muslims into the Congress party. The Vidarbha Provincial Congress, meeting at Akola, promptly formed a committee for the purpose, its members being Abdul Wahab, Brijlal Biyani, Dr Patwardhan and Durgabai Joshi. At Nagpur, P.K. Salve, a Christian Congressman, and five Muslims formed another committee. Maulavi Abdur Rauf Khan of Mahvi in Raipur, the other defeated Congress Muslim candidate, appealed to the Muslims to join the Congress. All these attempts ended in failure; only a few prominent lawyers of Berar joined the Congress.[42]

Soon the local Leaguers stopped even this modest development. The secretariat of the Berar Muslim League issued a press statement, warning the Muslims 'against the suicidal consequences of joining the Congress' and inviting for themselves 'religious, social and cultural difficulties'; it urged the poor Muslims, in particular, to keep clear of socialist-minded Congressmen's 'sudden love' for them. Some Muslim leaders demanded that the Congress accept Jinnah's fourteen points before hoping to enrol Muslims in the party.[43]

But then, the League was not yet a strong party in the province, there being divisions in its ranks, and some leaders being even prone to 'scandalous' activities to promote their personal interests, not the party's objects. Jinnah's personal intervention in the provincial party affairs was urgently required to frustrate 'the new game of the Congress' to encourage the provincial Leaguers to take a line independent of the one dictated by the national leadership of the party.[44] The Congress mass Muslim contact movement was viewed as a challenge to the League seeking to unite all the Muslims by playing on their communal feelings.

Shariff, the Law Minister, was the principal campaigner for the Congress. Clad head to foot in 'spotless *khaddar*', instead of his accustomed suits and boots,[45] he went about places, urging the

Muslims to fight shoulder to shoulder with Congressmen for the country's freedom, and assuring them that 'the more sacrifices they make . . . the more they would be qualifying themselves for their share of rights and privileges in the country'.[46] However, Shariff's advocacy for the Congress and condemnation of the League cost one dear and served the other well. It only spread fear among the Muslim mass that 'the nationalistic revival of the Congress' meant, in fact, 'the revivalistic nationalism of the Hindu.'[47] Shariff attracted no cheers but jeers in most public meetings he addressed; black flag demonstrations greeted the 'turn coat', the 'Congress *maulavi*', as the Muslim press lampooned him. At Amravati particularly, he was in a very 'apologetic mood', while vainly trying to justify his becoming a Congressman. Iftikar Ali, the MLA from Jabalpur, once his favourite follower and now his bitterest critic, ridiculed him as a 'Congress Muslim', who was not a true Muslim at all, for he could not, unlike a true Muslim and a Leaguer, publicly declare that he was 'a Muslim first and an Indian afterwards', and that for a true Muslim, religion and politics were inseparable, the latter being subordinate to the former.[48]

After the 1937 elections and due to Jinnah's personal efforts, the Muslim League was fast transformed from virtually a moribund body into a strong political force in the country.[49] The League in the CP and Berar too swelled in membership and popularity till by the end of 1939, it could justly claim to represent almost all Muslims in the province. The League message reached even small towns and villages through newly set up local branches of the party, and due to the exertions of roving professional propagandists sent regularly by the party's national leadership. By September 1938, 23,000 members had been enrolled in the provincial League.[50]

Jinnah himself visited important places in the province in 1938 and 1939; his 'progressively unreasonable' speeches, the observation of the Palestine Day and his own birthday, besides the death anniversary of Muhammad Ali at many places, kept Muslim enthusiasm in the province in 'fever heat'. Local Muslim Leaguers undertook tours in Muslim majority provinces—NWFP, Punjab and Sindh, for example—as members of the national committees of the party which, besides enhancing their personal political image, helped them mobilize the Muslim mass for the League cause.[51]

At annual sessions of the League after 1937, the condition of the Muslims in the CP and Berar figured prominently. Rauf Shah dilated on the 'disabilities and hardships' of the Muslims of his province at the Lucknow session of the party (October 1937) where resolutions were passed regarding communal riots in the province. At the next session of the League in Patna, Rauf Shah listed the Muslim grievances regarding inadequate employment in public services, discriminations in respect of educational opportunities and restrictions on cow slaughter imposed by the Congress government.[52]

All this yielded good results for the League, besides discrediting the Congress further among the Muslims. The League not only made an impressive showing at elections to local bodies but also in winning all by-elections for Muslim seats in the Provincial Assembly,[53] defeating at places Congress Muslims in straight contests. Jinnah himself persuaded a non-Congress Muslim candidate for the Narsingpur-Sagar seat to withdraw in favour of the League candidate, thus ensuring the latter's easy victory despite hard campaigning by Pathan Red Shirt volunteers for the Congress Muslim candidate.[54] The end of the Congress rule in November 1939 also saw the virtual end of all effective opposition to the League's claim to represent the entire Muslim community of the province. Most local momin leaders, in particular, now chose rather to fall in line with the League than persist in their futile challenges to it.[55]

The Hindu Mahasabha's electoral rout rather than dispiriting it stung it to more vigorous activity. The President of the party, Vinayak Damodar Savarkar, toured the province, condemning the Congress for its pro-Muslim policy. The annual session of the party in Nagpur in December 1937 was a 'sensational success', as the Governor himself testified; 'immense crowds' watched an aeroplane scattering flowers from the sky, and RSS volunteers displaying their skills in *lathi* exercises.[56]

Savarkar called upon the Hindus to assert their right to play music before mosques and strengthen themselves by military training. To him the *Shuddhi* Movement was 'not only a cultural and religious, but a political necessity' for the Hindu population, increased by reconversion, would also increase the prospect of more Hindu voters and legislators, thus adding to the political power of the community. For him the Indian nation was 'merely the English synonym for the Hindu nation' because 'to us', he said, 'Hindus, Hindustan and India mean one and the same thing'; 'We are Indians because we are Hindus and vice-versa'.[57] In June 1939, Savarkar addressed the party's provincial conference at Jabalpur, strongly pleading for Hindu unity.[58]

Provincial Mahasabha leaders, Moonje, Dr L.V. Paranjpe, Balashastry Hardas, M.G. Chitnavis, Pachlegaonkar and J.P. Verma, set up local branches of the party and enrolled now members. They attacked the 'timid policy' of the Congress which, in emboldening the Muslims to cause communal riots, was a 'blot of cowardice and scandal on the provincial administration'. Hindu unity and militancy to counter Muslim aggressiveness was the constant refrain of the Mahasabha pronouncements as also the party's call to economically boycott the Muslims.[59] In August 1939 Chitnavis, the Mahasabha MLA, speaking at a public meeting in Nagpur congratulated the young mahar who made a bid on the Minister Shariff's life and who had been released on bail before undergoing a jail sentence.[60]

All along, the RSS was closely associated with the Mahasabha activities; its rejection of the Gandhian creed of non-violence and espousal of the 'policy of strike first' instead, was stressed by not only the ever-bellicose Moonje, but even by the old pro-government, liberal of the liberals Moropant Joshi, as well. Joshi admitted the RSS being a Hindu communal organization, but justified its activities as intended to defend Hindu interests.[61] By 1939, the RSS had about 130 branches in the province, counting among its sympathizers even high-ranking government officers, as reported by the Premier Ravi Shankar Shukla himself to the Governor.[62]

Not to be outdone, the Muslims also set up voluntary organizations like the Sirat Committee, the Muslim National Guard, the Urdu Lashkar, and the Muslim League Volunteer Corps. Trained in arms, members of these organizations all 'redolent of communalism' and some reportedly financed by the Nizam's government, added to the worry of the Congress government.[63] The provincial Muslim League used these organizations to broaden its mass base.

III

Between October 1937 and September 1939, there were eleven riots in the province, the serious ones being at Nagpur, Jabalpur, Raipur, Murtizapur, Khamgaon and Malkapur, occurring mostly during the Holi and Muharram.[64] Conversion of Hindu Backward Class men, particularly Mahars, to Islam and their reconversion to Hinduism by the Arya Samajists created tension at Wardha while the activities of the Muslim *akhadas*, the RSS cadres, and the Mahasabhites aggravated the conflict of creeds at Katni, Burhanpur, Hoshangabad, and Narsingpur. When desecretion of temples and mosques fed the fire of religious frenzy, the local Muslim press charged the police with deliberate inaction and even covert complicity in Muslim harassment by the Hindus. This received wide publicity in the Muslim press in Delhi and UP Muslim MLAs condemned police indifference when local Congress leaders accompanied music playing Hindu religious processions going by mosques in wanton disregard of both existing local conventions and government regulations against such practice.[65] The Hindu Mahasabha too condemned what it called 'communalized' administration following 'communalized politics'; it accused the Congress government of prejudice when picking on Mahasabha workers for harsh punishment.[66]

Muslim MLAs, even Congressman Shariff among them, repeatedly raised the issue of riots in the Assembly; they were sore that Shukla, the Premier, turned down their suggestion to set up either local conciliation boards or a provincial committee to enquire into the festering communal problem on the plea that the earlier Akola Order was enough for the purpose. The apparently lackadaisical disposal of the case of a riot at Jabalpur in October 1937 angered the Muslims further; the Congress government seemed more concerned over how to save the public image of the Minister, D.P. Mishra, who was involved in the case, than how to douse the communal fire.[67]

Two incidents in particular, had much to do with the Hindu-Muslim tension during the Congress rule; one, the Zafar Hussain case, and the other, the Chandur-Biswa riot; the first discredited Premier Khare, and the second, Shukla, his successor.[68] The Muslim League exploited both the incidents. Shariff, the Law Minister in Khare cabinet, ordered the release of Khan Bahadur Zafar Hussain, Inspector of Schools, Berar Circle, then undergoing sentence for the crime of raping a minor Backward Class Hindu girl at Wardha. Ignoring the fact that Shariff had not consulted him before taking the step, Khare stood by his colleague when bitterly condemned by the enraged Hindu public and then asked for an explanation by the Congress High Command. Anasuyabai Kale, a Congress woman MLA, led a mammoth procession to the Assembly demanding Shariff's immediate ouster—a demand more vociferously vented at a large public meeting in Nagpur, where Khare was humiliated by shoes and brickbats raining on him, and Shariff narrowly escaped a murder bid by an infuriated Mahar Sitaram Gaikwad.[69]

In the melee that followed 116 persons were injured, T.J. Kedar, an MLA, seeking to defend Shariff, among them.[70] The echo of the incident reverberated through places far and wide—Wasim, Mandla, Khandwa, Burhanpur, Sagar and Harsad for example, polarizing the local Hindu and Muslim public opinion in communal lines.

Unfazed, Khare prevailed over the agitated Congress MLAs to accept Shariff's apology and then tried to persuade the Congress High Command to drop the matter treating Shariff's action as but 'an error of judgement and not perversity', there being, as he said, 'nothing dishonest' in whatever he did.[72] Keen on quickly drawing a veil ever the matter, Khare, then at odds with his prickly Hindi-speaking colleagues,[73] tried even to make light of Zafar Hussain's crime by doubting his victim's innocence;[74] he also tried to downplay the mounting agitation against the issue saying that it was mostly confined to anti-Congress political groups—meaning mainly the Mahasabha detractors of his ministry.[75] However, Khare failed to save Shariff. Unconvinced by the Premier's pleadings and already uneasy over reports of Shariff having released some other Muslim criminals as well,[76] the Congress High Command ordered Shariff's dismissal after a retired High Court Judge, who went into the case, pronounced the Minister's action unjustified.[77]

The case dented Khare's public image. It also reinforced the League's propaganda that the Congress government treated the Muslim and Hindu offenders differently as exemplified in two more cases. In the Muslim girl poisoning case at Hoshangabad, the Hindu offender was promptly released by the government although the High Court had earlier turned down his appeal against conviction.[78] A similar case in Bihar involving a resourceful Hindu culprit and a hapless Muslim victim had ended in an equally prompt release of the offender under the orders of the Congress Premier of Bihar himself, despite the Patna High Court having confirmed the conviction.[79]

At Chandur-Biswa in Yeotmal district, one Jagdeo Patil, a local Congress leader, was murdered in broad day light by a Muslim mob. Premier Shukla ordered the immediate transfer of the local police chief, a Muslim, despite the Governor's 'repeated and most earnest advice'. Almost the entire Muslim male population of the place—including some fourteen year old boys—was rounded up; a heavy punitive fine was imposed on the local Muslims alone, the Governor himself considering the crime an atrocious one.[80] The sessions court sentenced six Muslims to death and twenty four Muslims to transportation for life—'savage sentences', which left the Governor shocked.[81] However, on appeal, the High Court set aside the convictions, charging the prosecuting witnesses with having told 'fantastic lies' and dismissing the police contention that the Muslims alone had caused the trouble. Justice Vivian Bose passed severe strictures on the method of police investigation preceding the arrest of the Muslim offenders.[82] The case made national news, putting the Shukla ministry in poor light besides adding some more punch to the League's attacks on the Congress party.

For the Muslims the Congress ministry's worst act was the implementation of its rural education programme. It became the rallying cry for not only the Muslims of the province but also their coreligionists all over the country. Named 'vidyamandir' and drawn up with the advice of Dr Zakir Hussain, the celebrated Gandhian educationist, the scheme aimed at providing literacy to 24,000 villages, local people donating lands for the schools and local committees, elected by adult suffrage, managing them. Besides learning the three Rs, and being trained in spinning, weaving, rope and toy making as well, pupils were to be engaged in community welfare work such as rural sanitation and agricultural development.[83]

The scheme was designed to generate a spirit of self-help and mass involvement, local people to construct the school buildings themselves and keep them going with the proceeds of agricultural farms attached to the schools. Teachers were required to take a solemn pledge to serve the schools for twenty five years with a fixed remuneration of Rs. 15 per month, their mission being village uplift besides instilling in their pupils 'a national outlook to all the activities of a village.[83a]

Through the scheme the Congress ministry was to implement the Gandhian programme of rural reconstruction, using each 'vidyamandir' as the nodal point of the activities of the medical, health, cooperative, agriculture, and veterinary departments of the government. The 'vidyamandirs' would thus function as not just rural primary schools but as 'important social centres' for the local people to discuss 'national, social as well as educational issues'; they would be the 'radiating source of light and learning in villages', serving as models for all round rural development. It was expected to be the Congress government's main instrument 'to make village life interesting and happy and relieve the people from the misery in which they are living today'.[84]

Muslim agitation against the vidyamandir scheme soon escalated into a country wide organized campaign. The arguments were that since 'mandir' represented 'a place for idol worship', no Muslim boy could study in a 'vidyamandir'; rural schools would be of little use for the Muslims, mostly a town-living people; Hindus would monopolise the managing committees of these rural schools because the minority Muslims could never be elected to the committees, contesting from general constituencies provided for the purpose.[85]

Muslims refused to do anything with the Gandhian educational programme, for it posed a threat to the very identity of the Muslims as a distinct community. Muslims viewed the programme as a device to merge them into the fold of Hindu culture. If a boy joined a school run on Gandhian ideas, he would come out of it as 'anything but a Muslim, nourished with anti-Muslim ideas, nurtured in religious sentiments and with an absolutely inferiority complex'. Abdur Rahman Khan, the League MLA, urged the Muslims to beware of 'another Macaulay trap under which Muslims would be Muslims only in name but Hindus in culture and ideology.'[86]

Muslims all over the province observed 14 September 1938 as the anti-'vidyamandir' day. Abbas Ali Kamal led a large Muslim procession to the Assembly, while a bonfire of Gandhi caps organized by Abdul Majid symbolized the swelling Muslim anger against Gandhi, now branded by Maulana Abdul Natiq, once an ardent Gandhi admirer, as the greatest enemy of the Muslims.[87] Determined to stage a satyagraha, the Muslims were virtually on a war path. Even the *Hitavada* blamed the Shukla ministry for its tactlessness in provoking the Muslims and advised it to change the 'singularly unfortunate' name of the educational scheme—'an extremely simple concession' to make to pacify the enraged community.[88]

The anti-'vidyamandir' agitation increased the Muslim League's influence in the CP and Berar; it was also made use of by the party's provincial leaders to build up their personal image. The League working committee, meeting in Karachi in October 1938, supported the agitation, deciding to send to Nagpur the party's General Secretary, Liaquat Ali Khan, to take stock of the Muslim feelings in the province. Liaquat Ali, meeting Shukla in Nagpur, wrested from him an assurance that the question of 'giving an impetus to Muslim education' would be considered at a meeting of representative Muslims with the Premier on 7-8 February 1939.[89]

But the ministry, acting on its earlier decision, launched the scheme on 26 January 1939, the Independence Day,[90] which provoked the radicals in the provincial League under Khan Bahadur Nawab Siddiqui Ali Khan, Member, Central Legislative Assembly, to launch a satyagraha and court arrest.[91] The moderate Leaguers, led by Abdur Rauf Shah and Abdur Rahman Khan, both MLAs, condemned this precipitate step and pleaded for restraint till Liaquat Ali Khan's scheduled meeting with Shukla took place on 7-8 February. In fact, the national leadership of the League also took the provincial moderate Leaguer's stand. The hawkish Siddiqui made much of the apparently mild policy of Rauf Shah, his rival in provincial League politics, who was hooted in Muslim meetings while Siddiqui's stock soared high.[92]

However, the Muslim satyagraha in Nagpur was soon called off following a settlement between Shukla and Liaquat Ali Khan who was assisted by local MLAs. Shukla agreed to a primary education scheme for the Muslims named Anjuman-ul-Ilm or Madina-ul-Ilm, providing for rural schools founded and funded by local Muslims.[93]

Even this gesture proved small relief for Shukla. By now opposition to the 'vidyamandir' scheme and Gandhi's Wardha programme of education[94] had already cut across party lines among the Muslims in the whole country. The All India Muslim Educational Conference, the Jamat-ul-Ulema Hind, the Ameer-i-Shariat, Bihar and Majlis-e-Ahrar, all had joined the League denunciation of the Congress educational scheme.[95] Even some non-Congress Hindu MLAs supported the Muslims: for example, the ousted Premier Khare, by then bearing strong grudges against Shukla, the Congress party, and Gandhi, Kedar, the Vice-Chancellor of Nagpur University and a Khare loyalist, B.G. Khaparde of the Berar Nationalist Party and later the Vice-President of the All India Hindu Mahasabha, D.D. Rajurkar, leader of the pro-government Independent Party formed by Raghavendra Rao, R.G. Ghadichore and D.K. Bhagat, MLAs representing the Backward Classes.[96]

Dismissing the 'vidyamandir' scheme as 'chimerical', Kedar scoffed at 'this banyan tree education' in which 'every man in the rural areas will come forward with a blanket on his shoulders and with a *charkha* and *takli* in his hands'. Khaparde wondered why the Congress government was determined to 'foist the scheme on the province'—the scheme in which 'the teacher will be tilling his land and the boys, instead of learning, will be picking up the weeds in his field'. Rajurkar demanded its immediate abandonment, it being 'purely a party propaganda', besides 'a waste of public time, public energy and public money': it had been 'creating chaos' all over the country due to the swelling Muslim opposition to it. He warned that the programme 'instead of spreading literacy' would 'prove to be a curse on the education of the province'. Ghadichore and Bhagat joined the Muslim and other non-Congress MLAs in voting against the motion on the scheme moved by the Education Minister.[97]

Even the 'Congressite Muslim', Shariff, though deploring that 'prejudice had gone too far against the Congress', opposed the 'vidyamandir' scheme on 'national grounds': separate denominational schools for Hindu and Muslim children would 'only foster disunity and keep us divided for all time', driving the clash of creeds even to the level of school children.[98] The Urdu press sneered at Shukla's modification of the 'vidyamandir' scheme to accommodate Muslim interests; it was condemned as 'an educational Communal Award', exposing the Congress ministry's failure to launch a common educational programme for the Hindus and Muslims.[99] Since no Muslim landowner donated any land for Muslim rural schools, the Madina-ul-Ilm scheme could not take off[100]—a fact which reinforced the League propaganda that the Congress primary education programme was really intended to benefit the Hindus alone.

IV

Although the reorganized provincial Muslim League posed no great threat to the political dominance of the Congress, it created problems for the Congress ministry by articulating and focussing the Muslim hostility to its functioning. And this hostility was made an all-India issue by the Muslim League when giving the fullest publicity to the Pirpur Committee's report.[101] The Committee went round the province in June 1938 collecting from a cross section of the local Muslims evidences of their harassment by the Congress government, and urging them to join the League.[102] Identifying the accumulated grievances of the Muslims, the Pirpur Committee concluded with convicting clarity that 'Muslims in no other province have suffered so much as in the Central Provinces and Berar'.[103]

The Committee levelled about forty charges against the Congress ministry which were fully endorsed later by another committee—Fazlul Haq Committee—which too made a similar enquiry into Muslim grievances.[104]

Economic disabilities of the Muslims under the Congress rule were as apparent as their deprivation from a just share in public employment, so ran the Muslim charge. Restrictions on the slaughter and sale of cattle 'under cover of economic and sanitary grounds' had hit hard Muslim butchers and cattle traders. Many Muslim *bidi* workers had been sacked by their Hindu employees as punishment for having voted for Muslim candidates in the recent elections. Economic boycott of poor Muslim *tangawallas* and taxi drivers had persisted as had the government's denial of financial assistance to Muslims who owned small manufacturing units. Muslims had been systematically weeded out of employment, both private and pubic, not excepting even many honorary magistrates. Muslim employees in municipalities and other local bodies had been coerced either to enrol in the Congress party or at least to leave the League.[105]

The Pirport report condemned the Wardha scheme of education. It would

> ... involve giving education a religious garb. It will clearly imply the welding of two nations into one synthetic culture by means of a system of primary education and will only facilitate the conversion of the youth to the ideals of the Congress.[106]

Promotion of Nagari at the cost of Urdu, compelling Muslim pupils to worship Gandhi's portraits and statues in schools and to sing *Vande Mataram* were cited as glaring examples of the Congress attempt to 'systematically force Hindu culture and religion on the Muslims'. The Muslim League had already been condemning the Congress for 'foisting *Vande Mataram*' as the national anthem upon the country. They found the song to be, 'not only positively anti-Islamic and idolatrous in its inspiration and ideas but definitely subversive of the growth of genuine nationalism'.[107]

Its religious import was 'directed against the Muslims alone'. Muslim MLAs decided to walk out whenever the song was sung.[108]

Hindu ruffians attacking Muslim religious processions and desecrating Muslim holy places at will were attributed to not just police inactivity but police complicity. Action against some Urdu papers and Muslim public men on charge of fanning communalism clearly indicated the anti-Muslim bias of the Congress administration. The bias was clearer still in the progressive diminution of Muslim representation on local bodies, leaving the Muslims with no means to get their grievances redressed.[109]

This anti-Muslim bias in the administration was attributed by the Pirpur Committee to 'something like an identity of purpose between the Congress and the Hindu Mahasabha'; the Congress government was really the Mahasabha rule by proxy, Gandhi's *Ramrajya* being also the idealized *Hindurajya* of the Mahasabha.[110] The persisting connexion of some Maharashtrian Congressmen with the Mahasabha and the RSS despite the Congress party's official ban on such connexion was held out by the League MLAs as a vindication of their contention—'Scratch a Congressman and you will find him a Hindu Mahasabhite'.[111]

Provincial Congressmen themselves gave their League detractors a handle to brand them as communal-minded. Ignoring the fact that the Hindu Mahasabha had bitterly fought the Congress in the recent and earlier elections,[112] and had been constantly dubbing it as pro-Muslim and anti-Hindu, Khare, when Premier, had himself attended the civic reception of Savarkar, garlanding him.[113] He received accolades from both Moonje and Savarkar when setting up the first rifle club at Wardha,[114] thereby suggesting his adherence to the Mahasabha's ideal of militarization of the Hindus. Khare's colleague, Ramrao Deshmukh, the Public Works Department Minister, had sat through Savarkar's anti-Muslim tirades in a public meeting.[115] Vice-Chancellor Kedar, close to Khare, had conferred on Savarkar a D. Litt. (Honoris Causa) degree.[116]

Khare, on his own admission, and in common with most high caste Maharashtrians of the time, cherished an abiding admiration for the RSS although its involvement in communal riots was indeed common knowledge.

The RSS chief, Hedgewar, and a prominent leader, Dr Paranjpe, were his close associates in the Congress movement itself; the latter contesting him in the 1937 elections for the Nagpur seat in the Assembly did not affect their friendship nor did the RSS and the Mahasabha pulling together against the Congress in the elections worry him.[117]

Khare was close to many Responsivists, many of whom later turned Hindu Mahasabhites. He also had opposed the Communal Award when the Congress had officially adopted an ambivalent attitude towards it. Khare had brought into the provincial legislature a number of Responsivists-like Kedar, for example, who always opposed the Congress.[118] Involved like most high born Maharashtrians of the time in the Hindu unity movement, though not avowedly anti-Muslim in attitude,[119] Khare, after his ouster from the Congress party, became the President of the Hindu Mahasabha in 1949,[120] and then turned not only a bitter critic of the Muslim League but a zealous activist for the Hindu cause.

Not unnaturally, therefore, did the Pirpur Committee charge the Congress ministry with softness towards Mahasabha propagandists. The Congress government provided funds to the Hanuman Akhada in Amravati which the Muslims knew to have been the 'training ground for the Mahasabha',[121] and which the British government had kept a watch on, suspecting it to be a communal outfit.[122] Sarat Chandra Bose, brother of the then Congress President, Subhas Chandra Bose and Jawaharlal Nehru, the immediate past President of the Congress, attended a conference at Amravati where an impressive arch named after Savarkar had been put up.[123] This to the Muslims was the clinching proof of the 'complete identification between the so-called communal organisation of the Mahasabha and the oft-claimed "national institution" of the Congress'.[124]

However, most of the Muslim charges against the Congress ministry and particularly those levelled in the Pirpur and Fazlul Haq's reports, were rather the Muslim League's propaganda ploy than based on actual facts.[125] Neither official papers of the time nor private correspondence of policy makers then, including that of the Governor, Sir Francis Wylie, supported the allegations. The Shukla ministry's press communique was an effective refutation of all the charges, while Wylie regarded them as rather tendentious.[126]

The Congress ministry's press statement made it clear that Muslim representation in local bodies had not been reduced but remained mostly as before, the new government adhering to the established policy of nomination of Muslims also. The regulations restricting the slaughter of animals antedated the assumption of power by the Congress party, and so the new ministry could not be faulted for the resultant difficulties suffered by Muslim butchers.[127]

The Shukla ministry had really not been soft towards the Hindu Mahasabha and the RSS as borne out by Wylie's report to the Viceroy, Lord Linlithgow. The Mahasabha-controlled press and the party's activists like J.P. Verma had indeed been punished by fines and jail sentences; besides, when Shukla, sharing other Gandhians' suspicion that the 'RSS and such secret societies' were 'likely to support Bose' (who had fallen out with Gandhi and other top leaders of the Congress), thought of banning the RSS the Governor welcomed it as being 'a knock on Bose'.[128] Shukla was up against the Khaksars too, and the Governor, knowing it to be a communal organization and bitterly anti-League, did not object.[129]

In fact, the persistence of communal troubles during the Congress rule was not because of any want of administrative measures to prevent their recurrence, but inspite of them. The government's home department had scrupulously followed the rule book in maintaining law and order: it had been closely monitoring the activities of all communal organizations and political propagandists; the police had made minute reporting of all speeches from public platforms; the press, both Hindu and Muslim, had been subjected to strict restrictions; a blanket ban had also been imposed on slogan shouting near any place of worship besides sharp vigilance maintained on such places to prevent their misuse as armouries; strong warnings had been given against any government employee showing communal bias while discharging official duties.

The government had stated that it would not allow any 'innovations in the celebrations of festivals', such as taking out processions wherever they had not been 'the established feature of a festival'. No carrying of *lathis* nor playing of music was allowed if they were 'contrary to custom'; the police rounded up anti-social men as a preemptive measure against riots and clamped punitive fines on trouble mongers.[130] The Shukla government also released from jails some Muslims involved in riots at Jabalpur 'as a further sop to the Muslim community'.[131] Moreover, Khare, when Premier, had indeed scored a point over the Muslim MLAs by pointing out that communal riots had also occurred in Bengal and the Punjab, then not ruled by the Congress party.[132]

The Shukla ministry's press communiqué disproved the Pirpur Committee's allegation that the Congress was biased against Muslim education. The number of Urdu schools in the province, their distribution in the Urdu speaking tracts, and official provision for their maintenance and inspection proved the allegation wrong. The government disclaimed any intention to force the Muslim pupils to sing *Vande Mataram*; it ordered an enquiry into the reported case of Muslim pupils having been compelled to worship an image of Gandhi in a school at Chandur.[133]

Ironically enough, knowing well the Muslim abhorrence for *Vande Mataram*, Governor Gowan invariably stood up along with others when it was sung on public occasions,[134] thus, in effect, recognizing it as the national song. Besides, it was common knowledge that between 1905 and 1920, the song had been sung in innumerable meetings, many attended by Jinnah and other Muslim leaders, all Leaguers now,[135] and none ever protesting then.

That the Muslims reaped no benefit from the Congress rural educational programme was due more to their prejudice against it than to any Congress design. The Muslims were free to donate lands for their schools as the Hindus were for their 'vidyamandirs'; they could name their schools *bait-ul-Ilm* or whatever suited the purpose besides getting their wards instructed in either Urdu or Nagari, the teachers having been trained in both the languages.[136] Yet the Muslims had taken no advantage of the scheme, no land having been given by Muslim landowners for Muslim schools in rural areas.

Interestingly enough, this worst misdeed of the Congress ministry, as alleged by the Muslim leaders, received fulsome praise from contemporary British authorities as its best achievement. Reginald Coupland, no friend of the Congress, hailed the Congress rural educational programme as 'the most enlightened and encouraging feature of the new regime'. He regretted the Muslim attack on this 'great educational programme' as being 'somewhat ironical'.[137] Even Wylie had a 'sneaking liking for it', although he knew that it would 'certainly fail' due to Muslim opposition.[138] Sir John Sergeant, Educational Commissioner of the Government of India, had great admiration for Gandhi's Wardha Educational Scheme, while the Jamia Millia Islamia, the most important Muslim nationalist educational institution in India, was all in its favour.[139] Sir Hugh Bomford, Acting Governor of the province, wondered why the local Muslims, who were fluent in Hindi, made a fetish of education in Urdu for their children, when their coreligionists in the UP preferred Hindi primary schools to Urdu schools although the latter were many in number.[140]

When the Congress rule in the province was about to be over, a bill confirming and regulating the vidya mandir scheme was introduced in the Assembly by the Education Minister. Every Muslim MLA present and some of their Hindu colleagues, Khare including, opposed it.[141] But after the Congress rule ended, Governor Wylie kept the scheme going. In 1939 there were in the province 93 'vidyamandirs' with 2,469 pupils in them; in 1940, when the Governor ruled the province, the number of schools had fallen to 62, but the student enrolment in them had risen to 2,786; the cost of running the schools then was Rs. 62,000 per year, while the annual income from the farms attached to them was Rs. 51,200 only. The government thought it fit to meet the deficit,[142] no doubt seeing the merit of the programme initiated by the Congress ministry.

V

The British Governor's antipathy towards the Congress party, as reflected in their uneasy relations with Congress ministers, provided another dimension to the communal problem. Gowan first used the Muslims, the Muslim MLAs in particular, to prevent the Congress candidates from winning the election easily, and then from assuming power as the majority party in the Assembly, and, finally, to create difficulties in the Congress ministry's functioning smoothly. G.A. Khan, the Muslim Commissioner of Nagpur, kept the Governor posted with Congress activities during the elections,[143] while Raghavendra Rao used his Muslim connection to help the Governor against the Congress. With the Muslims in the Assembly, Gowan built up an anti-Congress bloc which he wished to be strong; he took an active interest in the Muslim constituencies which he wanted the Rao loyalists to win.

But it was Wylie, Gowan's successor, who bore the strongest prejudice against the Congress ministers, whom he dismissed as 'perhaps the poorest lot in all India'. To him, they were a bunch of 'deep-dyed' communalists whose administrative incompetence was matched by proneness to nepotism and corruption besides intriguing proclivities. They were men 'of very ordinary status and extremely limited attainments'; unable to look beyond their noses, they suffered from an acute inferiority complex while dealing, particularly, with senior officers.[144]

There could indeed be no easy solution to the communal problem when the Governor and his ministers held conflicting views on its character, causes, and responsibility and on the measures to tackle it. The 1935 constitution no doubt gave the elected ministers the responsibility for governance but it also left the Governors with the ultimate authority to determine both the scale and scope of ministerial responsibility for the administration. This became apparent in the context of tackling the communal problem.

To Wylie the ministers appeared eager to exculpate Hindu offenders from criminal cases and implicate the Muslim suspects in them. Shukla would rather remain inactive during communal riots than give up, under the Governor's pressure, his tendency to blame the Muslims alone for them; he would let riot cases in the court linger when unable to prosecute only the Muslims as guilty. Wylie had strong grounds to doubt if the Shukla ministry was sincere in solving the communal problem for the Premier and his colleagues harboured a strong anti-Muslim bias.

Wylie knew the Ministers, Shukla above all, being prone to discriminate against Muslim officers deserving promotion in service and to punish apparently erring Muslim police officers before official enquiries established either their deliberate lukewarmness in dealing with riots or their complicity in the aggravation of the troubles.[145]

D.P. Mishra's insistence on the transfer of Niaz Ahmad Khan, a police officer at Jabalpur, created a cabinet crisis of sorts when Premier Khare threatened rather to resign than succumb to Mishra's pressure to do an act which he held as both unfair and unjustified.[146] His colleagues grumbling, Khare confirmed Imam-ur-Rahim, the only Muslim ICS officer then in the province.[147] Wylie also knew that Khare opposed his colleagues' wish to punish Muslims merely on suspicion, besides their vindictiveness towards Muslim officers in general. Seeking to reburfish the Congress image among the Muslims, Khare advised his colleagues to function in such a manner as to win back the trust and confidence of the minority community.[148]

Wylie had some other evidences of the anti-Muslim bias of Shukla and his colleagues. Though indisposed, Shukla had rushed to Chandur-Biswa—a place not easy to reach—to attend the funeral of Jagdeo Patil, the slain local Congress leader, when the matter was sub-judice; he had insisted on the penal transfer of the local police officer, a Muslim, against whom he bore an earlier grudge.[149] D.S. Mehta, the Law Minister, took an 'intimate interest' in the Hoshangabad Panwala case because the offender was a Hindu and the victim a Muslim woman. The Minister had no word to condemn the murder attempt on Shariff, a fellow Congressman and his own predecessor; rather he compared Sitaram Gaekwad, the culprit, 'with some of the great heroes of history who had defended the honour of their womankind', as Wylie sarcastically reported to Linlithgow.[150]

Wylie attributed the government's inability to tackle the communal problem to the 'blatant attempts' at ministerial interference with the routine work of executive and police officers, and consequently the latter's inability—at times even unwillingness—to exercise their accustomed discretionary powers to deal with the law and order problem. The Ministers relied more on local Congressman's reports than local officers' assessment of the problem. Shukla was known to have had his favourites in the police service to implicitly rely on; this demoralised others in the service.[151]

Holding Shukla responsible for the nagging communal problem, Wylie often threatened to exercise his own special powers for the purpose;[152] he also kept up his private communication with local British officers.[153] Wylie was a determined defender of Muslim interests if ever threatened by what he suspected as his ministers' prejudice against the community.[154]

All this, besides exposing the Governor's want of confidence in his ministry, militated against the tradition which the new constitution was supposed to set: popularly elected ministers' responsibility for good governance of the province. Wylie rejected Shukla's recommendation that the Goonda Act be rigorously enforced to round up all trouble makers, actual and potential; he also rejected as 'disingenuous' the ministerial suggestion that a law be passed to prevent the use of mosques as platforms for incendiary communal speeches and as places for the storage of arms during riots.[155]

The ministers on their part were fully aware of the Governor's prejudice against them and the Congress party, and his softness for the Muslims—and this when the divergence between the League's and the Congress' attitude towards Indian politics had sharpened in the context of the growing convergence of the League's and the British government's approach towards it. This was focussed best in the Hyderabad Satyagraha in 1938–9.

The Satyagraha was launched by the Arya Samjists as a protest against the persecution of the Hindus by the Nizam's government. Forcible conversion of Hindus to Islam, imposition of Urdu on Hindu students and neglect of Hindu shrines in the state were evidences of what the Arya Samajists condemned as the Nizam's anti-Hindu policy. Hindus of the CP and Berar were agitated over tales of atrocities on their coreligionists which figured prominently in the fiery speeches of the Hindu Mahasabha activists who made common cause with the Arya Samajists. The Mahasabha's strong support of the movement was aimed at extending its influence when the Congress was yet to come out openly in defence of the Hindus suffering in a Muslim state.

At the annual session of the Mahasabha in Nagpur in October 1938, resolutions were passed supporting the satyagraha, followed by a 'formal declaration of war' against the Hyderabad state. Khare, then keen on settling scores with Shukla, condemned the Congress ministry's inaction regarding the satyagraha, ignoring some Congressmen's plea against such open condemnation. He contributed to the fund raised in the Mahasabha meeting for the satyagraha and congratulated Dr Paranjpe, his old friend and Mahasabha leader, on leading the first batch of satyagrahis to Hyderabad.[156] Vice-Chancellor Kedar, thrown out from the Congress like Khare, admitted to Nagpur colleges about two hundred Hindu students, earlier expelled from the Osmania University for singing *Vande Mataram*.[157]

Wylie wondered if the general public opinion strongly favouring the Mahasabha stand on the satyagraha would soon force the Congress ministry to openly come out in support of the Hindu cause.[158] The RSS did not plunge headlong into the movement, but its members were free to be involved in it in their individual capacity.[159] The Berar-Hyderabad border became sensitive with batches of satyagrahis from all across the country about to march into Hyderabad and the Nizam's troops, besides local Muslims, massed on the border to oppose the march.[160]

The satyagraha exacerbated communal feelings in the province when, at the instances of the Mahasabha, Hyderabad Day was observed widely. Muslims of Akola brought out processions at night opposing the Satyagraha while the local Arya Samajists organized *prabhat pheris* in its support. A branch office of the Hyderabad State Congress was set up in Nagpur under A.G. Deshpande, a Mahasabha leader of Aurangabad, followed by a Hyderabad Satyagraha Committee to despatch batches of satyagrahis to Hyderabad. All the more worked up now, Muslims under Samiullah Khan urged the Governor for his intervention to stop the Arya Samaj volunteers from crossing the Berar border.[161]

All this put the Congress ministry into a difficult situation. It could neither openly support the satyagraha, in the face of the Governor's stern warnings nor, in deference to the Governor's wish, prevent the Arya Samajists from crowding on the border, thereby giving a handle to the Mahasabhaites to further damage the Congress image among the Hindus in general.

The Governor firmly believed that all his ministers were in

sympathy with the Hindu sufferers in Hyderabad;[162] the Hindu grievances were indeed genuine as the Governor admitted himself. Many Hindu shrines in Hyderabad had really been in ruins due to official indifference and Urdu had in fact been imposed on Hindu students.[163] Wylie admitted being unable to blame the Hindus of Hyderabad for their grouses against the Muslim Nizam's government when he could take no exception to the Muslims of the CP and Berar protesting against the Hindu Congress rule. He was certain that restrictions on the Hindu religion in Hyderabad were 'undoubtedly actuated by communal considerations'.[164]

Meanwhile, the Shukla ministry had decided to move the Crown's representative in Hyderabad, laying before him the Hindu grievances and adding a warning that a civil war might soon break out in the state if the grievances were left unredressed any longer. While disclaiming any support to the Hindu Mahasabha agitations in Hyderabad as being politically motivated, the ministry expressed its full sympathy for the Arya Samajists' resolve to protect and preserve the religious and cultural interests of the majority Hindus in Hyderabad, which the Nizam was allegedly bent on converting 'into a Muslim state per excellence'.[165]

Mishra, the Home Minister, appealed to the British government to uphold 'its reputation as a civilized government' by preventing the 'recrudescence of medievalism' in the premier Indian state.[166] The Speaker of the Provincial Assembly, Ghanashyam Gupta, who was also the President of the All India Aryan League and an ardent Arya Samajist, discussed the Hyderabad issue with the Governor before deciding to meet the Viceroy himself. However, the meeting did not come off, Wylie having succeeded in scuttling it.[167]

The Governor wanted no escalation of the communal problem in the Nizam's state caused by the defenders of Hindu interests in the CP and Berar. With the war clouds gathering on the European sky and the political situation in India worsening, the Nizam's friendliness was of great importance to the British Indian government. Suspecting the Congress ministry's deliberate remissness in tackling the tension on the Berar border, Wylie privately asked local British officers to take all measures necessary to ease the tension.[168] Meanwhile he kept up his pressure on the ministry to somehow defuse the situation, which as he reputedly told Shukla, had intensified Hindu-Muslim ill-feelings in the province at large.[169] The Muslim League's declared opposition to the Hyderabad Satyagraha and Linlithgow's policy to keep on well with the Muslim League at the time weighed heavily on the Governor's mind.[170]

VI

The Congress took the League allegations against its ministries seriously. Muslims all over India had indeed been impressed by the League propaganda; as a result, the Congress stock among the Muslims had been further affected. The Congress therefore suggested that the Muslim League charges be enquired into by Sir Maurice Gwyer, the Chief Justice of the Federal Court; Jinnah did not accept the challenge.[171]

Linlithgow, then at odds with the Congress, and intent on keeping Jinnah in good humour, privately asked the Governors of all Congress-ruled provinces to report on local Muslim grievances. In their reports no Governor indicted the Congress Ministers for patent Muslim baiting, least of all Wylie. Rather, Wylie's report clearly established the baselessness of the Muslim charges.[172]

The Governor knew that with Hindu ministers in power, Muslims of the province needed to 'walk very warily these days', but he also knew that the Muslim fear was rather overplayed and a make believe. Wylie found little substance in the Muslim charge that officers with 'Mahasabha leanings', who allegedly had done grave injustice to the Muslims, had been rewarded with out of turn promotions. There was no substance either in another Muslim charge that it were the Hindus who always started communal riots but more Muslims were jailed than Hindus because investigations into riots were invariably one-sided.[173]

Wylie knew Shukla having an 'undoubted tendency to promote Hindu culture'; in the education department, particularly, the Governor marked 'a definite tendency to favour Hindu language and culture'. Wylie even doubted Shukla's sincerity in implementing his agreement with Liaquat Ali Khan about Muslim education in rural areas; the Governor was also sore that despite his 'secret' advice, Shukla did not appoint a Muslim to any high position in the education department. Wylie claimed to have even warned Shukla about the swelling Muslim resentment over 'subtle attempts to impose a Hindu culture' on them—by providing for spinning in the school curriculum, for example. In regard to the 'vidyamandir' scheme, the Governor, anticipating certain Muslim opposition to it, had advised Shukla to go slow, though vainly. The Governor viewed the pro-Congress propaganda in the province having a 'strongly pro-Hindu flavour'.[174]

Still, Wylie saw no real threat of any palpable damage to Muslim cultural interests, for the community was wide awake to effectively defend them. He also knew that the Muslims had been using the vidya mandir scheme, in particular, as only 'a colourable pretext' and as 'the necessary peg' to hang their agitation against the Congress ministry.[175] In fact, in respect of cultural matters, the Muslims seemed to be rather over-reactive; they cried aloud before receiving 'any real hurt'. Besides, if Urdu could be pushed in Hyderabad, where the population was eighty per cent Hindu, Wylie wondered why the Congress government in the overwhelmingly Hindu province of the CP and Berar be blamed if it was 'manifestly out for the same game only the other way round'[176]—promoting Hindi and neglecting Urdu, the language of a 'minute percentage' of the local population.[177]

Unlike elsewhere, in the CP and Berar there was no need for the Governor's intervention to secure for the Muslims adequate government jobs. Numbering less than 4 per cent, Muslims in the province held some 22 per cent of the jobs.[178] There was no cause for suspicion either that 'Congress-minded' Muslims were being preferred for public employment, although it was well known that Mishra, the local self government Minister, favoured such Muslims as nominated members on such bodies.[179]

It is true that Shukla had no Muslim in his cabinet despite the Governor's pleadings on behalf of the community and his own admission that 'he would be better off with a Muslim Minister'. But the Premier could hardly go against the decision of Gandhi and Vallabhbhai Patel that a Muslim needed to be a Congressman before being taken into a Congress ministry[180]—and at that time Shariff's plight still worked as deterrent to any Muslim MLA repeating his political misadventure. Shariff had really been penny-wise and pound-foolish; he had won for a while a ministership but lost for good the trust of his own community.

Above all, Wylie himself held but a very poor opinion of the CP Muslims—'a very degraded set', who had no leader 'with either intelligence or influence'; worse were the Berar Muslims, 'a pathetic class', a 'dissipated' lot, ever dazzled by the remembered glories of their great ancestors, and 'permanently depressed in consequence'.

As for the Muslim MLAs, they were men of the 'cheapest sort', having no appreciation of all-India issues and being 'only concerned with communal squabbles interlarded with sordid intrigues for their own individual advantage.'[181]

This held good for Shariff as well, a Cambridge graduate and by now a veteran in provincial politics and twice a Minister. R.N. Banerjee, the Governor's Secretary, in a confidential dossier on provincial politicians described Shariff as a man of 'mediocre ability', having but 'a small practice at the bar'. He did much to promote the cause of his own community, appointing, when a Minister, a 'disproportionate number' of Muslims as Assistant Public Prosecutors without sufficient justification. He showed 'clemency rather liberally to Muslims', even acting in some cases as the counsel of the accused people and inviting, in consequence Governor Gowan's reprimands. Yet, while the Muslims kept disliking him as a turncoat, Congressmen suspected him as being communal minded.[182]

Taking all this into account, Wylie's considered opinion was that under the Congress rule, the Muslims may have suffered only some 'pinpricks', no 'really serious injustice'. For the 'quite baseless allegations' against the Congress ministry set out in the Pirport report, the Governor could find only one explanation: Muslim fear of 'perpetual domination' by the Hindus, resulting in their total exclusion from 'the control of affairs'. This fear, caused by the progressive Indianization of the administration, had been confirmed by the total Congress ascendancy in provincial politics after the 1937 elections.

The Governor sympathized with the fears of the Muslims but could see no way to mollify them. All that he could assure them of was his own firm belief that the Congress could not be 'too openly and blatantly communal' any more than the ministers could inflict any wanton injustice on the Muslims in the face of the British authorities' determination to stand by them. In fact, in course of their brief rule, the Congress Ministers had experienced well enough that Muslim interests being the British governor's growing concern, their protection was also his special responsibility.

Viceroy Linlithgow was convinced; there was really no 'positive evidence of real oppression' of the Muslims in any Congress-ruled province. To Leopold Amery, the Secretary of State for India, the Viceroy confided: 'I never took these complaints seriously, and I should be surprised if they did not prove to be psychological in character.'

Even the *Hitavada*, which often correctly projected the Muslim point of view, besides representing the moderate and balanced public opinion of the time, dismissed the Muslim allegations as 'imaginary grievances', while blaming the League for 'trying to manufacture an agitation out of a vacuum'. It found the Shukla government 'actuated by no communal virus against the Muslims' while advising it to be watchful towards some local bodies where Hindu communal intolerance had indeed shown up in respect of such 'trivial matters' as 'unnecessary insistence' on the worship of Gandhi in schools managed by these bodies.

Years later, Wylie had this to say: 'the accusations of gross anti-Muslim bias on the part of Congress ministers were, of course, moonshine'.[187] This clinching verdict was given in a spirit of detachment and reflection facilitated by great distance in both space and time. The remark was made at a seminar in London in 1968—thirty years after Wylie had ceased to be an eye-witness to, and involved in, whatever, good or bad, the first Congress ministry had done in the CP and Berar.

NOTES

1. *CPLA*, 4 Nov. 1939, p. 227; 7 Nov. 1939, pp. 282, 357, 393; 8 Nov. 1939, p. 459.
2. Earlier, Jinnah had written a letter to the *Times of India* (Bombay), 3 Oct. 1925 saying that he did not regard the Congress as a 'Hindu institution', cited in Ambedkar, *Pakistan or Partition of India*, pp. 312–13.
3. See Chapter III. B.R. Tomlinson, *Indian National Congress and the Raj, 1929–1942: The Penultimate Phase*, London, 1976, p. 173.
4. Gwyer and Appadorai, *Speeches and Documents*, pp. 128, 261–2.

   The GOI Act, 1935 provided for 15 seats for the CP and Berar in the lower house of the Federal legislature of which 3 were Muslim reserved seats. In the upper house, the provision was for 8 seats with 1 reserved for the Muslims. Ambedkar, *Pakistan or Partition*, p. 446.
5. The Muslim population was 3.5 per cent, 3.64 per cent and 3.92 per cent of the total population of the province, according to the 1911, 1921 and 1931 census, respectively.
6. During the Congress rule (1937–9), the Governors were Sir Hyde Gowan (1933–7), Sir Rugh Bamford (Acting) and Sir Francis Wylie (1938–40).
7. For the provincial League before 1937, see Chapter III.
8. HP File 18 Oct. 1936, FR, 2nd half of Oct. 1936; File 18 Dec. 1936, FR,

2nd half of Dec. 1936. *Hitavada*, 6 Jan. 1937. N.N. Mitra, *Indian Annual Register, 1936*, vol. II, Calcutta, 1936, pp. 273–4.

9. *Hitavada*, 12 Feb. 1937. Samiullah Khan had earlier strongly opposed Shaukat Ali's reorganising the provincial Muslim League. Along with about seventy five other Muslims, he had walked out of Muslim Political Conference which Shaukat Ali addressed in Nagpur in October 1936. When Yusuf Shariff was declared President of the reformed Provincial Muslim League, Samiullah joined Rauf Shah and became the Vice-President of the latter's board, rivalling the board of Sharif. Ibid.

   Samiullah Khan was earlier the Secretary of the Provincial Khilafat Committee and a Swarajist. In 1952–6, he was a member of the Rajya Sabha, He died in 1967.
10. HP File 18 Dec. 1936, FR, 1st half of Dec. 1936, *Hitavada*, 3 Feb. 1937.
11. Syed Ahmad of Sohagpur and Maulavi Abdur Rauf Khan of Mahvi in Raipur. Rauf Khan later joined the Congress Socialist Party.
12. The original Muslim League Board under Shariff, the rival Board under Rauf Shah. The Muslim Independents loyal to Rao and Congress Muslims. HP File 20/1936.
13. The papers were the *Muslim League Gazette, Mahvi, Al Burhan* and *Al Faruq*. *Hitavada*, 31 Jan. 1937. SP 280061, File 69/1937. Maharashtra Archives (Vidarbha) Elections Dept. File 36/1935–37: DCS Yeotmal and Akola to Commr. Berar, 29 Apr. 1936.
14. D.E.U. Baker, 'Foundations of Congress Raj in the Central Provinces and Berar, 1919–1937', Jai Prakash Mishra, ed., *Researches in Social Sciences (Professor Amreashwar Avasthi Felicitation Volume)*, Delhi, 1993, pp. 305–6, 315–16.
15. See Chapter III.
16. For example, Nawab Siddiqui Ali Khan won the election to the Central Legislative Assembly in 1934 with the local Congress party supporting him. He continued to be a member of the Assembly till 1947. A confidant of Jinnah, he later turned into the bitterest opponent of the Congress in the provincial politics and led the radical Muslim League leaders against their moderate colleagues in the party. He wrote his autobiography, *Be Tegh Sipahi* (in Urdu), Karachi, 1971.
17. In 1929 Akbar Ali Ahmad Ali was a member of the Katol Taluka Congress Committee and Karan Ali Bhambabhai was on the Nagpur District Congress Committee. Samiullah Khan was also on this committee for several years. In 1926, Moonje, the Responsivist leader, contesting Abhyankar, the Congressman, for a seat in the central Assembly, made attempts at winning over Muslims; his associate, Dr. Cholkar, achieved a measure of success in the attempt. D.P. Mishra, *Living an Era*, p. 95.
18. For Muslim Swarajists see Chapter III. Abid Ali Siraj of Wardha was a delegate to the Congress session at Gaya in 1923. HP File 7/1923.
19. Tajuddin of Jabalpur was a member of the League committee to work out the Congress-League scheme finalized at Lucknow in 1916. Pirzada, *Foundations of Pakistan*, vol. I, p. 410. Syed Abdur Rauf Shah of Yeotmal,

the permanent President of the provincial League after 1937 was earlier a member of the League committee to formulate the Muslim demand for their adequate representation on all elective bodies and in public services. Sheikh Abdul Qadir and Muhammad Yusuf Shariff were members of the League committee to frame a scheme of constitutional advance for presentation to the Indian Statutory Commission. Anisuddin Ahmad, Muhammad Abdul Qadir, Maulana Abdul Natiq, Muhammad Yasin, and Ghulam Mohinuddin were appointed members of a provincial committee set up by the League for the same purpose. Khan Bahadur Wilayatullah was elected a Vice President of the Muslim League at its 23rd session (Nov. 1933). Jinnah asked him and Yusuf Shariff to reorganize the party in the province. Ibid., vol. II, pp. 28, 71, 103, 228, 232. Samiullah Khan was a member of the Muslim Activities Committee set up by the League in its annual session at Lahore in May 1924.

H.N. Mitra, ed., *Indian Quarterly Register, April–June 1924*, p. 663.

In the 40-member Central Committee of the Muslim League representing different provinces and regions, Berar, Central India and Ajmer together sent two members. Pirzada, Ibid., p. 29.

20. *CPLA*, 6 Nov. 1939, p. 280.
21. P.N. Chopra, ed. *Towards Freedom*, New Delhi, 1985, p. 515, quoting from Linlithgow Collections.
22. HP File 18 Apr. 1937, FR, 2nd half of April 1937.
23. SP 280121, pp. 30, 33, Notes from personal files of DCs: W. Grigson, DC Jabalpur, to Hyde Gowan, Governor, 1 Nov. and 1 Dec. 1936. In a private letter to Lord Linlithgow, the Viceroy, Gowan wrote: 'Both Govind Das and Mishra have so long combined sexual aberration with successful careers in politics that unless either goes to jail, the interruption would only be temporary'. Letter, 6 July 1937, cited in Chopra, *Towards Freedom*, p. 723. Govind Das, a Marwari merchant and a landowner of Jabalpur, joined the Congress in 1920. In 1923 he became a member of the Central Legislative Assembly, and two years later won a seat in the Council of State. He was an important political figure in central Indian politics. B. Hooja, *A Life Dedicated: Biography of Govind Das* (Delhi, 1956).

    D.P. Mishra of Jabalpur, a staunch Congressman served a jail sentence for participating in the Non-Cooperation Movement. After Govind Das, his political mentor, he was elected to the Central Assembly. He consolidated the Congress influence in the Hindi speaking Mahakoshal area of the CP and Berar. He wrote his autobiography *Living An Era*. See also *Samarpit Ardha Sati: Pandit Dwaraka Prasad Mishra Abhinandan Granth*, New Delhi, 1970.
24. SP 280060, Extracts from newspapers, April 1936; 280063, File 78-II of 1936, *Nishpriha* (Nagpur), 10 April 1936.
25. *Hitavada*, 8, 27, Jan. 1937. HP File 18 Jan. 1937, FR, 1st half of Jan. 1937.
26. HD Reforms File 31/37–Feb. 1937, enclosing *East India Constitutional Reforms: Elections showing the Results of Elections in India, 1937 (cmd. 5589/1937)*. *Hitavada*, 10 Mar. 1937.

27. Ibid, 5, 12 Feb., 9 April 1937. Samiullah Khan, a Khilafatist and a Congressman, was for long a member of the Nagpur City Congress Committee and CP Congress (Marathi) Subjects Committee. He worked in close concert with Abhyankar, Moonje and Jamnalal Bajaj, a Marwari businessman of Wardha and a confidant of Gandhi. Samiullah was the Vice-President of the CP Political Conference of which Dr Khare was the President. He controlled the Nagpur Textile Union, working in close concert with Khare and R.S. Ruikar, a prominent trade unionist and labour leader of central India, extending the Congress influence among workers in cotton mills and railways. In 1937, prior to the elections, he joined the Muslim League. HP File 7/1923; HP, FR, 1st half of March 1924, 1st half of Dec. 1927, 2nd half of Feb. 1929.
28. Gowan had dismissed as an 'incredible boast' the Congress assertion that it would win 65 out of 112 seats. The Governor had predicted the Congress winning at best 35 seats. J. Glendevon, *The Viceroy at Bay: Lord Linlithgow in India*, London, 1971, p. 49
29. *Hitavada*, 31 Mar. 1937. Muslims belonging to both Rauf Shah and Shariff's camps joined Rao's party.
30. See Chapter IV. His other colleagues were B.G. Khaparde and Raja Dharmarao Bhujangarao of Aheri.
31. *Hitavada*, 31 Mar., 9 Apr. 1937. Shariff and Rizvi were old political rivals in provincial Muslim politics. *CPLA*, vol. VIII, Aug. 1934, pp. 363, 368, 405. See also Chapter IV for Rao-Rizvi relationship.
32. *Hitavada*, 26 Mar. 1937.
33. Khare joined the Congress in 1918 as a lieutenant of Abhyankar. He was a member of the provincial legislative Council twice under the Montford scheme. Though deeply influenced by Tilak like all other Maharashtrian Brahmin leaders of his time, Khare became a follower of Gandhi and worked for the uplift of the Depressed Class Hindus. In 1923–9, he was a member of the Swarajist Party. After Abhyankar's death in 1935, Khare was elected unopposed to the Central Assembly, becoming the foremost Maharashtrian Congress leader in the province. He wrote his autobiography, *My Political Memoirs or Autobiography* (Nagpur, 1971). K.S. Kshirsagar, 'Dr N.B. Khare, Neo-Tilakite and Hindu Mahasabhite, 1882–1970', in P.L. Joshi, ed., *Political Ideas and Leadership*, pp. 121–32.
34. *Hitavada*, 13 June 1937.
35. J.R. Joshi, *Dr Kedar Yanche Charitra* (Life of Dr Kedar, in Marathi), Nagpur, 1956, p. 191. Kedar was a close associate of Khare and a Minister in 1928.
36. Chopra, *Towards Freedom* p. 722, Gowan to Linlithgow, 10 Nov. 1938.
37. *Hitavada*, 11, 18 July, 17 Aug. 1937.
38. In his letter to Jinnah, Shariff pointed out that Ahmad Syed, a member of the League Central Parliamentary Board, was also a member of the Congress party and had canvassed for it in the elections. Shariff asserted that a Muslim Congressman could also promote the interest of his community. Yakub Hasan, PWD Minister in the Congress cabinet in Madras,

was a founder member of the Muslim League and also a member of the executive committee of the League. Being a Leaguer, he remained also a staunch Congressman. *Hitavada*, 5 Sept., 20 Oct. 1937. HP File 18 Aug. 1937, FR, 1st half of Aug. 1937.

In UP, Muhammad Hafiz Ibrahim, elected on League ticket, joined the Congress and became a Minister. B.B. Mishra, *Indian political Parties*, Delhi, 1976, p. 425.

The CP Muslim League Parliamentary Board, headed by Shariff, passed a resolution urging him not to resign as an MLA. The Board strongly criticized the League Central Parliamentary Board and its President, stressing that the resolution of the League at Lucknow would be detrimental to national interest besides isolating the Muslim community from the mainstream of the national movement. Shariff's Board exhorted the Muslims to cooperate with the Congress in the country's Freedom Movement. It also set up a committee for the purpose. *Hitavada*, 12 Nov. 1937.

39. Letter of Maulavi Syed Bashir Ahmad of Talegaon Dashasar to Gandhi, and Gandhi's reply, saying that he did not view it morally wrong for the Congress to have made Shariff a Minister. Ibid., 13 Oct. 1937.

    C.R. Reddy, MLC, Madras and Vice-Chancellor of Andhra University, criticized the Congress for making Muslims, elected on League ticket, Ministers. 'It was, as though, separate electorate, admitted by the front door, was throttled in the backyard'. Naturally, he added, 'the Muslims resented this as a wily attack on the integrity of their organization, as seducing their members from their proper allegiance and spreading demoralisation'. *Congress in Office* (Madras, 1940), pp. 45–6.

40. Non-Congress groups were, besides the Muslims, the Independents, the non-Brahmins, and the Independent Labour Party members. The Hindu Mahasabha, Europeans and Anglo-Indians had one member each in the Assembly. *Hitavada*, 28 Feb. 1937.
41. *CPLA*, 5 April 1939, pp. 979, 989–90; 8 Aug. 1939, p. 320; 4 Nov. 1939, pp. 163, 169; 6 Nov. 1939, pp. 163, 169, 402.
42. *Hitavada*,14 April, 11 and 16 June, 24 Oct., 7, 12 Nov., 3 Dec. 1937. Syed Ahmad, President of the Mahakoshal Congress, was more successful than all others; in Jabalpur, where he was active, out of 1,165 men enrolled in the party, 324 were Muslims. Maulana Chiraguddin was another Muslim leader in the Mahakoshal Congress. Ibid., 14 April, 24 Oct., 7 Nov. 1937. HP, File 18 Nov. 1937, FR, 1st half of Nov. 1937. Reddy condemned the Congress mass contact movement among the Muslims as a 'blunder', an attempt to extirpate Muslim unity and identity and absorbing them into the Congress. *Congress in Office*, p. 46.
43. Chopra, *Towards Freedom*, p. 722, Gowan to Linlithgow, 6 July 1937. *Hitavada*, 23 April, 9 and 25 June 1937.
44. Ayesha Jalal, *The Sole Spokesman: Jinnah, the Muslim League and the Demand for Pakistan*, Cambridge, 1985, p. 44 fn.
45. *Hitavada*, 16 July, 7 Nov. 1937.
46. *CPLA*, 8 Nov. 1939, p. 450. Also Ibid., p. 459; 12 April 1939, p. 1137;

Hitavada, 18 July, 29 Sept. 1937. SP 280063, File 159 of 1937: *Jaddo Jehad* (Nagpur), 5 Jan. 1937.

47. Reddy, *Congress in Office*, p. 69.
48. *CPLA*, 8 Nov. 1939, p. 459; also Ibid., 12 Apr. 1939, p. 1137. *Hitavada*, 8 July, 29 Sept., 1937. SP 280063, File 159 of 1937: *Jaddo Jehad*, 5 Jan. 1937. Jinnah dismissed Congress Muslims as 'traitors, cranks, supermen or lunatics', quoted in Jamiluddin Ahmad, *Some Recent speeches and Writings of Mr Jinnah*, Lahore, 1946, pp. 25, 154, 225, 428.
49. Before the 1937 elections the League had no mass base. It was 'almost defunct' till 1934, and for long 'lived on paper' only, Choudhry Khaliquzzaman, *Pathway to Pakistan*, pp. 137, 139. Z.H. Zaidi, 'Aspects of the Development of Muslim League Politics, 1937–47', C.H. Philips and M.D. Wainwright, eds., *The Partition of India Policies and Perspectives, 1935–47*, London, 1970, pp. 245–6, Pirzada, vol. I, *Foundations*, pp. lxvi-lxviii.
50. HP File 8 Mar. 1938, FR, 2nd half of March 1938; 18 June 1938, FR, 1st and 2nd half of June 1938; 18 Aug. 1937, FR, 1st half of Aug. 1937; 18 Oct. 1937, FR, 2nd half of Oct. 1937; 18 Nov. 1937, FR, 1st half of Nov. 1937.

    Gowher Rizvi, *Linlithgow and India: A Study of the British Policy and the Political Impasse in India, 1936–43*, London, 1978, p. 124. Zaidi, 'Aspects of the Development', pp. 268–9.
51. SP 280068, pp. 31–3, 37–42, Chief Secy's Note on communalism, 10 Nov. 1938, IGP's Note, 13 Nov. 1938, Report on Muslim communalism by Y.A. Oakley, Asst. to DIG of Police, 8 Nov. 1938. SP 280070, pp. 125–28; SP 280071, pp. 126–30, Muslim League meeting, 10 June 1939; SP 280072, p. 150, Growth of communal feeling, speech of Siddiqui Ali Khan, 7 Aug. 1939. HP File 18 Jan. 1938, FR, 1st half of Jan. 1938.

    Abdur Rauf Shah and Ghulam Hussain, League leaders of the province, became members of the party's national committees. G. Allama, *Pakistan Movement, Historic Documents*, Karachi, 1967, pp. 124, 152, 153, 173.
52. Pirzada, *Foundations*, vol. II, pp. 275, 278, 298, 305, 312, 313.
53. The League won both the by-elections held between 1 Jan. 1938 and 12 Sept. 1942. Reginald Coupland, *Indian Politics, 1936–42*, London, 1944, p. 333.

    In 1939, the League won 30 seats in municipal elections and the Congress won 275. HP 18 Jan. 1939, FR, 1st half of Jan. 1939.

    In Nagpur municipal elections in 1937, Hindus solidly voted for Congress Muslims in Hindu wards, but these men received no such support in Muslim wards. *Hitavada*, 23 Dec. 1937.
54. HP File 18 Jan. 1938, FR, 2nd half of Jan. 1938; 18 Feb. 1938, FR, 2nd half of Feb. 1938.
55. The Momin Association of Nagpur had condemned the Muslim League Council for not including any momin in it. HP 18 June 1938, FR, 1st half of June 1938.
56. LD, Reel no. 2196, Wylie to Linlithgow, 11 Jan. 1939. HP File 18 Dec. 1937, FR, 1st half of Dec. 1937.
57. Quoted in Khursheed Kamal, *A Documentary Record of the Congress*

Government, 1937–39 related to Muslims under Congress rule (Islamabad, 1988), vol. II, pp. 126–7. V.D. Savarkar, *Ratnagiri Parva*, vol. I, *1924–37* (in Marathi), Bombay, 1972, pp. 120, 123, 152, J.M. Deb, *Blood and Tears* Bombay, 1945, pp. 145–6. HP File 18 Dec. 1937, FR, 1st half of Dec. 1937. *Hitavada*, 22, 26 Dec. 1937.

58. SP 280071, Files 204–23.
59. SP 280068, pp. 24–42, Report on the communal situation by the CSCPB, IGP and Y.A. Oakley, Nov. 1938, SP 280071, pp. 130–42. HP File 18 July 1938, FR, 2nd half of July 1938.

    Curiously enough, many Congressmen of Wardha appealed to the Mahasabha leaders not to condemn the Congress in their resolution. Many Congressmen had strong association with the Mahasabha. LP, Reel no. 2196, Wylie to Linlithgow, 11 Jan. 1939.
60. HP File 18 Aug. 1939, FR, 2nd half of Aug. 1939. Chitnavis was the son of the pro-Government liberal leader, Gangadharrao Chitnavis. For murder bid on Shariff see p. 158 later.
61. SP 280072, Special Branch Report on the RSS, 29 May 1939.
62. Ibid. File 289/1939. LP, Reel no. 2196, Shukla's Note, 23 May 1939.
63. SP 280068, pp. 31–3, 37–42, Report on the communal situation in the province, Nov. 1938.
64. Coupland, *The Constitutional Problem in India*, pp. 130, 131 fn. LP, Reel no. 2196, Wylie to Linlithgow, 23 Mar. 1939. HP File 18 Oct. 1937, FR, 1st half of Oct. 1937. SP 280070, File 127/1939.
65. HP File 18 June 1936, FR, 2nd half of June 1936; 18 Oct. 1937, FR, 2nd half of Oct. 1937; 18 Nov. 1937, FR, 1st and 2nd half of Nov. 1937. *CPLA*, 19 Sept. 1938, pp. 214, 216.
66. SP 280067, File 197, pp. 29–33.
67. *CPLA*, 18 Apr. 1939, p. 1481; 19 April 1939, pp. 1541–2.

    The Akola Order (1926) was viewed by the Muslims as being favourable to the Hindus. See Chapter IV.

    Mishra had allegedly raped a Muslim woman, Hasina by name, who was later married off to Mishra's car driver Naidu. There was a great public outcry over this incident, compromising Mishra's public image. For Mishra's version of the incident see his *Living An Era*, pp. 262–4.
68. Khare was the Premier for a year (July 1937–July 1938), when following acute differences with his Hindi speaking cabinet colleagues, Shukla and Mishra, and the Congress High Command supporting the latter, he resigned. Shukla then became premier. Khare's differences with the Congress leadership, particularly Vallabhbhai Patel and Gandhi, intensified, leading to his expulsion from the Congress in October 1938. Hereafter Khare not only became the bitterest critic of the Congress but joined the anti-Congress groups in provincial politics, even acting in close concert with the Governors of the province. Khare, *My Defence* Nagpur, 1938; *C.P. Ministerial Crisis* Allahabad, 1938; See also Khare's *Autobiography*, p. 254, and Baker, *Changing Political Leadership*, pp. 177–85. HP File 1938, FR, 2nd half of July 1938.

69. HP File 18 Mar. 1938, FR, 2nd half of March 1938. LC, Reel no. 2194, Bomford, Actg. Governor, to Linlithgow, 7 April 1938. Joshi, *Kedar's Biography*, pp. 193–4.

    Raghavendra Rao, as Home Member before the elections, had noted in a file that he would consider the question of reducing Zafar Hussain's sentence if and when he would make an appeal accordingly. Hussain was 46 years old and had served the sentence for less than a year when Shariff ordered his release. His wife died of heart failure, leaving four minor children, the youngest being only two years old. Khare Papers, File no. 108.
70. On Kedar see his biography by Joshi, *Kedar's Biography*.
71. HP File 18 March 1938, FR, 2nd half of March 1938.
72. Khare Papers, File no. 108 (XIII): Khare to Patel, 25 Mar. 1938 in reply to Patel's letters to him, 9 and 14 March 1938.
73. For Khare's strained relations with his Hindi speaking cabinet colleagues see Baker, *Changing Political Leadership*, p. 177–85.
74. Perhaps hoping to minimise the gravity of the crime, Khare gave out that he did not believe—unlike almost all others—that the minor girl had no earlier sexual experience at all. Khare Papers, File no. 108 (XIII), Khare to Patel, 25 Mar. 1938.
75. Ibid. The Governor had endorsed Shariff's release of Zafar, a point stressed by Khare. Ibid.
76. Ibid., File no. 108 (XV): Patel to Khare, 14 Mar. 1938; Khare to S.C. Bose (Congress President), 10 Apr. 1938. Shariff did not consult his colleagues when setting free Muslims prisoners. Joshi, *Kedar's Biography*, p. 192. Shariff and Kedar were friends, both being earlier members of the Peoples Party formed by the latter, and both being Khare loyalists.
77. Tomlinson, *Indian National Congress*, p. 92; Coupland, *The Constitutional Problems*, p. 124.
78. A Hindu betelshop owner had poisoned his customer, a Muslim woman. CPLA, 6 Nov. 1939, p. 281.
79. The culprit—Baban—a relative of the Raja of Amawan in Munghyr district in Bihar, had been sentenced to ten years imprisonment on a charge of unnatural offence and murder. He was released under orders of the Congress Premier of Bihar after only a few months of imprisonment; 'the Premier was amply rewarded by the Raja'. Anonymous letter from Patna to Shariff, 5 Apr. 1938, Khare Papers, File no. 108 (XII).
80. MA Police Dept., File nos. 6-2/1939 and 6-2/1940. LP, Reel no. 2196, Wylie to Linlithgow, 18 April 1939.
81. MA Police Dept., File nos. 6-2/1940, 13-44/1940. The Governor thought that in arresting 'ferociously' the almost entire Muslim male population, the government acted in a 'revengeful manner'. He personally intervened to get 43 persons acquitted. Ibid.
82. Ibid., File no. 6-1/1941. The Muslim League representing against the collection of fine, the Governor suspended its collection. He also withdrew the punitive police soon after the Congress ministry resigned. Ibid.
83. Government of CP and Berar, *Vidya Mandir Scheme—A way to the spread*

of free and compulsory mass education with a fixed period, Nagpur, 1938. Mitra, *Indian Annual Register, 1937*, vol. I, pp. 288, 344.

83a. *Vidya Mandir Scheme*, p. 15.

84. K. Mojumdar, 'The Congress Ministry in the Central Provinces and Berar, 1937–9: The Communal Problem', P.K. Mishra, ed., *Aspects of Indian History and Historiography*, New Delhi, 1996, pp. 30–4.

85. *CPLA*, 1 Nov. 1939, pp. 25–6; 2 Nov. 1939, p. 73.

86. Ibid., 14 Aug. 1939, pp. 783, 786; also vol. IV, Sept.–Oct. 1938, pp. 58–9.

87. HP File 18 Sept. 1938, FR, 2nd half of Sept. 1938. Abbas Ali Kamal, a Bohra Muslim (1906–87), served on Nagpur Municipal Corporation for many years before and after Indian independence. He was closely associated with Nagpur University and served as President, Nag-Vidarbha Chamber of Commerce.

    Abdul Majid Leader (1896–1963) joined the Khilafat Movement in 1920 and participated in the Congress Flag Satyagraha in 1923, for which he served a jail sentence. Till 1936, he was pro-Congress; then he became an ardent Leaguer. He served the Nagpur Municipal Corporation for years both before and after 1947. Sharfuddin Sahil, *Nagpur Ka Muslim*, pp. 175–6, 178–80.

88. *Hitavada*, 15 Jan. 1939.

89. SP 280069, pp. 43–6: Chief Secy's Note on Muslim satyagraha at Nagpur, and Press Communique issued by the Government, 10 Feb. 1939.

90. On 26 Jan. 1939, Jawaharlal Nehru unfurled the Congress flag on the bank of the river Ravi in the Punjab. The Congress celebrated that day every year as the Independence Day.

91. Siddiqui Ali Khan's *Autobiography*.

92. *Hitavada*, 27 Jan. 1939. Khursheed Kamal, *A Documentary Record of the Congress Government*, p. 165.

93. *Hitawada*, 12 Feb. 1939. LP, Reel no. 2196, Wylie to Linlithgow, 22 Feb. 1939.

94. 'Vidyamandir' scheme was a part of the Wardha Education Programme which was condemned by the League's Kamal Yar Jang Committee as being 'essentially communal' in character. See also Coupland, *The Constitutional Problem*, p. 191.

    Azizul Haq, Vice-Chancellor, University of Calcutta and later Indian High Commissioner in London, in his report (1942) strongly condemned the Wardha Education Programme. Ibid., p. 186.

95. Majlis-i-Ahrar, founded in the Punjab in 1931, by Mazhar Ali Khan and Maulana Ataullah Shah Bukhari, was a pro-Congress organization. Jinnah disliked its radical social programmes. Zaidi, Aspects of Development, p. 260. B.B. Mishra, *Indian Political Parties*, pp. 596–8.

96. *CPLA*, 1 Nov. 1939, p. 26.

97. Ibid., pp. 10, 14, 15, 26, 42, 71, 77, 91; 2 Nov. 1939, p. 92.

98. Ibid., 1 Nov. 1939, pp. 33, 38. Earlier, deposing before the Indian Statutory Commission in Nagpur, Shariff had opposed separate denominational schools for Muslims.

99. SP 280069, p. 68, *Jaddo Jehad,* 19 Feb. 1939. Abdur Rahman Khan, League MLA, said that Zakir Hussain himself had reservations about the scheme being named 'vidyamandir'. *CPLA*, 14 Aug. 1939, p. 591.
100. Ibid., 1 Nov. 1939, p. 91.
101. *Report of the Enquiry Committee appointed by the Council of the All India Muslim League to enquire into Muslim grievances in Congress Provinces,* Lucknow, 15 Nov. 1938. It was headed by Raja Syed Mohammad Mehdi of Pirpur.
102. HP, File 18 June 1938, FR, 1st half of June 1938.
103. *Pirpur Committee Report,* p. 53.
104. The Report came out in Dec. 1939 under the title *Muslim Sufferings under Congress Rule*, Calcutta, 1939, See also Padmasha, *Indian National Congress and the Muslims,* New Delhi, 1985, 2nd edn., pp. 133–8, Correspondence between Fazlul Haq and Jawaharlal Nehru, Nov.–Dec. 1939.
105. Mojumdar, 'The Congress Ministry', pp. 35–8.
106. Quoted in A.M. Zaidi, ed., *The Demand for Pakistan*, New Delhi 1978, p. 585. The scheme aimed at 'supplanting all other religions by a new religion—Gandhism'. Ibid.
107. *Pirpur Committee Report,* pp. 20, 21, 55, 57. A.M. Zaidi, *The Demand*, pp. 57–8.
108. Coupland, *The Constitutional Problem*, p. 102. In a League meeting at Raipur, Muslims resolved not to stand up when the song was sung in the Assembly. HP File 18 Sept. 1939, FR, 2nd half of Sept. 1939.
109. Padmasha, *Indian National Congress*, pp. 133–9. Out of the 15,000 elected members on the 83 local bodies in the province, less than half a dozen were Muslims, and only a dozen Muslims were on the staff of these bodies, ran the Muslim MLAs' charge. *CPLA,* Sept.–Oct. 1938, vol. IV, p. 535; 12 April 1939, pp. 1121–9. The Muslim MLAs' demand for separate electorates for local bodies was supported by Ghadichore, the Depressed Class MLA. Ibid., p. 1137.
110. Pirpur Committee Report, pp. 11–12.
111. *CPLA*, 17 Mar. 1939, p. 141: speech of Abdur Rahman Khan, League MLA. Ibid., 12 Apr. 1939, p. 1122: speech of Hidayat Ali, League MLA. Khare said that even after the ban (*Hitavada*, 9 Feb. 1939), 'individual Congressmen' attended meetings addressed by Savarkar, *Pirpur Committee Report*, p. 61.
112. Lorry leads of Congressmen disturbed Mahasabha meetings and Moonje had to be given police protection. HP File 4 Sept. 1937, FR, 2nd half of Jan. 1937. In the 1926 election for the Central Assembly, Moonje, then a Responsivist, had a bitter contest with Abhyankar, the Congress leader, who lost the election. In 1934 election for the Central Assembly, the two again fought, Abhyankar winning the election.
113. Central Provinces Secret—Abstract of Intelligence, 1939, vol. LIV, p. 10.
114. *Sawadhan* (Nagpur), July 1938, cited in Suhas Pendke, 'Leadership of Dr N.B. Khare', u npublished Ph.D. thesis, Nagpur University, July 1991,

p. 144. In May 1938 he laid a bill in the Assembly and suggested to the Congress Working Committee that a para-military force of 2,000 men be raised in the province. The bill was dropped when two months later he resigned. Ibid., p. 147.

115. HP File 18 Dec. 1937, FR, 1st half of Dec. 1937. Ramrao Deshmukh was in the Responsivist party led by Moonje before, like Aney, a fellow Berari, also a Responsivist, he 'infiltrated into Congress' during the Civil Disobedience Movement. D.P. Mishra, *Living An Era*, p. 252.
116. LP, Reel no. 2196, Wylie to Linlithgow, 20 Jan. 1939. Kedar was also a Responsivist once. Ibid.
117. Khare, *Political Memoirs*, pp. 213–15, *Hitavada*, 27 Jan. 1937. Khare pleaded with Henry Twynum, the Governor after Wylie, for the release of Tukdoji Maharaj, closely associated with the RSS, who was suspected to have been involved in disturbances at Chimur during the August rebellion, 1942, Khare, *Memoirs*, pp. 191–2.See Chapter IV for RSS involvement in Chimur disturbances.
118. D.P. Mishra, *Living An Era*, pp. 252, 255.
119. The Governor's Secretary found Khare 'certainly not as anti-Muhammadan as one or two of his colleagues' in the cabinet he headed. His official actions showed no marked communalism, unlike those of his colleagues, Shukla, in particular. LP, Reel no. 2196, R.N. Banerjee to G. Laithwaite, Secy. to the GG, 26 Aug. 1939.

    Khare, along with Moonje and Hedgewar, was a signatory to the Hindu-Muslim agreement at Nagpur in 1925. See Chapter IV.

    In 1927, Khare spoke on Hindu-Muslim unity at several places like Abhyankar. Central Provinces Abstract of Intelligence, vol. XXXVIII/ 1927.
120. Khare was President of the Mahasabha for two years, 1949–51. For his admiration for the RSS see his *Memoirs*, pp. 213–16.
121. *Pirpur Committee Report*, p. 61.
122. Chapter IV.
123. *Pirpur Committee Report*, p. 61.
124. Ibid., p. 12. In the late 1920s, the growing influence of the Mahasabhites on a section of the Congress leadership (such as in Lajpat Rai, M.R. Jayakar and Moonje) led Shaukat Ali to wonder if the Congress had become 'an adjunct of the Hindu Mahasabha'. Letter to M.A. Ansari, 19 May 1929 cited in Mushirul Hasan, ed., *Communal and Pan-Islamic Trends in Colonial India*, New Delhi, 1981, p. 213
125. 'The League was trying to convince neither the British nor the Congress; its propaganda was meant for 'home consumption', i.e. for the Muslims. In this it achieved remarkable success. Most Muslims believed the charges to be true and turned bitterly anti-Congress. Rizvi, *Linlithgow and India*. pp. 101–2.
126. LP. Reel no. 2196, Wylie to Linlithgow, 18 Apr. 1939. Hitavada, 10 Feb. 1939. Rizvi, *Linlithgow*, pp. 102–5.
127. C.P. Government's Press Note, *Hitavada*, 10 Feb. 1939.

128. LP, Reel no. 2196, Wylie to Linlithgow, 22 May 1939. Bose reportedly sent emissaries to Hedgewar in 1939, perhaps seeking his help for an armed uprising. Bose did not meet Hedgewar for the latter was in death bed. The Government viewed Bose as the most dangerous political activist. N.H. Palkar, *Dr. Hegdewar*, p. 354.

    Mahasabhites charged Premier Khare with disturbing their meetings by hired hooligans, even some Muslims among them. SP 280067, File nos. 82 to 97, pp. 29-33. HP File 18 Feb. 1938, FR, 2nd half of Feb. 1938.
129. LP, Reel no. 2196, Wylie to Linlithgow, 22 May 1939.
130. MAPM, File 778/1937, C.M. Trivedi, CSCPB, to all DCs, 20 June 1939, 5 Aug. 1938, Press Communique, 30 Aug. 1938, 22 June 1939, confidential Letter to all DCs, 20 Dec. 1937, 2 April 1938.
131. LP, Reel no. 2195, vol. II, 1938, Wylie to Lord Brabourne, Actg. Viceroy, 18 Aug. 1938.
132. *CPLA*, 29 March 1938, p. 81.
133. Ibid., 11 April 1939, p. 1040.
134. *Hitavada*, 10 Feb. 1939.
135. Philips and Wainwright, p. 161.
136. CP Government's Press Note, *Hitavada*, 10 Feb. 1939,
137. Coupland *The Constitutional Problem*, pp. 148, 191.
138. LP, Reel no. 2195, Wylie to Linlithgow, 29 Dec. 1938.
139. J.M. Deb, *Blood and Tears*, p. 110.
140. LP, Reel no. 2196, Bomford to Linlithgow, 23 March 1938.
141. *CPLA*, 2 Nov. 1939, p. 91.
142. Coupland, *The Constitutional Problem*, pp. 148, 190.
143. SP 280063, File no. 78-II/1936.
144. LP, Reel no. 2194, Wylie to Linlithgow, 7, 10 June 1938; Reel no. 2196, Wylie to Linlithgow, 23 Mar. 1939. Banerjee, Secy. to Governor, wrote to Laithwaite, Secy. to Viceroy (26 Aug. 1939) that Shukla had in him 'marked communalism'; he was 'definitely anti-Muhammadan and anti-Maharashtrian'; he favoured his caste men, Kanyakubja brahmins; besides, he was 'a by-word for dilateriness, not attending to files for weeks and months'. D.S. Mehta, the Finance Minister under Shukla, was 'not above communalism and favouritism'. D.P. Mishra, Home Minister, was 'a past master in the art of political intrigue and wire-pulling', though 'undoubtedly clever and quick in the uptake'. LP, Reel no. 2196. Gowan also found Shukla, when a Minister in Khare cabinet, 'a great disappointment', 'the laziest minister of the lot'.

    In contrast, Khare appeared to the Governor's Secretary, as 'an intelligent man who showed considerable capacity for administrative business'; he was 'not unreasonable in his outlook and showed much freedom form vindictiveness'. Khare was found 'honest and straight forward, with no marked communalism in his official action'; however, he was 'volatile and indecisive in nature, weak and anxious to please all'. Patel was hostile to Khare and incited D.P. Mishra against him. Gowan held Premier Khare in great respect. Banerjee to Laithwaite, 26 Aug. 1939, LP, Reel no. 2196.

145. LP, Reel no. 2196, Wylie to Linlithgow, 23 March, 18 April, 23 June, 6 July 1939.
146. LP, Reel no. 2194, Bomford to Linlithgow, 7 April 1938; Reel no. 2196, Wylie to Linlithgow, 6 July 1939, Banerjee to Laithwaite, 26 Aug. 1939. Mishra bore a strong grudge against the Muslim officer who was investigating the Hasina case. The officer had to go on leave when Mishra and Shukla practically forced Khare to conduct an enquiry against him. LP, Reel no. 2194, Bomford to Linlithgow, 23 Mar. 1938.
147. Khare in a statement given on 15 January 1940 confirmed his former colleagues' grudges against Niaz Ahmad and Imam-ur-Rahim. He also asked Nehru to come down to Nagpur 'to be shocked to find what the CP ministry had done in regard to the Muslims'. Khursheed Kamal, *Documentary Record*, vol. I, pp. 134–5. However, Khare, then expelled from the Congress and having scores to settle with Shukla and Mishra, was eager even to cut his own nose to spite their face. He bitterly opposed whatever Shukla and Mishra did as Ministers. Mojumdar, 'The Congress Ministry', p. 39.
148. LP, Reel no. 2194, Wylie to Brabourne, 22–5 June 1938.
149. Ibid., Real no. 2196, Wylie to Linlithgow, 23 March 1939. Earlier Shukla had tried to transfer the officer, blaming him for failure to control riots. Wylie had stayed the transfer. Ibid. See also LP, Reel no. 2196, 18 April 1939; Reel no. 2197, Governor Twynum to Linlithgow, 22 Aug. 1940.
150. LP, Reel no. 2196, Wylie to Linlithgow, 8 Aug. 1939.
151. Ibid, Wylie to Linlithgow, 18 April 1939, also 23 March, 23 June 1939.
152. Ibid., Wylie to Linlithgow, Telg. 7 June 1939.
153. Ibid., Wylie to Linlithgow, 23 June 1939.
154. Ibid., Wylie to Linlithgow, 6 July 1939.
155. Ibid., Wylie to Linlithgow, 22 May and 8 Aug. 1939. The mosques were used for League propaganda. Nicholas Mansergh, ed., *The Transfer of Power, 1942–47*, vol. VII, Document no. 62.

    The Shukla ministry claimed to do no more than strictly adhere to the earlier Akola Order. Neutrality in respect of religion would be observed, but when religious demands conflicted with the civil rights of individuals to use public thoroughfares, the government would uphold the latter. In respect of Berar, the Government would normally respect the local convention of no music on public roads flanked by mosques, but it also would exercise its right to restrict music by either community 'whether in respect of hours, proximity or volume, each restriction varying according to circumstances of time and place.' *CPLA*, 16 March 1939, p. 76.
156. LP, Reel no. 2196, Wylie to Linlithgow, 11 Jan. 1939. Central Provinces Secret Abstract of Intelligence, vol. LII/1939, no. 1, p. 664; vol. LIV, 1939, p. 81.
157. LP, Reel no. 2196, Wylie to Linlithgow, 11 Jan. 1939. This appeared as a symbolic act of solidarity with the Hindu cause in Hyderabad. Ibid., Wylie to Linlithgow, 20 Jan. 1939.
158. Ibid., Wylie to Linlithgow, 11 Jan. 1939.

159. Deshpande, 'Militant Nationalism', p. 104.
160. HP File 42/2 of 1938, 42/3 of 1939: DIB's Report on the Hyderabad agitation.
161. HP File 18 Dec. 1938, FR, 1st half of Dec. 1938; File 18 Jan. 1939, FR, 1st and 2nd half of Jan. 1939; File 18 Feb. 1939, FR, 1st half of Feb. 1939; File 18 April 1939, FR, 1st half of April 1939; File 18 May 1939, FR, 1st half of May 1939; File 18 Nov. 1939, FR, 2nd half of Nov. 1939.
162. LP, Reel no. 2196, Wylie to Linlithgow, Telg. 4 June 1939. Bharukha, the Minister for Industry, was eager to go as a volunteer. Ibid., Wylie to Linlithgow, 22 Feb. 1939. Swami Ramanand Tirtha, 'D.P. Mishra and Hyderabad Freedom Movement', *Samarpit Ardhasati,* p. 162.
163. LP, Reel no. 2196, Wylie to Linlithgow, 23 June 1939. The French Bishop in Nagpur had told Wylie about the condition of Hindu temples in Hyderabad; the Viceroy too knew this. Ibid., Linlithgow to Wylie, 3 July 1939.
164. Ibid., Wylie to Linlithgow, Telg. 10 June 1939. In Hyderabad state 85 per cent Hindus held only 20 per cent of government jobs while 10 per cent Muslims held 72 per cent of the jobs. Deshpande, 'Militant Nationalism', p. 160.
165. SP 280070, pp. 71–7.
166. Ibid., pp. 76–7, D.P. Mishra's Note, 13 June 1939. Mojumdar, 'The Congress Ministry', pp. 34–5.
167. LP, Reel no. 2196, Wylie to Linlithgow, Telg. 10 June 1939.
168. Ibid., Wylie to Linlithgow, Telg. 7 June 1939; also his letter, 23 June 1939.
169. Ibid., also his Telg. 4 June 1939.
170. The Muslim League Working Committee meeting at Meerat on 26 March 1939 condemned the Hyderabad Satyagraha. G. Allama, *Pakistan Movement*, pp. 166–7.
171. Rizvi, *Linlithgow and India*, p. 101.
172. Ibid., pp. 102–5. LP, Reel no. 2196, Wylie to Linlithgow, 18 April 1939. Sir Ziauddin Ahmad, Member Central Assembly, raised the issue of Muslim harassment in Congress provinces, Marquis of Zetland, Secy. of State, also asked Linlithgow about the matter. LP, Reel no. 2196, Linlithgow to Wylie, 14 Jan., 10 June 1939.
173. Ibid., Wylie to Linlithgow, 18 April 1939. Wylie also reported that 'Quite a first class' police officer. Tara Chand, the Nagpur city police chief, who was universally trusted by the Hindus and Muslims alike, became very unpopular with the latter when he took strong action against a few Muslim rioteers. Ibid., Wylie to Linlithgow, 23 July 1939.
174. Ibid., Wylie to Linlithgow, 18 April 1939. Also Reel no. 2195, vol. II, Wylie to Linlithgow, 29 Dec. 1938.
175. Ibid., Reel no. 2196, Wylie to Linlithgow, 8 Feb. 1939.
176. Ibid., Wylie to Linlithgow, 18 April 1939.
177. Ibid., Wylie to Linlithgow, 23 July 1939.
178. Ibid., Wylie to Linlithgow, 18 April 1939.
179. Ibid., Wylie to Linlithgow, 23 June 1939.

180. Ibid., Wylie to Linlithgow, 18 April 1939.
181. Ibid., Wylie to Linlithgow, 23 June 1939.
182. Ibid., Banerjee to Laithwaite, 26 Aug. 1939. Also LP, Reel no. 2194, Bomford to Linlithgow, 23 March 1938.
183. Ibid., Reel no. 2196, Wylie to Linlithgow, 18 April and 23 July 1939.
184. Ibid., Wylie to Linlithgow, 18 April 1939.
185. Quoted in Rizvi, *Linlithgow*, pp. 102 *et seq*. Rajmohan Gandhi, *Patel*, Ahmedabad, 1990, p. 289. B. Shiva Rao, 'India, 1935–47', in Philips and Wainwright, p. 420.
186. *Hitavada*, 12 Feb. 1939.
187. F. Wylie, 'Federal Negotiations in India, 1935–39 and After', in Philips and Wainwright, p. 523.

CHAPTER VI

Communal Politics, 1939–1947

In the war years and after communalism in the CP and Berar was more a complex issue influenced by the developments in national politics than a festering law and order problem caused by local Hindu-Muslim clashes. The Muslim element in provincial politics assumed added importance when the. Muslim League established itself as the strongest representative organization of the community, and Jinnah its sole spokesman, the government recognizing him as such.

The sharpening Congress-League conflict at the national level set the tone of Hindu-Muslim relations at the regional sphere. Muslims drawn closer to the League appeared to the local Hindus as being driven farther from the nationalist cause championed by the Congress. Muslim non-participation in Congress-led movements in the province reinforced the impression that they were inspired by only narrow, selfish, and communal interests—the impression sedulously fostered by the Hindu Mahasabha and the RSS. Added to this was the disgrace suffered by Muslim Congress leaders at the hands of their correligionists.

In the war years, the government's pro-League attitude was as evident as its anti-Congress posture. Governors Wylie and Henry Twynum used the Muslims as a pliable pressure group against the troublesome Congress, 'a predominantly Hindu party', as Twynum described it.[1]

The end of the Congress administration in November 1939 was for the Muslims a liberating progress from the majority Hindu tyranny to the safe rule of the Governor—and so a cause for celebration.[2] The League MLAs rejected the Congress contention that the government needed to have consulted the party before dragging the country to the war. They moved a resolution urging the government to make no commitment regarding the constitutional progress without the approval of the Muslim League. The resolution was vehemently opposed, Yusuf Shariff, the Muslim Congress MLA, fully supporting the opposition.[3]

With the exception of a few, the Muslims showed no interest in the individual satyagraha launched by the Congress in 1940-1;[4] from the Quit India Movement that followed, they held themselves severely aloof[5] throughout Berar. Only at small places (like Chimur, Ashti, Deoli, and Peth Ahmadpur) a few Muslims were involved in the local mob killing some government employees and destroying government property.[6] Muslims took no part in the annual Congress celebration of the Independence Day—26 January—nor in the agitations over INA officers' trial.[7] The provincial Muslim League formed Muslim defence committees for protection from apprehended Congress attacks during the August disturbances, 1942.[8]

II

Generally speaking, during the war years when the Governor ruled, communal bitterness did not invariably flare up into any major blazé nor did tensions at places always escalate into full-scale riots. In 1940–1, there were some incidents at Katni, Mandla, Itarsi, Pachmadi, Dhamtari, and Mehkar. A somewhat graver incident at Burhanpur left fifty three Hindus and eighteen Muslims injured as a result of police firing. A lathicharge on the Muslims at Khamgaon in May 1939 and at Akola in January 1942 during muharram enraged them and they demanded a judicial enquiry.[10] In December 1939 Jabalpur witnessed a riot.[11] Khaksars, wearing military uniforms, paraded the streets at Burhanpur, Malkapur, Akola, and Amravati while RSS volunteers flaunted the Hindu might by staging lathi drills with a view to scaring the Muslims.[12] Hindu and Muslim 'martyr' days were observed to keep alive the memory of killings in riots that took place years back.[13]

In 1941, a riot at Amravati,[14] leading to eight deaths, needed deployment of military police to restore peace. Hindu ruffians ransacked the homes of Muslim League leaders, Hidayat Ali and Sharifuddin, while the Muslim DSP, K.M. Hussain's strong steps were attributed by Hindu leaders to his anti-Hindu prejudice.[15] Moropant Joshi, the former Home Member, charged the officer with 'not acting fairly' in respect of the Hindus and took exception to his 'constant companionship' of Muslim legislators.[16] The League leaders in their turn blamed Hindu police officers, Tarachand and Pandit, for their anti-Muslim bias.[17] B.G. Khaparde, the Hindu Mahasabha leader, was suspected of sowing among Hindu policemen disloyalty to their Muslim superiors.[18] The Governor heeded to the Muslim demand for an official enquiry into the riot, setting aside the Berar Commissioner's opposition to what he disliked as washing dirty linen in public.

Leaguers and Arya Samajists, many paid propagandists, engaged themselves in slanging matches. Rumours about Hindu sufferings in Hyderabad, Dacca, Bombay, and Ahmedabad received wide currency and ready credence. Police flagmarched in Nagpur, Jabalpur, and Akola as a precautionary measure.[20] Riots united the Muslims and increased the influence of League leaders in particular. But no Hindu unity resulted from the Mahasabha and RSS activities; the Congress opposed both, deprecating their use of religious sentiments to build up political strength;[21] and it was the Congress which at the time influenced the Hindu elites most.

Unlike in the Congress regime, officers under the Governor's rule were free from fear of political interference, and freer to use their own authority to tackle the communal problem. The government banned the publication of 'exaggerated and sensational' reports on communal disturbances while refraining from any 'wholesale interference with the liberties of the general public'.[22] Firmly upholding all local customs and practices regarding religious rights and practices, the officers also upheld the people's right to represent to the government and to seek judicial redress.[23] Local officers dealt with communal incidents with their accustomed impartiality, despite charges of partisanship and display of their religious bias.

Thus at Lonar in Buldana district a small riot broke out in February 1942 over a Muslim objection to the planting of a banyan tree by the Hindus on the route of the *tazia* procession during muharram. B.V. Deo, the Brahmin sub-divisional magistrate, got the tree uprooted, satisfied that it had 'no special importance or sacredness' whatsoever, and that the Hindus had planted it 'with the distinct idea of putting an obstacle in the way of the *tazias*' and 'only as a pretext for picking up quarrels' with the Muslims.[24] M.R. Joshi, another brahmin officer, convicted some Hindus for a communal riot at Mehkar in Buldana dictrict[25] immediately before the country's independence when anti-Muslim feelings ran high among the Hindus in general.

K.M. Ahmad, the Muslim DC of Akola, upheld the Hindu objection to Muslims taking cows for slaughter through Hindu localities, defying local convention against such provocative action.[26] Later he also exposed the hollowness in the Muslim propaganda that Hindu officers were rather soft towards Hindu miscreants.[27] Najibuddin, a Muslim first class magistrate at Akola, ordered a lathicharge on a Muslim procession in January 1942 that left seventy Muslims injured, provoking Muslim and even some Hindu protests.

Local officers on most occasions adhered strictly to the existing ban on any innovations in respect to religious celebrations like playing of music where it was banned or changing the customary route of religious processions. However, at times, old religious customs and conventions came in for new interpretation by local authorities whose action was influenced by the existing conditions and not by the practice upheld by their predecessors decades ago. For example, at Darwa in Yeotmal district, the home of a Hindu had within its precincts the tomb of a Muslim saint where for many years Muslims had been offering prayers. In June 1941, local Hindus, led by Aney, now a member of the Viceroy's Executive Council and a determined defender of Hindu interests, represented to the government against the practice; it was stopped by the local authorities to the detriment of Hindu-Muslim relations at the place.[29]

However, at times the officers themselves differed on the interpretation of existing orders to deal with local communal problems. This was most apparent in the case of the Fatterkheda mosque incident in Buldana in 1941. Local Hindus asserted their right to take music playing dasserah processions before the mosque; Muslims opposed it because no such processions had ever gone past the mosque since its construction more than three and a half centuries ago. For local officers it was a test case of a conflict between the civil right of the Hindus and an established convention favourable to the Muslims. While the DC would uphold the convention banning music before the mosque at all times, the Divisional Commissioner saw no reason to restrict the civil rights of the men to use the public road, irrespective of whether the men played music when traversing it and disturbed the Muslims praying in the mosque. The Hindus produced a judgement of the Allahabad High Court to clinch their contention. The DC and the Commissioner then asked the Hindus and Muslims to obtain fresh court orders either permitting the exercise of civil rights by the former or restricting it for the sake of upholding the old convention which suited the latter.[30] Similar was the case in two mosques at Anjani Buzruk, a village in Buldana district, where too, the DC found it hard to convince the Hindus that a local tradition indeed banned music before the mosques.[31]

Generally speaking, during the war the government wanted people's strict adherence to local conventions, whatever be the court rulings, local authorities given a free hand to regulate religious processions for the sake of communal peace.[32] The government imposed no general ban on the entry of political propagandists from outside the province, mainly Hyderabad, although it was they who most stoked the communal fire. There was no ban either on the Hindus celebrating the Shivaji day or the anniversary of the revolt of 1857;[33] but overt incitement to communal hatred through the press and rumour mongering were restrained by timely admonitions.[34]

Communal peace hinged mainly on the efficiency of local officers as came out clearly during war years. The DC of Akola had an excellent rapport with both the local Mahasabhites and Leaguers. The Mahasabhites gave him an undertaking against anti-Pakistan slogans while taking out processions through Muslim localities. The Leaguers in their turn fully appreciated the DC's periodical warnings to some Muslim riffraffs making provocative speeches. The 'tolerant attitude' of the two communities led the DC to hope that 'politico-communal propaganda in Akola will be conducted on constitutional and peaceful lines'.[35] The DC welcomed the Leaguers' decision to shift the headquarters of the party from Nagpur to Akola where communal troubles were unlikely to break out during religious celebrations.[36]

It was at Akola that Muslim butchers undertook not to kill cows on Mahavir Jayanti, a holy day for the Jains, who agreed to compensate the butchers for their loss in business.[37] 'Moderation, perfect discipline and orderliness' marked the provincial League session at Akola in March 1941, for which the DC extended all facilities.[38] He attended an official dinner and even a *mushaira*, though knowing no Urdu at all. Significantly, some prominent Hindu barristers attended the session as invitees.[39]

There were a few other signs of improvement in the communal situation. Unlike in the Congress rule, municipal elections now not only passed off generally peacefully but at places in Akola district, Mahasabha and League candidates, both anti-Congress, entered into agreements for sharing seats and avoiding contests.[40] At Khamgaon municipal elections, Congressmen teamed up with even local Leaguers to prevent the Mahasabha winning seats.[41] In Jabalpur municipal elections, P.C. Bose, the losing Hindu Forward Bloc candidate, had the informal League support.[42]

At Amravati too the DC, J.W. Meldrun, was fairly successful in maintaining communal peace. In September 1942, he could effect a long-term agreement between Hindu and Muslim leaders against taking out any religious processions till the war was over. Instead of processions, feeding the poor marked religious celebrations. Meldrun encouraged moderate Muslim leaders, Sharifuddin and Hidayat Ali, to assert themselves against their extremist rivals seeking to defame them for having made the agreement. Several Muslim leaders valued the DC's support for winning local elections.[43] But it also needs stressing that the fact that the entire Berar division was for most part in 1941 'extremely quiet'[44] was in no small measure due to the Congress efforts to promote communal harmony and the exertions of the veteran liberal, Moropant Joshi, to the same end.

III

The exigencies of the war obliged the government to soft-pedal both the League and the Hindu Mahasabha whose cooperation it valued for war operations, apart from meeting the Congress challenge.[46] The government also winked at the spread of other communal voluntary organizations—the RSS, the Khaksars, the Ahrars, the Muslim National Guards, the Urdu Lashkar, and the Sirat Conference, for example, though restraining them from any violent activity using the Defence of India rules for the purpose. During the Quit India Movement the war committees were used to 'unostentatiously mobilize' public support against the Congress.[46a]

Unlike the Congress, the League and the Mahasabha helped the government in army recruitment, though for different reasons. For the local Leaguers it was the best pro-government stance to adopt; for the Mahasabha, it was the best opportunity to militarize the Hindus for a stern reckoning with the Muslims in future.[47] In the local war committees formed by the government, the Leaguers and the Mahasabhites fought their own battles of mutual denunciations which the authorities chose to ignore.[48]

The government also winked at the provocative speeches of Khaparde, the Mahasabha leader, for his prosecution would 'probably considerably hamper the local war effort', as the DC, Amravati warned.[49] His membership of the war committees did not deter Khaparde from leading a movement at Amravati against the government's ban on Mahasabha activities at Bhagalpur where a riot had broken out.[50] Earlier, while contesting for a seat in the Central Legislative Assembly, vacated by Aney, Khaparde had adopted while electioneering a 'strong Hindu stance'.[51]

The government was also aware of Khaparde having 'got his knife into the local police' at Amravati, many of them Muslims; and so no wonder, he proved less helpful in tackling the local communal problem than the League leaders[53] whom the government could more easily manage through the Muslim DSP, Hussain, in particular. In Berar, it was the Mahasabha rather than the League which required close watching.[54] Leaders like V.N. Deshpande, R.V. Wagh and R. Jiwaji, all of Nagpur, kept 'poisoning the atmosphere at Amravati' by urging the Hindus to socially and economically boycott the Muslims.[55]

Mahasabhaites coming to Berar from Hyderabad unleashed a vitriolic attack on Gandhi's 'bania politics'[56] which had harmed the general Hindu interests. Moonje condemned the Congress for its 'mistaken' policy and the League for its Pakistan scheme. The Mahasabha observed 22 December 1939 as the day of deliverance from the Congress misrule.[57] It collected donations for the Dacca Fund set up by Savarkar to help the local Hindus and the Hinduism Defence Fund created for the protection of Hindu interests in general and Mahasabhites in particular.[58]

The Mahasabha spread rumours of about four thousand Hindu pilgrims having died of arsenic poisoning in a fair at Tandura in the Hyderabad state, as also about the Nizam recruiting Pathans and Afghans for intrusion into Berar if the war turned worse for Britain.[59] The Mahasabha celebrated 22 October as the Hindu Rashtra Day when condoling the Hind sufferings in Hyderabad; it idolized Shivaji and the Sikh Gurus who fought the Muslim rulers.[60] Brahmin speakers of the Mahasabha emphasized the need for Hindu unity, seeking to promote it by organizing Hindu national festivals as opposed to festivals which were caste-specific. They made repeated reference to depressed classes as Hindus, though 'not very enthusiastically'.[61]

The Mahasabha demanded redistribution of local body electorates to end what it condemned as over-representation of Muslims. The combination of depressed class Hindus with local Muslims in local body elections threatened the existing hegemony of the 'Brahmin-Bania group' in municipalities.[62] The Mahasabha and the League competed in voting on communal lines during local body elections in Berar. Demanding a ban on the Koran, Mahasabha leaders paraded Muslims reconverted to Hinduism.[63] The government did not interfere with Savarkar's many visits to the province, for responsive cooperation with the government in the war was his stand while consistent opposition was the Congress call.[64] The government watched the Mahasabha trouncing the Congress at Khamgaon municipal elections, although it indicated 'turbulent Hindusm'.[65]

During the war some voluntary organizations of the deepest communal dye spread their wings far and wide in the province and beyond. The government updated its information on the RSS, the Khaksars, and some other organizations, their aims and objects, their membership, financial condition and the castes and communities they represented; their activities were closely monitored, not interfered with.[66]

Police report had it that the RSS was 'undoubtedly gaining strength' in different districts.[66a] In 1939, there were 130 *shakhas* all over the province, Nagpur district having 32 of them with 3,000 members; all over India there were 350 branches with 40,000 members. In 1942 there were 48 branches in Nagpur city alone and about 30 elsewhere in Nagpur district, the total membership being 7000. In 1944, 44 new branches had been set up all over India, the cadres numbering a little over 34,000, counting among them many old Congressmen, particularly followers of Aney who had actively participated in the Civil Disobedience Movement (1930–3).[67] The RSS extended its membership among non-Brahmins, who, by 1943, constituted about 30 to 40 per cent of its 76,000 members, of whom 50 per cent belonged to the province.[68]

During the war, the RSS avoided any overt political activity.[69] Its members served on war committees, cooperating in army recruitment drives.[70] In keeping with the government's 'friendly arrangement' with it, the RSS also acquiesced in the government's ban on the use of military uniforms and performance of drills and military exercises.[70a] Both Hedgewar and his successor, M.S. Golwalkar, scrupulously avoided giving any provocation to the government while steadfastly promoting the cause of Hindu unity and militancy.[71] The RSS built up a 'private army' for the freedom of the country, surrounding its activities with 'an intriguing secrecy'.[72] Golwalkar encouraged the enrolment of reliable and young government servants, particularly teachers, in the RSS organization which avoided taking any direct part either in anti-Pakistan movement or communal unity efforts.[73]

However, despite disclaimers, the RSS cadres in their individual capacity were involved in some violent activities during the Quit India Movement. Tukdoji Maharaj, a religious recluse closely associated with the RSS and having a large 'militant following', was at Chimur immediately before the disturbances that caused the killing of some government employees. The government apprehended Tukdoji and banned his visit to Chanda for six months.[74]

The RSS was never declared an illegal organization though subjected to restrictions of the Camps and Parades (control) Order, 1944.[75] The government was not unaware of the 'general policy' of the RSS 'to disguise their military camps and parades as camps for physical exercises', but apart from watching its activities with 'utmost vigilance', it imposed no restrictions on the camps. The RSS had, in fact, issued a circular removing military training from its curriculum and abolishing all posts connected with military training.[76]

But then, the government turned down the Berar Commissioner, M.I. Rahim's suggestion that camps for physical exercises be also banned, convinced as he was that the RSS was a semi-military organization. Rahim even wanted to ban the annual camp of Rashtriya Sevika Samity, the women's wing of the RSS, at Akola, although both the DC and the DSP disfavoured the step. Flag salutation, physical training, intellectual discussions, training in spinning, household duties, cleaning toilets, and sweeping streets and lanes were some of the camp activities. However, the police were free to inspect RSS camps which at times were held away from the district headquarters to avoid a close watch on them by the police. The government classified the RSS men into violent and non-violent ones, the former to be promptly arrested.[77]

The government knew about some Congressmen taking an active part in RSS activities but chose to ignore it;[78] it also knew of the differences between Hedgewar and Moonje when the latter raised a militant outfit, Ramsena, and listed Hedgewar as one of its patrons without his consent.[79] The RSS now appeared to the government as being an independent organization not affiliated to any political or communal organization though retaining its 'definite communal objects'.[80]

Muslim voluntary organizations became active after the Muslim League was reorganized during the 1937 elections. Muslim National Guard, an organization 'purely of a communal nature'[81] was set up at Katni, Sagar, Burhanpur, and Berar, all inhabiting a large Muslim population, in 1939 when the Muslim League stepped up its activities in the province. The Muslim League Volunteer Corps was raised in Nagpur and Jabalpur. Most Muslim voluntary organizations received financial support of the Nizam's government besides being active during elections.[82] However, the Muslim National Guards lay low in 1943–4 partly due to a warning given to it by the government against its reorganization on the lines set by the League at its Karachi session in December 1943.[83]

IV

Hindu-Muslim relations in 1939–45 had much to do with the impact of the Muslim League on the local Muslims and the reaction it caused among the Mahasabhites, the RSS volunteers and the Congressmen. The League grew from strength to strength, the process accelerated by Jinnah's regular visits to the province, the collection of money for the Jinnah Fund and the organization of many Muslim conferences,[84] both regional and national. Pakistan Day (20 March) was observed every year by all the branches of the provincial League in districts and meetings addressed by Muslim national leaders. By September 1938, 23,000 members had been enrolled and in 1943, 33,541 new members.[85] In May 1939, 49 new branches of the party had been set up with 25,000 members. The League made special efforts to enrol women members.[86]

In January 1940 Fazlul Haq, the Premier of Bengal, addressed the Jabalpur district Muslim League conference; he lambasted the erstwhile Congress ministry as a 'worthless self-serving group' and criticized the Governor for allowing such men to hold the ministerial posts at all. He likened the Congress and the Mahasabha with dogs, the latter being the barking ones. Haq demanded a Royal Commission to go into the grievances of the Muslims of Jabalpur who had allegedly suffered during the Congress rule.[87] Fazlul Haq having 'once again run amuck' was commented upon by the *Hitavada*.[88]

Nawab Muhammad Ismail Khan of Delhi in his Presidential

speech at the annual conference of the provincial League at Nagpur in March 1940 opposed the idea of a Constituent Assembly for fear of a Hindu majority in it. He blamed the government for placating the Congress instead of safeguarding minority Muslim interests. Besides urging the Muslims to join the League in large numbers, and thereby strengthening Jinnah's hands, he demanded that no Muslim in the Indian army be ordered to fight the correligionists and no constitution be adopted for the country unless it was accepted by both the Hindus and Muslims. Resolutions were adopted in the conference denouncing Maulana Azad and urging the government to provide for the use of Urdu in all offices; introduction of communal electorates for all local body elections was also a demand put forth in the conference.

In April 1941, Jinnah, his sister, Fatima Jinnah, Liaquat Ali Khan, Raja of Muhammadabad, Amir Ahmad Khan, and Malik Barakat Ali attended the meeting of the All India Muslim Students Federation at Nagpur which aroused great enthusiasm among the local Muslims. A point stressed by Jinnah was that the small Muslim minority of the province were systematically 'terrorised and cowed down' by the overwhelming Hindu majority.[90] All India States Muslim League conferences were also held at Nagpur and Jabalpur in 1943 and 1944 where Hindu rulers of central Indian states were condemned for oppressing their Muslim subjects.[91] In April 1944 Azizul Haq addressed the 53rd session of the All India Muslim Educational Conference.[92]

As elsewhere, in the CP and Berar too, the League made use of mosques and maulavis for party propaganda while urging the Muslims to support the Pakistan scheme as being not only a political necessity for the community but as their religious obligation as well.[93]

The activities of the provincial League no doubt reflected the policies and programmes of the national leadership of the party, but at times some local Leaguers' bellicosity caused not a little embarrassment to the party's national body. Nawab Siddiqui Ali Khan, for long a member of the Central Legislative Assembly and the most thrusting member of the provincial League, accused the Governor of 'flattering the Congress leaders beyond limits'. He even appealed to the Nizam for help to save the Muslims of the CP and Berar from what he condemned as Hindu atrocities. Not satisfied with the provincial League's decision to appoint a committee to go into the

Muslim grievances, he repeated Fazlul Haq's demand for a Royal Commission to enquire into them.[94]

Siddiqui Ali Khan hit newspaper headlines when he got involved in the Sataranjpura mosque incident at Nagpur in September 1940. The incident exposed the government's reluctance to annoy the League and its supreme Leader, Jinnah, who needed to be kept in good humour while the war was on. A Muslim mob, instigated by Siddiqui Ali Khan, manhandled Tarachand, the Hindu police officer of Nagpur, accusing him of having desecrated the mosque. The local government had to release Siddiqui, Jinnah's confidant, from jail and drop criminal cases against him and his associates, Viceroy Linlithgow buckling under Jinnah's pressure and himself pressurising a grumbling Governor.

Jinnah's emissary, Haji Abbas Sattar Ishaq, a colleague of Siddiqui in the Central Assembly and a member of the League's Central Working Committee, gave an undertaking to the Governor, committing the local Muslims to good behaviour in future. C.M. Trivedi, the Chief Secretary, himself went to the jail to coax an obdurate Siddiqui to offer just a formal apology while Ishaq advised the Muslims to approach government officers for redressal of their grievances instead of plunging themselves into 'unconstitutional agitations.[96]

In fact, many local Leaguers were themselves rather tired of Siddiqui's 'obstinacy and unreasonableness', but in the interests of the party they had to 'save him from his own folly'.[97] More embitterment in Congress-League relations resulted from the humiliation suffered by Maulavi Maqbul Ahmad of Seoni, a Congress leader, at the hands of local Leaguers who took serous exception to his remark that Jinnah had but a poor knowledge of the Koran.[98] His condemnation of the Pakistan scheme at public meetings further enraged the Leaguers.[99] Meetings addressed by nationalist Muslims accompanied by Red Shirt volunteers were boycotted by the Muslims who attended in large numbers the meetings arranged by League leaders to condemn the activities of the nationalist Muslims.[100]

The government's reluctance to annoy the League was also clear from the steps it took against the Khaksars, who were bitterly anti-League. The DC foiled the Khaksar attempt at staging a big rally at the provincial League conference at Akola in March 1940 in deference to the local Leaguers' strong opposition to the Khaksars.[101] The Khaksar movement was kept under surveillance after the organization was banned in 1941 when a Khaksar made a bid on Jinnah's life. The police flushed out many Khaksars from their hideouts—mostly mosques—at Elichpur, Amravati and Nagpur. British political officers in Hyderabad, Indore and other central Indian states prevented the local Khaksars from going to Nagpur, where, with the good offices of Yusuf Shariff, the government made an agreement with the Khaksars. The men surrendered to the police and left Nagpur.[102] By July 1941, the organization was 'as good as dead'. The Khaksars were mostly of the 'lowest riffraff classes', quite 'incapable of any organized effort' to influence the local public which, in fact, took 'very little interest' in whatever still remained of the movement after 1941.[103]

In 1943, the government lifted the ban on the movement when its leader Allama Mashriqui gave an undertaking against his men wearing military uniforms and badges. The Khaksars then began reorganizing themselves with the government resolved to prevent any violation of Mashriqui's undertaking by his zealous followers in the province. Khaksar-League ill-feelings persisted especially at Amravati and Burhanpur.[104]

After the war, when Congress-League relations further deteriorated, the Khaksars made a special effort to enlist Hindus in their ranks, stressing Hindu-Muslim unity. They blamed Jinnah for creating a party of fanatics and for failing to resolve the constitutional impasse. Demanding that Jinnah again meet Gandhi for a settlement, the Khaksars warned the League supremo that Muslims would be forced to seek a new Leader if he refused to see Gandhi.[105] At a meeting held at Amravati in December 1944, Congressmen and Communists congratulated the local Khaksars on their efforts to promote communal unity; at places many Congress-minded students acted in concert with the Khaksars. The Ahrar party also wanted the League to make up with the Congress.[106]

There was another reason why during the war the government needed to keep on good terms with the League: to prevent uneasiness spreading among Muslims over the British policy towards Islamic countries. This was particularly necessary when the League's national leadership decided to observe 1 November 1940 as a day of protest against the allied powers' policy towards Muslim states in West Asia and to register the Indian Muslims' sympathy for the states.[107] It was indeed no small relief for the CP and Berar government when Rashid Ali's pro-German movement in Iraq and the

Turko-Afghan treaty passed off almost unnoticed by the local Muslims, although there was some excitement over the Arab-Jewish conflict over Palestine. The government deployed its Muslim officers and the League leaders to explain Britain's Iraq policy to prominent Muslim leaders of the province.[108] Rauf Shah, the provincial League chief, proved particularly helpful in restraining the Berar Muslims from any agitation over the Iraq issue.[109] Imam-ur-Rahim, the Officiating Secretary to the government, and Abdul Razak, the Muslim Independent MLA, provided the government with information on the reaction of the local Muslims to the situation in Muslim countries in West Asia during the war.[110] Governor Twynum admitted that he needed to 'tread extremely warily in connection with any developments in the Middle East.[111] Naturally, in such a situation Siddiqui Ali Khan, the 'tub thumper', exciting the Muslims on the Iraq issue with a view to bolstering his own image, caused the government considerable irritation.[112]

V

Governors Wylie and Twynum were not only hostile to the Congress but partial to the League and the Muslim community in general. They made political use of the fourteen Muslim MLAs—of whom ten were Leaguers[113]—against Congressmen in the Assembly, investing them with an importance they had never acquired before. Wylie repeatedly advised Shukla to include a Muslim in his cabinet only to be told that the Congress high command had decided that a Muslim MLA could not be considered for a ministership unless he crossed over to the Congress party, and that now was virtually impossible. The Governor knew for sure that no Muslim MLA would risk Yusuf Shariff's political fate for the allurement of a ministership in a Congress cabinet; and Shariff himself though still tied to the Congress chariot, was definitely barred from a ministerial berth by the Congress national leadership's decision against him.[114]

Wylie then encouraged Khare, the ousted predecessor of Shukla and now expelled from the Congress party, to bring down the Shukla cabinet and form a non-Congress coalition ministry with the support of the Independent Party, Muslim MLAs, and some supposedly dissident Congressmen.[115] Khare, eager to turn the table on Shukla, assured the Governor of his ability to cause defections from the Congress party,[116] banking mainly on fellow Maharashtrian MLAs who shared his grudges against Shukla, D.P. Mishra, and the Mahakoshal group of Hindi-speaking Congressmen who dominated the party at the time. For about four years, from November 1939 when the Shukla ministry resigned, to July 1943, when the tide of the war turned definitely in favour of the allied powers, Governors Wylie and Twynum kept conniving with Khare to somehow cobble up a non-Congress coalition ministry. Khare on his part kept luring the Muslim MLAs, among others, to his projected pro-government ministry.

Khare failed in his object; he could not garner the support needed to survive a no-confidence motion which the majority Congress party was certain to move against his ministry. Wylie left the province in May 1940, sore that Khare was only 'deluding himself'[117] when making tall claims of mustering adequate support among legislators for his ministry.

Before his governorship of the CP and Berar, Henry Twynum had served in Bengal as the Chief Secretary, counting among his friends prominent League leaders—Fazlul Haq, Khwaja Nazimuddin, and Shahid Surhawardy. Towards communal disputes his attitude was rather pro-Muslim; on the issue of music before mosques, for example, he regarded 'the Muslim case the more reasonable', the Hindus being more provocative. He wanted a total ban on music before all mosques during prayer hours, not in respect to only the mosques specifically listed either in Hindu-Muslim agreements at places or in executive orders prevalent at others. He was against any 'rigid acceptance of the common law principle' that all were free to use public highways as they pleased, although he was aware that even most ICS and IP officers of the province favoured upholding the citizen's right to use highways without any restriction whatsoever.[118] He had all sympathy for the Muslims who, being small in number, 'appear always in the role of aggressors',[119] although local officers—many British among them—blamed the Muslims as much as the Hindus for causing communal troubles.

More than Wylie, Twynum personally preferred the restoration of ministerial administration to the continuation of the Governor's rule during the war; the government's war efforts, he hoped, had better prospects of success when a ministry was in place. But the League was wholly opposed to the idea, Jinnah holding firmly that Muslim interests were secure under the Governor's administration rather than under a Hindu majority rule. Linlithgow would in no way annoy Jinnah when the Congress troubled the government to no end.

This set the background in which Twynum persisted in his attempts at ministry making. For quite a while he shared Khare's hope that many Congress MLAs, who reportedly disliked the party high command's decision against forming another ministry and who sorely missed the legislator's allowance (Rs. 75 a month),[120] would before long flock behind Khare, allured by the prospect of regaining political power. When Khare gave him a list of sixty-one MLAs who were likely to support him,[121] the Governor was overjoyed at the 'tremendous stride' made by the legislators 'in the direction of breaking away from the present policy of the Congress'.[122] For Khare, fully cooperating with the government's war efforts, the Governor had all good words: he was a 'broad minded likeable little man who, though probably weak' was 'very tenacious of purpose as his attitude towards the present high command and his former colleagues'[123] clearly indicated. Twynum looked fondly forward to the day when Khare would return to power instead of 'Shukla, Mishra and Co.'.[124] Khare perfectly fitted into the Governor's scheme of breaking the Congress hegemony in provincial politics.

Khare and Twynum met several times to work out their strategy,[125] the Governor taking upon himself the task of coaxing some Muslim MLAs into Khare's cabinet. W.V. Grigson, Secretary to the Governor, and Khan Bahadur Abdur Rahman Khan, the League MLA and Publicity Secretary of the provincial League, discussed the matter, Grigson pleading that the League, by joining the cabinet, would provide security to Muslim interests, besides setting an example of Hindu-Muslim cooperation in running the provincial administration.[126]

In fact, of the ten League MLAs, Khare and Twynum could be sure of winning over just one, Rizvi, through his mentor, Raghavendra Rao's good offices. All the rest, it was well known, 'would blindly follow Jinnah whatever their personal views',[127] and Jinnah was firmly opposed to the resurrection of the 'dead constitutional scheme'[128]—the Government of India Act, 1935 under which a ministerial administration could again be set up in the province. Abdur Rahman echoed what Jinnah had already made known: Muslims felt far happier under the Governor's rule; he added that under the existing rule, the government's war winning efforts had been far more successful than they could be under a restored ministerial administration.[129]

Nevertheless, Abdur Rahman promised to take the matter up with Jinnah when Grigson persisted, assuring him that the Governor would himself finalize with Khare the terms and conditions under which the Muslims could join the new Khare cabinet.[130] However, the provincial League leaders knew well that no matter what the Governor and Khare said to the contrary, a ministry of small non-Congress groups in the Assembly would fall like ninepins when challenged by the dominant Congress party which alone could provide a stable government to the province. And if the Congress returned to power, it would mete out a vengeful treatment to the Muslims for backing Khare in his futile attempts at forming an anti-Congress ministry. In such a situation the Governor, despite his sympathy for the Muslims but because of constitutional constraints, could do very little to protect the Muslims.[131] In fact, Muslims still grudged that the Governor had not protected them adequately when they were mistreated by the Congress ministry in 1937–9. Twynum was disappointed when even Khare's bait of two ministerial berths to the Muslims in a cabinet of five failed to offset the League legislators' fear of Jinnah's wrath if they swallowed the bait.[132]

In January 1941 Khare and Twynum stepped up their efforts at ministry making when many Congressmen had been jailed for participation in the individual satyagraha; a non-Congress ministry now ran little risk of facing a no-confidence motion in the Assembly.[133] But the Muslim MLAs were still hesitant, particularly after knowing that Aney backed Khare in the ministry making project. Muslims were acutely suspicious of Aney, who, besides being closely associated with the Hindu Mahasabha, the RSS, and the Hindu unity movement in general, had, as a member of the Viceroy's Executive Council, consistently opposed the return of Berar to the Nizam[134]—a fond object of all the Muslims. In fact, Muslims of the province had no faith in any Hindu leader except Raghavendra Rao, now away from provincial politics but still wielding considerable influence among the non-Congress elite, particularly the Muslims.[135] Both Khare and Twynum sought his good offices to persuade the non-Congress and Muslim MLAs to help form the Khare ministry.[136] Khare wrote to Jinnah assuring him of the 'comprehensive plan' of his ministry to protect Muslim interests.[137]

However, all the efforts of Khare and Twynum came a cropper due to unfavourable reactions of both Linlithgow and Jinnah. The Viceroy was 'dead against affording any support to the kind of manoeuvres'[138] which was needed to cobble up a minority non-Congress ministry and then keep it going. Such a ministry of small groups had indeed 'no real degree of stability' nor 'a prospect of reasonable performance'; it would fail to facilitate the government's war efforts,[139] the object for which the governor had been trying to set up a ministry. Such was the view of the Secretary of State too.[140]

As for Jinnah, Khare's offer though tempting, was not free from some risk. Initially, Jinnah was not wholly averse to being 'bought over'[141] by Khare; two Muslims in a cabinet of five would indeed be a great political gain for the League. But Jinnah was wary, Khare's real intentions being still unclear to him. Jinnah distrusted all Congressmen including Khare. He knew that Khare was hostile only to the Congress high command, not to the party itself. He also knew that Khare had sympathizers, mainly fellow Maharashtrians, in the Congress party whose support he sought to draw on to form a ministry.

Therefore, before committing himself, Jinnah needed to be convinced that Khare had actually formed an altogether new party and made its members known through the press. Jinnah warned Rauf Shah and Abdur Rahman Khan against 'putting themselves too much in Khare's hands' and acting in a haste.[142] He knew that there were in the provincial League some who were eager for ministership. Jinnah's cautious approach to the League's political prospects in the CP and Berar was in part influenced by the problems created at the time by his partymen in Bengal, Sind, and Assam.[143] Jinnah decided to temporize, asking his men to keep talking to both Khare and the Governor and buy time.

Rauf Shah and Abdur Rahman Khan met both Khare and Grigson several times, insisting that the ministry be a 'composite' one instead of a mere coalition, so that no major policy decision could be taken by it without prior concurrence of all its constituent parties.[144] Khare assured the League leaders that no decision affecting Muslim interests would be taken by his ministry without taking the Muslim League into confidence.[145] He also requested Rauf Shah to raise at the League working committee meeting in Delhi the issue of the party joining his ministry. However, considering Jinnah's choleric character and Rauf Shah's mild temperament, Khare had doubts if the latter could at all muster sufficient courage to raise the matter at the League meeting.[146] As for Jinnah, he ignored Khare's letters to him in which, besides claiming support of many MLAs, Khare had also stressed two facts: as a Premier he had risked his colleagues' wrath to protect Muslim interests and prevent injustice to them;[147] and even prominent Leaguers of the province like Samiullah Khan and Maulana Abdul Natiq had publicly denounced the Congress high command for the bad treatment to Khare,[148] thus suggesting their sympathy for him.

Khare persisted with patient tenacity. He saw Linlithgow more than once but failed to remove the Viceroy's deep seated aversion to 'playing with minority ministries' and 'manoeuvrings in support of a particular faction or outlook' in provincial politics, despite his sympathy for the 'restlessness of the Liberals and men like Dr Khare'.[149]

Desperate, but still clinging to his hope of becoming the Premier again, Khare now requested Twynum to at least ensure that if at Jinnah's behest the League did not join his ministry, it should at least stay neutral whenever he faced a no confidence motion in the Assembly.[150]

However, by now much time had already passed, and Twynum's interest in a minority ministry had definitely flagged. He saw that Khare, 'the incorrigible optimist'[151] had for more than two years indulged in 'some sort of wishful thinking', trying to build up his ministry 'on sand'.[152] Khare had actually received only promises, no solid support of any—not even that of his long time friend and former colleague, Ramrao Deshmukh, who in fact, was 'far from enthusiastic about the whole project'.[153] If anything, Khare had indeed proved himself a very poor judge of men when fondly hoping that he could cause desertions from the Congressmen in the Assembly to help him form the ministry.

In August 1942 the Congress launched the Quit India Movement when, more than ever before, the British government required being on good terms with the League which opposed the movement. Sometime before, Khwaja Nazimuddin, the prominent League leader and later Premier of Bengal, while touring the CP and Bear as a member of the Muslim Defence Council, had stayed with the Governor, Twynum, his friend, and had promised him help to keep the Muslims away from any Congress movement.[154] Twynum relied on Nazimuddin's promise.

Twynum made another move. His efforts to set up a pliable non-Congress ministry having come to nothing, he now toyed with the idea of appointing two non-official Indian advisors in his council,

Khare and Rauf Shah,[155] as a means of attaching the non-Congress forces closer to the government when the Congress movement had already strongly influenced the general public. Khare had in the meanwhile spurned the Congress offer of a reconciliation, having decided once and for all that his political future lay only as an opponent of the Congress. His followers in the province, calling themselves Responsivists, were by now 'more or less committed to the Government's aid by reason of their race, wealth, previous record or status'.[156] As for Rauf Shah, he, unlike his *bete noire,* Siddiqui Ali Khan, was a moderate Muslim, being on good terms with both Khare and Raghavendra Rao; keen on maintaining good terms with the Governor also, he, for a time at least, seemed not too enamoured of even the Pakistan idea.[157]

However, Twynum soon gave up this project too when the crisis created by the Congress passed off; exercising his own powers and rallying all non-Congress elements behind him, the Governor was able to suppress the Quit India Movement. He imposed punitive fines on Hindus alone, exempting the Muslims despite local officers—among them some British—disfavoured such an exemption.[158] This wilfully driven political wedge further divided the Hindus and Muslims, the latter now all the more distrusted as being hostile to national interests which the Congress championed.

In 1943, Twynum strongly recommending, Khare was made a member of the Viceroy's Executive Council—a 'fitting reward' for the 'valuable services' he rendered to the government.[159] Apart from helping in army recruitment,[160] Khare had given the authorities 'valuable information' about the Congress activities both inside and outside the province, including its attempts at disrupting communication links between places.[161]

Muslim MLAs remained a factor in provincial politics when T.J. Kedar made another attempt to form a non-Congress ministry with their help. Kedar, who took over from Khare the leadership of the Responsivist party, shared the latter's eagerness to be the Premier though having no comparable standing in provincial politics; above all, both among the Governor and the local Muslim elite, he, unlike Khare, had a very poor image. The Governor viewed him as 'a careerist, volatile and unscrupulous'[162] politician, while the Muslims knew him as but a political chameleon who had 'changed his party labels more often than his clothes'.[163] Kedar demurred giving two ministerial posts and two parliamentary secretaryships to the

Muslims which earlier Khare had conceded. Muslims were aware of his opposition to the Pakistan scheme, his efforts to win over Congressmen by offers of help to get their colleagues released from jail, and his attempts at tempting the non-Leaguer Muslims into his projected ministry. This 'most dangerous principle to set up Muslims against Muslims'[164] angered the League most when it was well known that Jinnah regarded all non-Leaguer Muslims as non-Muslims.

Curiously enough, a few among the local Leaguers were still eager to join Kedar's coalition ministry only if the acquiescence of the party's national leadership could somehow be secured. They were sorely disappointed; Rauf Shah received from Jinnah 'a bit of a raspberry'[165] which snuffed out his flickering hope of somehow becoming a minister. Jinnah sternly rebuked him for hankering to join a ministry of 'mere mushroom groups' and 'miscellaneous characters having no backing of a recognized organization or any real support of public men'—men who were 'just scrambling for ministerships as opportunists'. Rauf Shah confabulating with such men for an agreement before joining the ministry angered Jinnah further: 'you might as well enter into treaties and pacts with the lampposts', Jinnah thundered; the men being of no political standing whatsoever. Such a rag-tag ministry had no chance of survival in the face of certain opposition of the Congress in the Assembly, once it was reconvened. And it was the Congress which now counted most in provincial politics.

Jinnah sternly reminded Rauf Shah that he not only was the provincial League chief but held in his custody 'the reputation of the All India Muslim League' itself;[167] Jinnah also reminded him of the cardinal principle of the League: a provincial ministry had to have Muslims in it, and such Muslims must be none other than Leaguers. Jinnah knew that Kedar had been sounding the four non-League Muslim MLAs apart from Rauf Shah himself. Jinnah warned Rauf Shah against being wheedled into an agreement with anybody before submitting it to the League supremo himself.[168] Jinnah would prefer the provincial League MLAs sitting in opposition to their joining any 'make-shift ministry' which, devoid of any popular support, would have to depend entirely on the Governor and his Councillors for its survival.[169]

Jinnah also saw that Twynum was no longer keen on having a ministry. The Quit India Movement was over and with the USA joining the allied powers, the war had turned favourable for the latter. In this changed situation, the Governor would rather go slow, no longer directly encouraging the Leaguers to join a pro-government coalition ministry;[170] he really had no need for such a ministry now. This the Governor had already made clear to both Kedar and Abdur Rahman Khan when they had pressed him to openly support the ministry when formed.[171]

It was not unknown to Twynum that Kedar was just seeking to make use of the Muslim MLAs to realise his personal ambition, and this was known to the Muslims too.[172] The Governor was certain that Kedar would fail in his object because, however eager personally, no Muslim MLA would dare join the ministry in the face of Jinnah's disapproval. Abdur Rahman Khan had, in fact, told the Governor plainly that if any ministry were formed with no Muslim in it or any non-Leaguer Muslim in it, Muslims would be forced to stage such a strong reaction as would plunge the whole province into chaos.[173] Whether or not the Governor took the warning seriously, he used it to discourage Kedar from persisting with his effort.

Ultimately, Kedar, like Khare earlier, failed to garner the requisite support of legislators to form a viable ministry. Like Khare again, he importunated the Governor time and again to help him, even assuring Twynum that the ministry would give him no trouble whatsoever; that the men would be bound by no political principles but only by their personal aspirations and personal allegiance to him.[174] Having failed, again like Khare, to receive even a reply to his letter to Jinnah, Kedar gave up the hope of enlisting the League support to his scheme; he would settle for a non-Leaguer Muslim minister,[175] having presumably Yusuf Shariff in mind. Interestingly enough, Shariff had just resigned his Congress membership,[176] hoping for either a judgeship or a ministership in a coalition cabinet.[177] Shariff and Kedar were old friends and earlier members of the People's Party formed by Kedar. Besides, all along Shariff had kept up friendly relations with both Kedar and his mentor, Khare.

Twynum was indeed in a strong position, what with powerful politicians bending over backwards to seek his favour. He was aware of some Leaguers who had not taken kindly to Jinnah's directive; they still believed that 'a pliable and reasonably strong ministry' could be formed if only it could secure the Governor's 'active benevolence'[178] and stay in place by his pressure and patronage. But the Governor chose to bide his time, neither directly encouraging the power seekers nor openly discouraging them. He had to defer to the Viceroy's strong opinion about the matter. Linlithgow had never been enthusiastic about a ministry during the war; he had repeatedly asked Twynum to continue with his personal rule which had so long kept the 'general temper of the province low'.[179]

The Viceroy wanted nothing short of a stable ministry, if the Governor insisted on having a ministry at all to smoothly conduct war operations; there had never been any prospect of such a ministry as could be approved of by the Viceroy. All along the Viceroy had strong doubts if 'a ministry dominated by careerists and living in constant dread of the reappearance of the major Hindu political party (that is the Congress) would really be too strong a foundation to work at'.[180] He was particularly surprised over the 'inordinate demand' made by the Muslims as their price for supporting the ministry: two ministerships and two parliamentary secretaryships were indeed 'ludicrously in excess of' what they really deserved[181]—going by their ratio in the population of the province and their political strength.

This provided the *coup d' grace* to attempts at making a 'make-shift' ministry composed of Muslims and other non-Congress groups. Twynum had now no need to 'start something like the King's Party of George III'[182] to form a pliable ministry far less ensuring its survival 'by exerting gentle pressure through his officers on the many wavering personalities in local politics'.[183] The ministry making exercise laid bare the division among the self-seeking political elite and made the Governor's task easier during the trying times of the war.

VI

In post-war years two developments influenced both the course and character of communalism in the province: Congress political ascendancy in the province confirmed by its runaway victory in the elections of 1946; and the general Muslim acquiescence in the Congress rule despite the insoluble constitutional problems created by the clashing Congress and League national leaderships. Before long a section of the provincial Leaguers realized the futility of sniping at the Congress and the wisdom in reconciliation with the majority Hindu rule; only a small group of local Leaguers persisted in the policy of confrontation with the Congress mostly at the bidding of the League national leadership.

The provincial Congress leaders encouraged the process of reconciliation, reassuring the minority Muslims of security while taking all steps to prevent their involvement in communal troubles. Congressmen dealt with the Mahasabha challenge effectively and took care to prevent other Hindu communal groups from creating any great mischief.

Unlike in 1937, the election-eve scene in 1945–6 was far less tense despite the withdrawal of the Defence of India Rules to maintain public order.[184] Communal propaganda was on a much lower key, the only election issue being the League's Pakistan scheme and the constitutional impasse created by League-Congress differences.

All the three parties, the Congress, the League, and the Mahasabha, plunged headlong into the election fray, all enrolling new members by a determined recruitment drive and a sustained propaganda campaign. There were a few clashes between Congressmen and Mahasabhites,[185] Moonje, as ever, charging the Congress as pro-Muslim and soft towards the League; both the parties made use of the Ganapati festival for political propaganda.[186]

The League set up district election offices and a central camp at Jabalpur to train its cadres in electioneering techniques, political agitations and fund raising, each district being asked to donate a specific amount to the election fund.[187] A women's committee was created and volunteers sent to picket cinema halls at Amravati to prevent Muslim women from visiting them.[188] The provincial League issued an instruction to Muslims against attending meetings addressed by non-Leaguer Muslims.[189]

All the three parties had internal problems to sort out before going to the polls. The Mahasabha was jolted by Aney debunking the party's Hindu militarization policy while declaring that the Congress non-violent means was best suited to accelerate the nationalist cause.[190] Rebels caused problems for the dominant Mahakoshal group in the provincial Congress;[191] a prominent leader of the Vidarbha Congress, Manoharsha Awari undertook a fast, protesting against the list of candidates given the party ticket for the election.[192]

Personal rivalries added to the troubles of the faction-ridden provincial League. The old rasping quarrel between Rauf Shah and Siddiqui Ali Khan often exploded into the full public view, the moderate and extremist elements in the party ranging behind them respectively, besides the Berari and non-Berari groups. The Berari Leaguers requested Jinnah to set up a separate Berar unit of the party just as the Congress had done years ago.[193] During the elections, the Shia-Sunni conflict in the provincial League surfaced as did the Momin challenge to the League's claim of political primacy.[194] Abbas Ali Kamal, a Shia Leaguer of Nagpur, strongly grudged the nomination of Abdul Sattar Faruqui as the official League candidate for the Nagpur seat, setting aside the nomination of Kamal by the provincial League itself.[195] For this and some other instances of the 'despotic and unjustifiable attitude' of the party high command, A.S. Khan, a pleader of Chhindwara, President of the local League and an elected representative on the Muslim League Council, resigned the party.[196]

The momins were themselves a divided lot, some fully supporting the League when their leader Faruqui was given the party ticket[197] while others, their claim to the ticket ignored, continued with their opposition to the League. Anisuddin Ahmad condemned Faruqui as an incompetent man 'pushed up' by Congress minded *koshtis* of Burhanpur, Jabalpur, Kamptee, and Nagpur; he was 'an instrument in the hands of the Congress enemies' of the Muslim League.[198] The anti-Rauf Shah faction alleged that he and his ally, Abdur Rahman Khan, had in 1937 written to Maulana Azad, expressing their willingness to join the Congress if they were made ministers in the Congress cabinet.[199] Three rebel Leaguers opposed the official candidates, one, Muhammad Asghar Ali defeating the veteran Hifazat Ali for the Nimar seat.[200]

Yusuf Shariff, who had returned unheralded to the League in 1943, failed to politically redeem himself; he was denied the party ticket;[201] his political fate was indeed the seal of his character, promotion of personal interests alone motivating his changing political alignments.

Curiously enough, the rivalry between two League stalwarts, Burhan-ul-Haq, and Iftikar Ali, for the Jabalpur Muslim reserved seat had an unintended effect: a Hindu-Muslim fraternization for a while in the town so long notorious for communal troubles. Iftikar Ali now befriended D.P. Mishra, the former Minister, and the two led a huge procession shouting slogans for Hindu-Muslim unity.[202] Mishra also went to Burhanpur, equally notorious for communal strifes, to condemn the Pakistan idea and forge Hindu-Muslim amity.[203]

Nationalist Muslims of the province met at the home of Abdul

Rahman Khan, Secretary of the Jamait-ul-Ulema, Central Provinces, and decided to contest all the fourteen Muslim seats, forming a parliamentary board for the purpose.[204] However, much to the Leaguers' delight, nationalist Muslims created no impression on their community, which dismissed them as 'a big hoax'.[205] The CP Liberal Association's plea to the government to abolish the communal electoral system proved too late a cry in the wilderness.

The League won thirteen of the fourteen Muslim seats, routing mainly the Muslim Independents and Khaksars.[207] The one Muslim League rebel who won the election,[208] defeating the official candidate, soon returned to the party.[209] Many Khaksars now joined the League,[210] and the Momins chose to sink their differences with the League, resigning to the latter's increasing influence among all Muslims.[211] No Muslim contested from any general constituency, let alone any Leaguer.

The Congress came in on a flood of popularity, winning 94 of a total of 112 seats, but its two Muslim candidates lost to the Leaguers.[212] However, two other Muslim candidates won, one from the University constituency, and the other from a commerce constituency.[213] The Hindu Mahasabha, which contested all the seats, won just one, clearly suggesting that Hindu voters were all for the secular Congress party, no matter how able the Mahasabhites had been either in routing the Congress in municipal elections at places or rousing the Hindu hoodlums during communal riots at others. It was commonly believed that the RSS men did not vote for the Mahasabha,[214] the cold relationship between the top leadership of the two organizations being an important development in the war years and after.[215]

Immediately after the elections, there was an appearance of personal ambitions of some Muslim leaders getting the better of their feeling of communal solidarity. Rauf Shah's keenness to forge a Congress-League tie up and becoming a minister in a coalition cabinet was opposed by his detractors in the provincial League as was his bid to re-admit to the party the rebels who had contested the official candidates. Several prominent Leaguers demanded Rauf Shah's resignation as the chairman of the party's parliamentary board.[216]

Rauf Shah's hopes dashed when provincial Congressmen showed no interest in a coalition cabinet, despite, so claimed Rauf Shah, the Congress President Azad's interest[217] in such a cabinet. Whether or not such a coalition would have improved the communal situation in the province, it would have certainly broken the provincial League asunder, which had ever been faction-ridden and riven with personal jealousies between leaders.

Grudging acquiescence rather than willing acceptance was the initial League reaction to the new Congress government under Ravi Shankar Shukla. Prompted by the national leadership of the party, the provincial Leaguers at first sought to discredit the Congress rule by attributing communal tensions to official apathy and even incitement. Muslims were asked to trigger public panic by indulging in provocative cow slaughter and brick-batting whenever communal feelings ran high anywhere.[218] Rumours of thirty thousand Punjabi Muslims awaiting Jinnah's orders to sacrifice their lives for the cause of Islam created natural uneasiness in Hindu localities.[219] In the CP and Berar too, as elsewhere in the country, the League had already turned the Pakistan issue into a religious one, mosques being used for political propaganda.[220]

The Shukla government was both tough and tactful in dealing with the Muslim community. The general mood of the community itself seemed to have been changing on the eve of the election and more apparently after it. Thus Jabalpur and Nagpur witnessed an 'unprecedented spectacle' of Hindus and Muslims offering each other *pan-supari* during Dussehra and Id[220a] which was reciprocated later by the Muslims of Bilaspur where the Young Muslim Association held a function during dusserah. Some League leaders of Jabalpur and Nagpur opposed the process of reconciliation while local Communists supported it. The *Id Milat* at Amravati was attended by prominent Hindus. With Tukdoji Maharaj presiding over a meeting organized by the Rashtriya Yuvak Sangh, a Congress youth organization, a young Muslim installed a Ganesh idol, giving out a symbolic message of Hindu-Muslim unity.[220b]

There were clearer signs of improvement in the communal situation at the grassroots level. Viceroy Wavell's fear, in May 1946, of CP and Berar becoming a 'good third'[221] to the United Provinces and Bihar in respect of communal disturbances proved unfounded. Except at Badnera and Amravati, the League's Direct Action call (August 1946) and the killings in Calcutta and east Bengal districts passed off without much Muslim reaction elsewhere in the province. Muslims observed only a 'token' Direct Action Day on 16 August; they took out no large procession nor staged any hartal or picketing of Hindu shops. Muslim title holders did not give up their government titles as demanded by the League leadership. Most Muslims preferred security under the Congress government to risking its wrath; the fear of Hindu *Koshti* retaliation dampened the bellicosity of Muslim ruffians.[222] And all this despite the harangues of Faruqui, President of the Nagpur District Muslim League, against the Shukla government.[223]

At the directive of Maulana Azad, the Congress leader, a Muslim was elected unopposed on the Vidarbha Congress Committee.[224] Dr M.A. Latif Yazdani, once a staunch Leaguer, became the President of the Hindu Muslim Unity Board at Raipur besides sending a letter to Pethick-Lawrence, the Secretary of State for India, opposing the League's Pakistan scheme.[225] A section in the provincial League made critical comments on the League representatives in the interim government, expressing their misgivings about Liaquat Ali's competence.[226] Abbas Ali Kamal, earlier an ardent Leaguer and now fully reconciled to the Congress rule, won the election to the Vice-Presidentship of the Nagpur municipality, there being only 300 Muslims among his 3,300 electors.[227] He toured through Muslim localities, urging the people not to be swayed by the killings in Noakhali, Bombay, and Chhuprah.[228] Hindus and Muslims joined local Muslims at Damoh to celebrate for the first time the Prophet Muhammad's birthday, recalling the old Khilafat spirit.[229] In November 1946, local Congress and League leaders at Akola and Wassim addressed meetings together to prevent communal tensions. At places Hindu and Muslim leaders worked together to resolve disputes over the playing of music before mosques.[230] Finally some Muslim MLAs made impressive speeches when joining all others to celebrate the day of Independence.[231]

The Congress government kept the communal situation under complete control, the Home Minister, D.P. Mishra, taking all steps for the purpose.[232] No untoward incident followed when tales of Muslim atrocities on Hindus and Sikhs in the Punjab inflamed the Hindu public opinion, and refugees from the Punjab, Sind, and Hyderabad poured into the province followed by Muslim exodus from Berar to Hyderabad and the Muslim state of Bhopal.[233] The Hindu Mahasabha's observance of the Punjab Day and the League asking the Muslims to flee to Muslim states created no problem but some excitement among the Hindus and Muslims as did the rescue of some Hindu women from among some groups of Muslim evacuees stranded at railway stations.[234] Shukla himself visited Sagar to allay local Muslim fear of Hindu attack. He imposed a punitive police at Burhanpur following provocation to local Sikhs that led to a small riot at the place.[235]

VII

Berar was the only real problem of the Shukla government in the post-war years. Inhabited by a large Muslim population,[236] Berar districts had an acute and persisting communal problem. Riots rocked Badnera and Amravati in October–November 1946 as a Hindu reaction to Muslim atrocities in east Bengal. Police firing on a rampaging mob at Badnera took two lives;[237] local Congressmen and Leaguers freely indulged in rumour mongering which exacerbated the situation. The DC, G.L. Watson, urged strong measures: permanent posting of a punitive police force at the Amravati town, rigid implementation of the Goonda Act, and the externment of all suspicious characters from the district—to bring home to all that 'communal rioting does not pay'.[238]

The Muslim League used the Badnera and Amravati incidents to establish that the Congress government was as ever thoroughly anti-Muslim. The League's enquiry report sought to confirm that the local police, generally hostile to the Muslim community, acted at the bidding of the local Congressmen while targetting the Muslims alone for brutal action. Its conclusion was: 'the police was determined to annihilate the Muslims and curb down their spirit and to establish Hindu domination at Badnera'.[239] Hindu lawlessness had the 'encouragement or connivance of the Badnera police'.[240] The League found a clear correlation between Congress leaders' participation in the All India Physical Education Conference organized by the Hanuman Vyayam Prasarak Mandal at Amravati, the great excitement created among the local Hindus and the bloody riot that followed.[241] Shukla was condemned for his 'hymn of hate' against both the British government and the Muslims, whom he had been asking to 'pack up' and go to their 'dreamland, Pakistan'.[242]

Shukla gave a 'thundering reply' to League allegations, acting on Gandhi's suggestion.[243] The Berar Commissioner, C.J.W. Lillie's, enquiry into the police firing established that the Muslims were the aggressors who looted Hindu shops, thus justifying the police firing.

Intelligence reports had it that the League MLA, Hidayat Ali, gave open incitement to communalism.[244]

Berar's retrocession to the Nizam was another issue which had a bearing on the local Hindu-Muslim relations during the war and after. The Nizam had acquiesced in the perpetual lease of this rich cotton growing tract to the British government in 1902 without giving up his *de jure* sovereignty on it. His flag flew on ceremonial occasions all over the region and his birthday was celebrated as an official function. By an agreement in 1936, the Nizam secured the right to post his Agent at Amravati to safeguard the interests of his subjects in Berar when under ministerial rule in the province. Under the agreement he was entitled to be consulted when a Governor of the province was appointed and could object to the appointment of anyone as Governor recommended by an Indian ministry.[245]

The Nizam caused the British government some uneasiness—even annoyance—by periodical references to his sovereignty over Berar and at times by expecting its return to him as a reward for his services to the government—in the two wars, for example.

Public opinion in the province was clearly polarized on this issue, the Muslims favouring the Nizam's rule to be restored in Berar and the Hindus opposing it. In 1918, the Nizam had raised the issue with Edwin Montagu, the visiting Secretary of State for India, and encouraged general Muslim support for it, However, such support came first from Muslims outside Hyderabad,[246] not from his own subjects. The Nizam's move failed due to the lukewarmness, if not overt opposition, of the strong Hindu leadership of Berar. Both Ganesh Khaparde and Sripad Tambe refused to play into the hands of the Muslims for the Nizam's cause.[247] Tambe, ever a defender of Hindu interests, was concerned over Hyderabad having become a strong centre of Muslim influence due to the Aligarh movement, already 'pretty strong' there. The Nizam getting back Berar would stimulate the pan-Islamic movement and cause 'a great menace to the interests of the Hindus'.[248]

In 1924 the Berar issue provided a test case for the interpretation of paramountcy, Viceroy, Lord Reading, rejecting the Nizam's petition for Berar's return to him and the submission of the issue to an independent commission of enquiry to establish the tenability of his claim. Berar, becoming a strong centre of the Swarajists and Hindu Mahasabhites caused the Nizam considerable worry.[249]

In later years, with Hindu-Muslim relations worsening due to riots in Berar, its return to the Nizam became a cause for agitation by the Muslim League and counter-agitation by the Mahasabha. Local Congressmen too shared the general Hindu opposition to the return when Hindu sufferings in Hyderabad had already worked up the general Hindu sentiment and the Nizam's government had taken anti-Congress measures at the British government's behest.

The Berar issue gained a sharper focus during the final days of the Second World War and after when the Nizam again asserted his claim on the tract as a reward for his services during the war. While the Muslims, as ever, were united in their support to the claim, the Hindus, unlike before, were now divided on the issue. The division showed up in the conflicting stand taken by the local Brahmins and non-Brahmins, Maharashtrians and non-Maharashtrians and Beraris and non-Beraris.

All this came to the fore in June 1945 when the Prince of Berar toured the tract followed two years later by Sir Mirza Ismail, the Premier of Hyderabad. Both the visits had an undeclared but evident political purpose: to gauge the feelings of the Beraris to the Nizam's reasserted claim to the tract. While non-Brahmins and depressed class Hindus, both opposed to the brahmins, welcomed the Prince's visit, local authorities feared that the 'extreme Maharashtra Brahmin section of the Hindu Mahasabha' could create troubles when opposing the visit.[250]

However, among the Brahmin members of the Mahasabha there were deep differences between the Beraris and non-Beraris on the issue of the Prince's visit. At the Mahasabha's national body's session at Akola, Kulkarni, Joglekar, and Phadke, all Brahmins but none a Berari, made house to house propaganda for boycotting the visit and urged the people to stage black flag demonstration against the visit.[251] Some Mahasabha leaders represented to Aney, a strong champion of the interests of Berar, that the Prince's visit should be opposed as an 'aggressive act of the Muslims', Hindus being exhorted to court arrest to prevent it.[252] Local authorities feared Hindu-Muslim clashes following reports of League leaders raising funds for organising receptions to the Prince and the Mahasabha President, Savarkar, touring Berar to organise Hindu opposition to the visit.[253]

But then, the provincial Hindu Mahasabha meeting at Bilaspur, overruled the party's decision at Akola to boycott the visit, the Maharashtrian members of the party being keen on the Prince's visit after satisfying themselves that it was 'not a veiled move for the retrocession of Berar' to the Nizam.[254] Khaparde, the Vice-President of the All India Hindu Mahasabha and the President of its provincial unit, and a Berari Brahmin, opposed the boycott resolution passed by the party's national body at Akola.[255]

This greatly incensed V.G. Deshpande, the General Secretary of the All India Hindu Mahasabha, and a non-Berari Brahmin, who held a secret meeting of partymen at Khamgaon to form a committee to organize the boycott of the visit which he knew for sure was politically motivated.[256] He strongly criticized Punjabrao Deshmukh, the foremost non-Brahmin Maharashtrian leader of Berar and former Minister, for allegedly supporting the Nizam's claim to Berar.[257] As for Berar Congress, contemporary official reports had it that most of them were rather indifferent to the Prince's visit, while a few like P.S. Patel, a prominent non-Brahmin MLA, openly supported it.[258] The Hindi speaking businessmen of Khamgaon took leading part in organizing the reception of the Prince as did Congress leaders of Amravati as well.[259] The DC Amravati reported that majority of the local Hindus were both unwilling to boycott the visit and unenthusiastic about the Mahasabha's boycott call.[260]

Actually, the Prince's visit passed off 'quietly and gracefully', local people showing 'nothing but respect and affection for the Prince' as indicated by the addresses presented to him. No communal outbreak marked the visit, local authorities having preserved perfect peace, receiving active cooperation of both Hindu and Muslim leaders; none really saw 'eye to eye with those advocating boycott'—practically non-Berari Maharashtrian Brahmins only. The Prince for himself discreetly avoided anything to suggest that he had any political bee in his bonnet.[261]

Sir Mirza Ismail's visit to Berar[262] in April 1947 deepened the differences between Hindu caste groups rather than intensifying Hindu-Muslim ill-feelings. The Mahars joined the Muslims in favouring Berar's return to the Nizam, one of their leaders, S.A. Khandare of Amravati, asserting that the Nizam was the 'rightful owner of Berar and legitimate claimant to it'. He assured Mirza Ismail that the 'good wishes of the Mahars went with the house of the Nizam'.[263] Khandare repeated the same sentiment at a meeting convened by Brijlal Biyani, a non-Brahmin Congress leader of Berar, The Berar Young Muslim Federation and the Berar Scheduled Caste Federation jointly presented a civic address to Mirza Ismail.[264]

Of all the Berar leaders, it was Punjabrao Deshmukh who made the most of the visit. He kept Mirza Ismail's company during a part of his tour, hosted him a lunch at his home in Amravati and arranged for him a grand reception by his Shivaji Education Society. In his welcome address, Deshmukh expressed his 'great debt of gratitude to the Muslims, both official and non-official, for their heartiest cooperation'[265] in his educational effort. However, the reception arranged by Deshmukh was 'a conspicuously non-Brahmin affair', as R.D. Bahl, the DC Amravati, clearly saw, Muslims, Depressed Class Hindus, and Christians, besides Maratha Kunbis, in great numbers attending the show.[266]

It was significant that the Hanuman Vyayam Prasarak Mandal, Amravati, the famous school for physical culture and education, an institution run by upper caste Hindus with strong links with the RSS and the Hindu Mahasabha, invited Mirza Ismail without the knowledge of Punjabrao Deshmukh. More significant was Mirza Ismail's not visiting the institution which disappointed its members who knew that the Hyderabad Premier gave interviews to many local leaders, mostly non-Brahmins and 'to a large number of Muslims of all degrees of eminence'.[267]

The Congress government of the province was not worried over any political fall-out of Mirza Ismail's visit, though it knew that 'ostensibly private', the visit was a means to keep alive the Nizam's claim to Berar.[268] While the League MLAs were ardent supporters of the claims, the general Hindu opinion was now better organized to resist it. This became apparent in the resolutions passed by many municipal committees, the Berar All Parties Conference, the Berar Chamber of Commerce, and the Bar Associations of Akola and Buldana.[269]

Even Punjabrao Deshmukh, by then a Congressman,[270] publicly referred to the Berar people being 'most genuinely apprehensive of retrocession' of the tract, warning that Berar's future had to be settled in accordance with its people's wishes.[271] Besides, local authorities assured the Shukla government that the many receptions held in honour of Mirza Ismail indicated rather the local people's accustomed civility to a visiting dignitary[272] than their eagerness to become the Nizam's subjects again[273]—Muslims and depressed class Hindus, excepting. Even the latter's proclaimed attachment to the Nizam sprang from their deep-seated hostility to the Brahmins, who led the anti-Nizam movement in Berar, than anything else. The strong Congress hold on Berar and the anti-League sentiment among

Hindus in general were secure enough guarantee against the Nizam reestablishing his rule in Berar.

All told, as Bahl correctly saw, Mirza Ismail's visit actually turned out to be rather 'a very confused affair' like a 'punch and Judy show with more than one person pulling the strings, usually in contrary directions.'[274] Local political bigwigs, often rivals, sought to show off their closeness to the Hyderabad Premier either to brighten their own image or to derive some more material gains.[275] Punjabrao, for example, got from Mirza Ismail a handsome donation for his education society, besides fully utilizing the visit to enhance his own political stature.[276]

Immediately before Independence, the Nizam made one more desperate attempt. He requested the British government to make a new treaty separating Berar from the CP and turning it over to him before leaving India. But then, with their hands full with many pressing cares at the time, the British decided to keep the Berar issue in the backburner till their 'paramountcy obligation' ceased in India and they left the country. Sir Frederick Burrows, the last British Governor of the CP and Berar, knew well that Mirza Ismail had been strongly influenced by the non-Brahmin leaders of Berar without suspecting that they wanted Berar as a separate province only to promote their own interests—not the Nizam's. And this Burrows pointedly told Mirza Ismail before turning down his entreaties for a new treaty.[277] At the same time, Lord Mountbatten, the Viceroy, also assured a worried Jawaharlal Nehru, the Prime Minister of the Interim Government, that the British had no intention to give Berar back to the Nizam before leaving India.[278]

The situation in Berar remained tense in the days immediately before and after Independence. Panic gripped many places following rumours of impending disorder and chaos. An exodus of Berari Muslims to Hyderabad had to be checked by strong measures and public appeal.[279] Some domoralization had set in among the local business community, mainly Hindus. Caste Hindus intensely disliked the depressed class Hindus' declared loyalty to the Nizam through their representative D.K. Bhagat, once an MLA.[280] By now, in the provincial politics a rift had developed between the non-Brahmin Maratha Kunbi leaders and Depressed Class leaders when many of the former joined the Congress party.

The Hindu Mahasabha drew up several representations to Premier Shukla, opposing the Nizam's suspected bid to create troubles in Berar and asking the Hindus to beware of the local Muslims.[281] The

Hindu no-retrocession demand was supported by all local organizations of Telhara, Murtizapur, Manglurpir, Shegaon, Khamgaon, Karanja, and Amravati. The Buldana municipal committee wanted the holding of a general referendum on the issue while the Berar All Parties Conference held out a warning that any treaty between the departing British authorities and the Nizam, effecting the retrocession, would not be binding on the people of Berar. Hindus appealed to Gandhi, Nehru, Patel, and J.B. Kriplani and even the Viceroy to consider the Berar people's strong sentiment over the issue.[282] By now the activities of the Razakars in Hyderabad and the Nizam's anti-Congress policies had further reinforced the Hindu determination to foil the Nizam's bid to take over Berar.

There were reports of Nizam's troops foraying into Berar districts and encouraging the settlement of some reservists of the Hyderabad state forces in tracts close to the Akola district. Hindu Mahasabha workers saw Nizam's troops particularly active at Muslim-inhabited Wasim. The Nizam's government made vitriolic propaganda about food scarcity in Berar and the Congress government's mismanagement of the problem.[284] All this assumed a sinister significance, justifying a strong representation with the Nizam's government. Local officers, however, saw no need for it, dismissing the latest developments as but a flash in the pan. Commissioner C.J.W. Lillie, who earlier had served in Hyderabad, and 'knew a little of local politics', attributed the developments to some 'extremist elements' in the Nizam's government, who, 'like the Bourbons of France... have learnt nothing and forgotten nothing'. He disfavoured taking the matter up with the Nizam, for the latest developments on the Berar border indicated nothing but 'excessive zeal by some subordinate military officers on the border'.[285] Home Minister Mishra, however, took it more seriously; he kept Vallabhbhai Patel, the Minster-in-Charge of States, posted with the developments on the Berar-Hyderabad border.[286] He addressed public meetings emphasizing the government's ability to foil the Nizam's scheme.[287]

VIII

A general anti-Muslim sentiment rankled in the Hindu mind even after Independence. The continuing general Muslim sympathy for Pakistan, the activities of the RSS and the Hindu Mahasabha, culminating in the assassination of Gandhi, the Pakistani invasion of

Kashmir and the Police Action in Hyderabad—all of this contributed to the sentiment.

Premier Shukla himself seemed to have been affected by the sentiment when he resolved to end the continuing Muslim over-representation in the public services, particularly in the police and revenue (executive)) departments. This over-representation, appearing as the colonial government's partiality to the Muslims, had periodically caused acrimonious debates in the provincial legislature. Shukla would cleanse the administration of the Muslims though publicly disclaiming any such intention.[289] He would use the existing rule of compulsorily retiring government employees who had served for twenty-five years or more; he would even pay compensation to 'oust' all non-CP Muslim personnel in the Special Armed Police and District Emergency Force 'who were yet to complete twenty five years of service'. He would also discharge Muslim cadets in the police training college, the government disfavouring their absorption in the provincial police force after they passed out of the college. He would 'oust' all Muslim employees recruited recently but yet to be confirmed in their services.[290]

However, Shukla failed in his scheme, the bureaucracy opposing it as being both legally untenable and administratively impracticable. High ranking officers, now mostly Indians, held that for his proven inefficiency alone could a government employee be sacked, whatever be his religious faith. However, the government could discourage any further Muslim recruitment so that their representation in the services was brought down to their proportion in the local population; but even that could be done not by any government order but by demi-official instruction to recruiting authorities so as to avoid legal complications, if challenged in the court.[291]

The Shukla government was also determined to weed out the League's lingering influence in the province after Independence. In fact, it was then clear that its cadre strength (49,049) was no indication of the party's political relevance.[291a] A few prominent Leaguers had gone away to Pakistan, but some returned soon, realising the wisdom of the old adage, 'a known devil is better than an unknown angel'. Most League leaders chose to live on in India, giving up their separatist feelings; some of them, still politically ambitious, turned pro-Congress, watching with no regret the fast withering away of their old party, now utterly irrelevant. Yusuf Shariff, Abdus Sattar Faruqui, and Muhammad Zaheer Warsi of

Kamptee (a member of the League's central committee) made sincere efforts to dissuade Muslim exodus to Pakistan and Hyderabad.[291b]

However, some Urdu schools continued to be 'a seminary of reactionary communal and League politics' and consequently, a potential 'social danger'.[292] Government's surveillance forced the men associated with the schools to escape to Hyderabad, leaving but a few others rendered wholly inactive for local politics but cherishing an undying sympathy for the League. Muslims working in the gun carriage factory at Jabalpur were closely watched and arms seized from some Muslim houses, including that of Siddiqui Ali Khan of Nagpur.[293]

The government maintained a strict watch on virtually the entire Muslim community in Berar, not excepting even the policemen,[294] some reportedly 'completely anti-Hindu'.[295] Following the Nizam's troop movements on the border, the entire administration of Berar, and particularly the neighbourhood of Chanda, was 'put on a war footing from the security point of view' in the months preceding the Hyderabad Police Action.[296] Local people were given training in arms by the army, and home guards deployed in villages to deal with Muslim intruders from Hyderabad, mostly cattle lifters.[297] S. Mushran, DC Akola, stayed in touch with Hyderabad State Congress leaders for information on military movements by the Nizam's government on the Berar boder.[298]

The government prepared a dossier on all Hindu and Muslim voluntary organizations with details on their activities and growth.[299] Mishra urged the Muslims to recognize that their greatest safeguard against insecurity lay in their 'complete merger in the majority community except in matters religious and cultural'.[300]

The communally-surcharged atmosphere in 1947–8 influenced even the official mind at times, high ranking Hindu officers, like their coreligionists everywhere, resenting the general Muslim bias for the new state of Pakistan and reported Muslim atrocities on Hindus at some places in the country.[301] This came out particularly among officers of Berar, still a troublesome tract. Thus, H.S. Kamath, the Commissioner, for example, while not wanting the Muslim community to suffer due to the Hindu boycott, both social and economic, held the Muslims themselves responsible for their woes. He noted:

The unfortunate fact has to be faced that Muslims as a community have, by their senseless support of Pakistan and all that it has meant, laid themselves open to suspicions of all kinds, and any suffering which this may bring about for them can be removed primarily by their own efforts in the opposite direction.[302]

Later, in November 1947, when Muslims were worsted in a riot at Pathrot in Amravati district, Bahl, DC Amravati, wanted to punish all rioteers, Hindus and Muslims. Kamath disapproved this before laying down what looked like a new administrative principle:

> We should not, I think, now follow the old practice of punishing both the guilty and the innocent by starting security proceedings in cases of this nature. It is infinitely more just to proceed only against that party against which there is prima facie proof of guilt.[303]

Going by official reports, Muslims were, of course, the aggressors, but Hindus, many Congress workers among them, were not wholly innocent either.[304] Bahl, a civilian trained in the colonial administrative tradition, faithfully reported facts to his superior. But Kamath, also a civilian and having had the same administrative training, chose to strike a new note in the administration which seemed to him justified by the changed political condition of the time. After Independence and with most Muslims of the province choosing to stay on in their hearth and home,[305] any demonstrative impartiality in governance was no longer such a political necessity for local officers as it had so long been under the foreign colonial rule—the least so when such impartiality bore the distinct appearance of appeasement of the minority community for the sake of stemming the surging tide of Indian nationalism spearheaded by the majority Hindus.

NOTES

1. LP Reel no. 2199, Twynum to Linlithgow, 5 Oct. 1942.
2. HP File 18 Dec. 1939, FR, 2nd half of Dec. 1939.
3. *CPLA*, 6 Nov. 1939, pp. 280–1; 8 Nov. 1939, pp. 446, 482.
4. MAPM, File 2 (723/1939–40), DC Akola to Commr. Berar, 26 Aug. 1940. Abdul Bari Muhammad Razak of Wun (Yeotmal district) was a Congress *satyagrahi*. Fazl Rahim, a pleader of Kamptee, another Congress satyagrahi, did propaganda work at Amravati. File 703/1940, Yeotmal weekly Report; 726/1940, Amravati weekly Report, Feb. 1941.

   In 1940, of the 163 'district agitators' listed by the police, only four were Muslims. In a revised list of 151 Congressmen who needed to be watched, only three were Muslims. Muhammad Ali Abdul Ali Bohra of Khamgaon, a Forward Block activist, had 'revolutionary tendencies'. MAPM File 2 (723)/ 1939–40, DC Buldana to Secy. PM (C.M. Trivedi), 25 Aug. 1940.

5. MAPM, File 1/1942, Divisional Fortnightly Confidential Reports for 1942, 2nd half of Aug. 1942.

   Rafiq Mian Zamir Mian of Nagpur and Sheikh Usman Sheikh Yakub were killed in the disturbances during the movement. Yaseem Khan Fateh Khan, Aziz Muhammad Faiz Muhammad were jailed for involvement in the movement. M.Y. Quddusi, 'Some freedom fighters of Vidarbha', *Hitavada*, 20 Aug. 1976.

   Munshi Abdul Qadir, a pro-Congress Muslim leader, participated in the movement. Sheikh Khaksar, Saiyad Chhotu, Muhammad Usman and Muhammad Hashim were killed in police firing. Sharafuddin Sahil, *Nagpur Ka Muslim*, pp. 196, 198.

6. Ten government employees lost their life in the August 1942 disturbances, among whom was Abdul Samad, a police constable at Ashti. MAPM, File 16-65/1946.
7. MAPM, File 3/1945, FR, 1st half of Dec. 1945. HP File 18 Sept. 1944, FR, 1st half of Sept. 1944.
8. HP File 18 June 1942, FR, 1st half of June 1942; 18 July 1942, FR, 1st half of July 1942; 18 April 1943, FR, 2nd half of April 1943.
9. MAPM, File 1940, FR, 1st and 2nd half of Jan., I half of Mar. 1940.

   LP Reel no. 2197, Wylie to Linlithgow, 10 Feb. 1940. The Governor held the Muslims 'solely responsible for the trouble', and imposed 'with great reluctance' a punitive fine on them after conducting a public enquiry. Ibid., 22 Jan., 10 Feb., 9 April 1940.

10. MAGAD, File no. 4a-33/1942.
11. LP Reel no. 2197, Wylie to Linlithgow, Tel. 30 March 1940, 9 April 1940.
12. Ibid., same to same, Telg. 30 March 1940.
13. MAPM, File 705/1940, Buldana Weekly Reports, March, April 1941.

   The Hindu Mahasabha held annual meetings at Chandur Biswa in honour of Jagdeo Patil, the slain Congress activist (Chapter V), who was compared with Bhagat Singh, the well-known revolutionary of the Punjab who was hanged in 1931. Ibid.

14. MAGAD, File 4-54/1941, Reports on Amravati riots, Sept.–Oct. 1941. MAPM, File 1/1942.
15. MAGAD, File 4-54/1941.
16. Ibid., Joshi to A.L. Layard, Commr. Berar, 27 Sept., 6 Oct. 1941.

   Rauf Shah said that when he went to school, his father had entrusted him to the care of Moropant Joshi, who, he regretted, had now turned anti-Muslim. Joshi presided over meetings of Hindus held to defend community interests.

17. Ibid.
18. Ibid., Layard to Trivedi, 27 Sept. 1941. Husain, an able officer, was obstinate and rather tactless. Ibid., Report on Amravati riot by D.G. Watson, DIG Police, Western Range, Sept. 1941.

19. Ibid, *Hitavada*, 2, 5 Nov. 1941. Hidayat Ali, the League MLA, made provocative communal speeches.
20. Ibid.
21. In Congress Sevadal meetings at Amravati, Savarkar and Moonje were criticized and the RSS condemned for inciting communalism. MAPM, File 726/1940, DC Amravati to Secy. PM, 4 Aug. 1941.
22. MAPM, File 778(2)/1937; also File 778/1936, Government Memorandum on action to be taken to prevent the occurrence of communal strifes, CS to all DCs, 20 Dec. 1937. Also File 122/1939, CS to all District Press Advisors and DMs, 13 Dec. 1939.
23. Ibid.
24. MAPM, File 10/1942, SDM, Buldana to DC Buldana, 1 Feb. 1942.
25. MAPM, File 18/1946–7, Joshi to Commr. Berar, 7 July 1947.
26. MAPM, File 1/1944.
27. Ibid., Also File 18/1946–7, DC Akola to Commr. Berar, 14 Nov. 1946.
28. MAPM, File 11/1942, L.R.S. Singh, DC Akola to Trivedi, 1 Feb. 1942, Commr. Berar to Secy. PM, 14 Feb. 1942. The Commr. of Berar held a public enquiry which was neither so elaborate as to exacerbate communal feelings nor so summary as to cause disappointment among local Muslims. Ibid.

    Brijlal Biyani (1895–1961), a prominent Congress leader of Akola and then a member of the Council of State, condemned the lathicharge and tried to restore communal peace. Ibid.
29. MAPM, File 7(740)/1941, Secy. PM to DC Yeotmal, 3 June 1941, DC Yeotmal to Secy. PM, 21 June 1941.
30. MAPM, File 9(738)/1941. The dispute was finally settled in 1946, Muslims allowing Hindus to play music before the mosque except during prayer hours determined by the DC. Abdur Rahman Khan, the League MLA, and D.N. Deshpande, a Mahasabha leader, did much to bring the settlement about. MAPM, File 1/1946.
31. MAPM, File 9(738)/1941.
32. Ibid., Secy. PM to Commr. Berar, 17 Nov. 1941.
33. MAPM, File 1/1941.
34. MAPM, File 704/1940, DC Akola to Trivedi, 18 May 1941.
35. Ibid.; also same to same, 28 Jan., 4 Feb. 1941.
36. Ibid., DC Akola to Trivedi, 21 Jan. 1941.
37. MAPM, File 1(746)/1941, FR, 1st half of April 1941.
38. MAPM, File 6(725)/1940–41, DC Akola to Secy. PM, 28 March 1941. HP File 18 March 1941, FR, 2nd half of March 1941.
39. MAPM, File 1(746)/1941, Berar Divisional Confidential Fortnightly Reports.
40. Ibid., FR, 1st half of April 1941.
41. Ibid., FR, 1st half of Oct. 1941. However, the Mahasabha won 13 out of 15 seats.
42. Ibid., FR, 2nd half of Oct. 1941.
43. MAPM, File 13/1942, DC Amravati to Secy. PM, 3 Oct. 1942; File 726/

1940, same to same, 1, 28 April 1941. However, by November 1942, the two factions had made up their differences. MAPM, File 1/1942, FR, 2nd half of Sept., 2nd half of Nov. 1942.

44. MAPM, File 1/1941, FR, 1st half of July 1941.
45. Ibid., FR, 2nd half of Sept. 1941.
46. MAPM, File 2(724)/1939–40, Secy. PM to all commrs., 1 Dec. 1939.

46a. SP 280122/1942, M-27, T.C. Jayaratnam, Secy. PM to Moldrun, 19 July 1942.

47. The object was 'not so much to help the war as to train the Hindus in the use of arms against future emergencies'. MAPM, File 1(746)/1941, FR, 2nd half of Dec. 1941 and 1st half of Jan. 1942. Moonje wanted the Hindus to join the army 'to balance Muslim strength' in it. MAPM, File 726/1940, M.J.R. Sullivan, DC Amravati, to Trivedi, 4 March 1941. Also MAPM, File 704/1940, DC Akola to Trivedi, 26 Feb. 1941.
48. MAPM, File 1/1942, Divisional Fortnightly Confidential Reports for 1942, 30 Dec. 1941.

    Muslim recruiting officers openly supported the League's Pakistan scheme, and the government ignored it. MAPM, File 704/1940, DC Akola to Trivedi, 26 Feb. 1941.

    Officially, the League was neither against the government's war operations nor openly in favour. In the CP and Berar Leaguers were members of the war committees despite Jinnah's opposition to such membership.
49. MAPM, File 2/1942, A.H. Layard, DC Amravati to Jayaratnam, 27 Jan. 1942. The same was the government's reaction to the strong anti-Muslim speeches of V.G. Deshpande, another Mahasabha leader. MAPM, File 108/1939, CS to DC Wardha, 2 Nov. 1939.
50. MAPM, File 1/1942. Also File 726/1940, DC Amravati to Secy. PM, 18 March 1941.
51. LP Reel no. 2199, Twynum to Linlithgow, 20 July 1942. The Mahasabha appealed to communalism freely, condemning the Pakistan scheme far more vigorously than the Congress. MAPM, File 704/1940, DC Akola to CS 27 April 1941.

    Khaparde made 'entirely unfair and unwarranted' propaganda against local Muslims. MAPM, File 726/1940, DC Amravati to Secy. PM, 18 March 1941, 1 April, 5 May 1941. Also File 1/1941, FR 30 Sept. 1941.
52. MAPM, File 726/1940, Layard to Trivedi, 19 May 1941. In 1947, of the 112 constables, there were 66 Muslims; out of 24 Head Constables, 6 were Muslims. MAGAD, File 29/1947 (Secret).
53. MAPM, File 726/1940, Sullivan to Trivedi, 1 April 1941. Khaparde's attitude during the Amravati riot (1941) was very objectionable. MAGAD, File 4-54/1941.
54. Sullivan, DC Amravati, praised the local League leaders for their co-operation in preserving peace. MAPM, File 726/1940, Sullivan to Trivedi, 5 May 1941.
55. Ibid., DC Amravati to Trivedi, 9 June 1941.

56. MAPM, File 108/1939.
57. HP File 18 Dec. 1939, FR, 1st half of Dec. 1939.
58. Ibid., Also MAPM, File 704/1940, DC Akola to Trivedi, 15 June 1941, Buldana Weekly Reports, Jan.-March 1941: File 705/1940, 726/1940, DC Amravati to Secy. PM, 28 April 1941; File 1703/1940, File 3/1945, FR, 2nd half of May 1945.
59. MAPM, File 704/1940, DC Akola to Trivedi, 29 June 1941.
60. MAPM, File 7(724)/1940, DC Buldana to Trivedi, 28 Oct. 1939. Moonje said 'our chief enemy and enemy no. one are the Muslims of the League, and I believe all our energy and attention should be directed towards preparing the Hindus to meet their menace'. LP Reel no. 2198, Twynum to Linlithgow, 22 June 1941, enclosing an intercepted letter of Moonje, 7 June 1941.
61. MAPM, File 1 (746)/1941, FR 30 April 1941.
62. MAPM, File 740/1940, Buldana Weekly Report, 18 Aug. 1941.
63. MAPM, File 704/1940, DC Akola to Trivedi, 18 March 1941. Mahasabha leader, Panchalegaonkar, claimed to have reconverted two hundred Muslims to Hinduism. HP File 18 April 1945, FR, 1st half of April 1945.
64. Deshpande, 'Militant Hinduism', p. 211. Mahasabha leaders demanded the restoration of the site of the Viswanath temple at Banaras on which a mosque stood. MAPM, File 108/1939.
65. LP, Reel no. 2198, Twynum to Linlithgow, 23 Oct. 1941.
66. MAPM, File 115/1939, Under Secretary, PM to all DCs, 8 Dec. 1939. Also MAPM, File 108/1939. These voluntary organisations were 'evidently intended for communal conflict'. Reginald Coupland, *Indian Politics* London, 1944, p. 51.

    In Amravati district, particularly, no definitive list of Hindu communal organizations could be drawn up because several members of the Kisan Sabhas, the Forward Block, the Congress, the Congress Socialist Party and even the Communist Party were also members of the Hindu Mahasabha and the Hanuman Vyyam Prasarak Mandal. MAPM, no. 2 (7247)/1939–40, DSP Amravari to DM Amravati, 19 Aug. 1940.

66a. MAPM, File 104 (889)/1941, FR, 2nd half of Oct. 1942. MAPM, File 926/1942, Letters from District officers to CS, Oct.–Nov. 1942. The RSS cadres in Yeotmal were mainly drawn from Aney's Congress Nationalist Party. Ibid.
67. MAPM, File 2 (723)/1939–40, DC Akola to Commr. Berar 26 Aug. 1940; MAPM, File (unnumbered), 1940, FR, 1st half of Sept. 1942, 2nd half of Oct. 1942; File 926/1942, DC Nagpur to CS, 16 Nov. 1942. SP 280072, Report of the Assistant to the DIG Police Special Branch , 29 May 1939. SP 280077/1944, Note on Voluntary Organizations in CP.

    In 1947 the RSS cadres in the province were 39,000 in number. *CPLA*, 18 March 1947, p. 641.

68. Deshpande, 'Militant Nationalism', p. 210.
69. Ibid., p. 104.
70. SP 280076, File 250/1943, Note by CS, 19 Sept. 1942.

70a.LP, Reel no. 2197, Twynum to Linlithgow, 22 Aug., 7 Sept. 1940. The Hanuman Vyyam Prasarak Mandal also followed suit. Ibid., same to same 21 Sept. 1940.

71. HP File 18 Oct. 1944, FR, 1st half of Oct. 1944. The police reports in 1944–5 made no reference to any direct RSS involvement in communal troubles. MAPM File 3/1945, FR, 1st half of Sept. 1945.

72. SP 280077, File no. 93/1944, Note on Voluntary Organizations in CP. The Hindu Mahasabha had in 1940 organised a cadre called Ramsena, and another called *Saktishali Dal* as a counterpoise to the Khaksars. MAPM, File 1940, FR, 2nd half of April 1942. HP, File 18 Jan. 1940, 1st half of Jan. 1940.

73. HP File 18 Oct. 1948, FR, 2nd half of Oct. 1943; File 18 Sept. 1944, FR, 1st half of Sept. 1944. SP 280077, File 93/1944, Note on Voluntary Organizations in CP.

74. MAPM, File 98(908)/1942. LP Reel no. 2199, Twynum to Linlithgow, 14 and 28 Nov. 1942. However, the police (Special Branch) found no direct connection between Tukdoji, the RSS and the Congress. J.P. Wheeler to G. Burgess, Secy. to Governor, 1 Oct. 1942 in Ibid (enclosure). K. Mojumdar, 'Chimur, 16 August 1942: Revolt at the grassroots, *Indo-British Review*, Madras, XVIII, no. 1, 1990, pp. 163–73.

    Tukdoji (1909–1968) participated in forest satyagraha during the Civil Disobedience Movement in the province. He advocated social reforms. P.L. Joshi, ed., *Political Ideas*, pp. 288–91.

    In Bombay several RSS men were arrested for sabotage during the Quit India Movement and for their suspected links with the Japanese. SP 280077/1944. DC Buldana feared RSS support to any anti-government movement launched by the Congress. His letter to CS in MAPM File 2(723)/1939–40. Also H.V. Sheshadri, ed., *RSS: A Vision in Action*, Bangalore, 1988, p. 22.

75. The Congress, the Muslim League, the Hindu Mahasabha and the Khaksars were also brought under the order. MAPM File, 53/1944–46; *CP and Berar Gazette*, 6 Oct. 1944. HP File 28 June 1945, Pol. (1) and K.W.

76. MAPM, File 1/1944–45; File 53/1944–46, CS to all DCs, 27 June 1945. HP, File 18 May 1943, FR, 1st half of May 1943.

77. In Oct. 1942 all DCs were asked to furnish reports on local RSS organizations. MAPM, File 926/1942. Also File 1/1945, Note on RSS by Commr. Berar, June 1945, DC Akola to Commr. Berar, DSP Akola to DC Akola, June 1945.

    Under a standing order of the government, all meetings held by the Congress, the League and the Mahasabha were attended by Intelligence Department staff. Later the order included the Hindustan Red Army, Scheduled Caste Federation and the Communist Party. MAPM, File 5/1946.

78. MAPM, File 104 (889)/1941, FR, 2nd half of Oct. 1942. However, several times in 1934–39 local RSS volunteers at Wardha had clashes with members of the Congress-dominated Pratap Vyayamshala, leading to the RSS men's prosecution by the government. MAPM, File 28/1939, S. Sanyal, DC Wardha, to H.C. Greenfield Commr. Nagpur, 13 April 1939.

79. Deshpande, 'Militant Nationalism', pp. 110, 224.
80. MAPM, File 926/1942, DC Nagpur to CS, 16 Nov. 1942. So long the government had viewed the RSS as being 'the striking force of the Mahasabha' and its very 'kernel'. Governor Twynum personally wanted to seize the RSS offices and its leaders. SP 280076, File 250/1943, Note by CS, 19 Sept. 1942.
81. SP 280072, Report of the Assistant to DIG Police Special Branch, 29 May 1939. HP File 18 Dec. 1939, FR, 2nd half of Dec. 1939. Muslim National Guards cooperated with government officers during the war. Ibid.

    Also HP File 18 Dec. 1937, FR, 1st half of Oct. 1937; 18 July 1942, FR, 1st half of July 1942. MAPM, File 1940, FR, 1st half of March 1940, 1st half of July 1942; File 1/1942, FR, 2nd half of Nov. 1942; File 3/1945, 1st half of Dec. 1945.
82. SP 280072, Report of the Asst. to DIG Police, SP 280068, File 31/1939, Note on Communalism by CS, 10 Nov. 1938.
83. SP 280077, File 93/1944. Khaksar membership decreased from 1226 to 1069 in 1943–4 due to its hostility towards the League. Ibid., Note on Voluntary Organisations in CP.
84. MAPM, File 1940, FR, 1st half of April 1940, 2nd half of March 1942. In the war years the League Working Committee met several times in Nagpur under Jinnah's Chairmanship. A.M. Zaidi, ed., *The Demand for Pakistan*, New Delhi, 1978, p. 333.
85. SP 280072, Report of the Asst. to DIG Police, Z.H. Zaidi, 'Aspects of the development of Muslim League policy, in Philips and Wainwright', p. 268. MAPM, File 740/1940, Akola District Weekly Reports, 22 July 1941. The League turned the war to good account. 'The war which nobody welcomes, proved to be a blessing in disguise. Meanwhile we did some spade work and then we were sufficiently strong not to be ignored completely.' Jamiluddin Ahmed, *Speeches and Writings of Jinnah*, vol. II, Lahore, 2nd edn. 1964, p. 245.
86. HP File 18 Feb. 1939, FR, 2nd half of Feb. 1939. For the League after 1937 see also Khalid Bin Sayeed, *Pakistan: The Formative Years*, Karachi, 1960, pp. 88–104.
87. HP File 18 Jan. 1940, FR, 1st half of Jan. 1940. LP Reel no. 2197, Wylie to Linlithgow, 22 Jan. 1940.
88. Ibid.
89. MAPM, File 1940, FR, 1st half of March 1940.
90. Zaidi, 'Aspects of the Development', p. 657.
91. HP File 18 October 1943, FR, 2nd half of Oct. 1943; 18 April 1944, FR, 2nd half of April 1994.
92. Ibid.
93. Nicholas Mansergh, ed., *Transfer of Power*, vol. VII, Document no. 62.
94. MAPM File 1940, FR, 1st half of Feb. 1940.
95. HP File 18 Sept. 1940, FR, 1st half of Sept. 1940; File 18 Nov. 1940, FR, 1st half of Nov. 1940. MAPM File 1940, I and 2nd half of Oct., 1st half of Nov., 1st half of Dec. 1940.

96. MAPM File 1940, FR, 1st half of Feb. 1940. HP File 18 Dec. 1940, FR, 2nd half of Dec. 1940. LP, Reel no. 2197, Twynum to Linlithgow, 7, 23 Oct., 10, 24 Nov., 10 and 21 Dec. 1940.
97. SP 280074, File 19/1942, Note by CS, 27 Dec. 1941.
98. MAPM, File 726/1940.
99. MAPM, File 704/1940, DC Akola to Secy. PM, 18 Feb. 1941; File 726/1940, DC Amravati to Trivedi, 11 Feb. 1941.
100. HP File 18 May 1940, FR, 2nd half of May 1940. Muhammad Hayat Azad of Wardha was a nationalist Muslim. *Hitavada*, 9 Oct. 1945.
101. MAPM, File 704/1940, DC Akola to Trivedi, 15, 23 June 1941. Ironically enough, Nawab Bahadur Yar Jang, the President-elect of the League session at Akola, was himself an all India Khaksar leader. Ibid., DC Akola to Trivedi , 4 March 1941.
102. HP File 18 June 1941, FR, 1st and 2nd half of June 1941. SP 280073, File 255/1941, Govt. of India to CSCPB, 20 June 1941, C.M. Trivedi's note on Khaksars in CP, 19 June 1941. MAPM, File 726/1940, DC Amravati to Secy. PM, 7, 14 July, 1941.
103. MAPM File 704/1940, DC Akola to Trivedi, 4 and 18 March 1941. SP 280063, File 255/1941, Trivedi's note on the Khaksars, SP 280077, File 93/1944, Note on voluntary organizations in CP. The government viewed the Khaksars as a 'dangerous organization which would be better ended than mended'. The Khaksars were suspected to have been strongly influenced by Hitler and his Nazi organization. Trivedi's note on Khaksars, enclosing GOI HD to CSCPB, 13 June 1941. Also LP, Reel no. 2198, Twynum to Linlithgow, 22 June 1941.
104. HP File 18 Aug. 1943, FR, 2nd half of Aug. 1943; 18 March 1944, FR, 1st half of March 1944. MAPM, File 3/1943, Jayaratnam (CS) to Meldrun, DC Amravati, 16 June 1943.
105. SP 280067, File 93/1944, Note on Voluntary Organizations in CP, op. cit.
106. HP File 18 Nov. 1944, FR, 1st half of Nov. 1944; File 18 Dec. 1944, FR, 1st half of Dec. 1944.
107. MAPM, File 80/1940.
108. LP, Reel no. 2198, W.V. Grigson, Secy. to Governor, to Gilbert Laithwaite, Secy. to Viceroy, 16 May 1941.
109. MAPM, File 80/1940, Trivedi to all DCs, 6 May 1941; DC Akola to Trivedi, 21 and 31 May 1941.
110. LP, Reel no. 2198, Twynum to Linlithgow, 28 May and 15 Sept. 1941.
111. Ibid.
112. Ibid. The Governor was prepared to have even a 'show down' with Siddiqui Ali Khan to frustrate his eagerness to hog the limelight over Britain's Iran and Iraq policy. Ibid. Also HP File 18 Sept. 1941, FR, 1st half of Sept. 1941.
113. The three others belonged to the Independent party led by Rajurkar, who opposed the Congress and was approached by the Governor to form a non-Congress ministry. LP Reel no. 2196, Wylie to Linlithgow, 4 Sept., 8 Nov. (Telg.) and 12 Nov. 1939.

114. LP, Reel no. 2196, Wylie to Linlithgow, 18 April 1939.
115. Ibid., same to same, 4, 8 Nov. (Telg.) and 12 Nov. 1939. The Independent Party had 18 members, Muslim League had 10, Khare claimed the support of 11 MLAs, assuring the Governor of securing the support of a few dissident Congressmen besides. Ibid., 4 and 12 Nov. 1939.
116. LP, Reel no. 2196, Wylie to Linlithgow, Telg. 4 Sept., 8 and 12 Nov. 1939.
117. LP, Reel no. 2197, Wylie to Linlithgow, Telg. 5 May 1940.
118. LP, Reel no. 2197, Twynum to Linlithgow, 21 Sept. 1940.
119. Ibid.
120. LP, Reel no. 2197, Twynum to Linlithgow, 19 July 1940.
121. Ibid., same to same, 22 Aug. 1940.
122. LP, Reel no. 2197, Twynum to Linlithgow, 22 Aug. 1940. Justice Vivian Bose of the Nagpur High Court opined that Khare 'played into the hands of the Governor and thereby created a gulf in the party'. He dismissed Khare's defamation case against his former Congress colleagues. LP, Reel no. 2199, G. Burgess, Secy. to Gov., to Laithwaite, 29 May 1942.
123. LP, Reel no. 2197, Twynum to Linlithgow, 22 Aug. 1940.
124. Ibid., same to same, 19 July 1940.
125. Ibid., same to same, 30 June, 7, 15, 19 July, 12, 22 Aug. and 17 Dec. 1940.
126. LP, Reel no. 2198, same to same, 26 Aug. 1941.
127. Ibid., enclosing Grigson's report on discussions with Abdur Rahman.
128. Ibid., Reel no. 2198, same to same, 26 Aug. 1941.
129. Ibid.
130. Ibid.
131. Ibid., same to same, 26 Aug. 1941. Grigson himself was keen on Khare ministry with Muslims in it. He hoped to garner support from several MLAs. Grigson's report of his discussions with Abdur Rahman.
132. Ibid.
133. Ibid. Reel no. 2198, same to same, 9 Jan. 1941. Khare called himself the 'Martin Luther' of the Congress. In December 1940 he formed the National Democratic Union to rally non-Congress elements. M.G. Datar, *Speeches and Statements of Dr N.B. Khare*, Nagpur, 1943, pp. 7, 76–9.
134. LP, Reel no. 2198, same to same, 26 Aug. 1941. Aney and Moonje were 'allied in thoughts'. Both were Responsivists. Aney's National Democratic Party was close to the Mahasabha. The RSS congratulated Aney on his membership of the Viceroy's Council. He presided over RSS meetings. He was helpful in army recruitment during the war. He criticized the Congress individual *Satyagraha* and the League's Pakistan scheme. LP, Reel no. 2197, Twynum to Linlithgow, 23 Oct. 1940; Ibid. Reel no. 2198, same to same, 10 Jan. 1941. MAPM, File 726/1940, DC Amravati to Secy. PM, 18 Aug., 28 April 1941; File 1(746)/1941, FR 31 July 1941. HP File 18 Aug. 1934, 2nd half of Aug. 1934.
135. LP Reel no. 2198, Twynum to Linlithgow, 26 Aug. 1941.
136. LP, Reel no. 2198, Twynum to Linlithgow, 3 Oct. 1941.
137. Ibid. same to same, 2 Sept. 1941, enclosing Khare to Jinnah, 30 Aug. 1941.

138. Ibid., Reel no. 2198, Linlithgow to Twynum, 20 Jan. 7 March 1941.
139. Ibid, Reel no. 2198, Linlithgow to Twynum, 20 Jan. and 7 March 1941. MAPM, File 3(866)/1943.
140. LP Reel no. 2198, Linlithgow to Twynum, 25-7 Nov. 1941.
141. LP, Reel no. 2198, Twynum to Linlithgow, 25 Sept. and 3 Oct. 1941.
142. LP, Reel no. 2199, same to same, 28 Jan. 1942.
143. Fazlul Haq of Bengal, Sikandar Hayat Khan of the Punjab and Sadullah Khan of Assam had many differences with Jinnah. Muslims in the CP and Berar held many meetings supporting Jinnah against the three men. MAPM, File 726/1940, DC Amravati to Secy. PM, 25 Aug. 1941; File 1(746)/1941, FR 15 Aug. 1941. Fazlul Haq was expelled from the League in Dec. 1941.
144. LP, Reel no. 2199, Twynum to Linlithgow, 13 Feb. 1942.
145. Ibid., same to same, 2 March 1942, and enclosure.
146. Ibid.
147. See Chapter V. Khare wrote to Jinnah that he would secure the support of 59 MLAs, including 10 Leaguers. Ibid., enclosing Khare to Jinnah, 7 Feb. 1942.
148. HP File 18 Aug. 1938, FR, 1st half of Aug. 1938.
149. LP, Reel no. 2198, Linlithgow to Twynum, 7 March, 6 Sept., 25–7 Nov. 1941.
150. Ibid., Reel no. 2199, Twynum to Linlithgow, 2 March 1942.
151. Ibid., same to same, 30 April 1942.
152. Ibid.
153. Ibid.
154. Ibid., same to same, 24 June 1942. HP File, 18 June 1942, FR, 1st half of June 1942.
155. Ibid., same to same, 12 Aug. 1942.
156. Ibid. The Congress High Command sent Dr Syed Mahmud to Nagpur to win Khare back to the Congress. Ibid.
157. Ibid., Reel no. 2198, same to same, 15 Sept. 1941. Rauf Shah struck Twynum as 'a particularly mild-mannered moderate little man'. Ibid. Twynum detested Siddiqui Ali Khan. Ibid.
158. MAPM, File 101(936)/1942, DC Nagpur to Commr. Nagpur, 10 Oct. 1942, Commr. Nagpur to CS, 19 Oct. 1942, DC Chanda to Commr. Nagpur, 18 Oct. 1942. Official enquiry established that at Chimur 'Muslims as a class did not keep aloof from the disturbances'. 'Muslims of Ashti took a 'leading part' in the local disturbances in which some government employees were killed by the mob. Ibid. Commr. Berar to CS, 14 Sept. 1942. The DC Wardha reported that half a dozen local Muslims were 'Congress-minded' and had taken part in the destruction of government property. Ibid. See also MAPM, File 1940, FR, 1st half of Sept. 1942; File 54(945)/1942, Press communiqué issued by the government, 15 Sept. 1942.

    In 1946 the Congress government of the province decided to refund the collective fines (roughly Rs. 3,41,500) to their payers. *CPLA*, vol. I, May 1946, p. 96. MAPM, File 1-5/1946, 1-10/1946.

159. LP, Reel no. 2200, Twynum to Linlithgow, 11 Jan. and 17 April 1943.
160. Khare was the Chief Warden of the ARP and the 'real active leader' in the National War Front. He was the main link between the non-official organization helping in the war operations and the Provincial War Committee of which he was the President.
161. LP, Reel no. 2199, Twynum to Linlithgow, 16 Aug., 2 Sept. and 13 Dec. 1942.
162. Ibid., Reel no. 2200, Twynum to Linlithgow, 23 June 1943.
163. Ibid., enclosing Abdur Rahman Khan to Secy. to Gov., 13 June 1943. D.P. Mishra condemned 'out and out opportunists like Kedar', when, along with several other Responsivists, (who had strong links with the Hindu Mahasabha and the RSS), Khare had inducted into the Congress to strengthen his own position in the provincial Congress. *Living an Era*, pp. 107, 251, 252.
164. LP, Reel no. 2200, Abdur Rahman to Secy. to Gov., 13 June 1943.
165. Ibid., Twynum to Linlithgow, 12-14 July 1943.
166. Ibid., enclosing an intercepted letter from Jinnah to Rauf Shah, 23 June 1943. There were 38 Congress MLAs in prison and 21 (supposedly) dissident Congressmen. There were seven small non-Congress groups; the League being the eighth. Also HP File 18 June 1943, FR, 2nd half of June 1943.
167. LP, Reel no. 2200, Twynum to Linlithgow, 12-14 July 1943.
168. Ibid., Jinnah's intercepted letter.
169. Ibid.
170. Ibid., Twynum to Linlithgow, 12-14 July 1943.
171 Ibid.
172. Ibid., Twynum to Linlithgow, 23 June 1943, enclosing Abdur Rahman to Secy. to Gov., 13 June 1943.
173. Ibid.
174. Ibid., Twynum to Linlithgow, 28 July 1943.
175. LP, Reel no. 2200, Twynum to Linlithgow, 28 July 1943.
176. Ibid.
177. LP, Reel no. 2200, Twynum to Linlithgow, 28 July 1943. HP File 18 July 1943, FR, 1st half of July 1943.
178. LP, Reel no. 2200, Twynum to Linlithgow, 28 July 1943.
179. Ibid. Linlithgow to Twynum, 30 June 1943.
180. Ibid.
181. Ibid.
182. Ibid., Twynum to Linlithgow, 28 July 1943, Linlithgow to Twynum, 15 June 1943.
183. Ibid., Twynum to Linlithgow, 28 July 1943. Thus the hope of forming a non-Congress ministry in the CP and Berar like the one formed in Orissa remained unrealised. Reginald Coupland, *The Constitutional Problem in India*, pt. III, *The Future of India*, Madras, 1944, p. 31.
184. SP 280078/1945.
185. HP File 18 Oct. 1945, FR, 2nd half of Oct. 1945. 93,112 primary members were enrolled in the Congress party in Berar, 30,000 in Raipur,

36,000 in Jabalpur, 21,000 at Hoshangabad. *Hitavada*, 11 and 23 Jan. 1946. MAPM, File 3/1945, FR, 1st half of Dec. 1945. The Hindu Mahasabha fixed a target of enrolling 20,000 members in Berar by 15 Oct. 1945. A parliamentary board of the party was set up to conduct elections in Berar. Ibid., FR, 1st half of Aug. 1945, 1st half of Sept. 1945.

Earlier, the Congress had not only fought the 1937 elections treating the Mahasabha as its main rival, but Khare and other Congressmen were then charged with employing hired hooligans to disturb Mahasabha meetings in Nagpur and Kamptee, from where Khare contested. Khare had allegedly got defamatory articles published to malign Moonje and J.P. Verma, Secretary of the Nagpur city unit of the Mahasabha, besides setting *goondas* on the latter. SP 280067/1938, pp. 29-34.

186. MAPM, File 3/1945, FR, 2nd half of Sept. 1945. HP File 18 Sept. 1945, FR, 1st half of Sept. 1945; File 18 Oct. 1945, 2nd half of Oct. 1945.
187. MAPM, File 3/1945, FR, 1st and 2nd half of Sept. 1945. HP File 18 Dec. 1945, FR, 2nd half of Dec. 1945. The provincial Muslim League set a target of one lakh for the election. HP File 18 Sept. 1945, FR, 1st half of Sept. 1945. The League's Pakistan propaganda in election meetings raised the communal temper high, local authorities apprehending incidents. MAPM, File 3/1945, FR, 1st half of Sept. 1945.
188. *Hitavada*, 26 Sept. 1945. The President was Begum Seth Muhammad Harun of Akola and the Vice President was Begum Siddiqui Hasan of Jabalpur. Also MAPM, File 3/1945, FR, 2nd half of Jan. 1945, 1st half of Feb. 1945.
189. HP 18 Nov. 1945, FR, 1st half of Nov. 1945.
190. MAPM, File 3/1945, 2nd half of Oct. 1945.
191. There were four Congress rebels. *Hitavada*, 2 March 1946.
192. *Hitavada*, 21 Feb. 1946.
193. MAPM, File 1940, FR, 1st and 2nd half of March 1940. Earlier Tajuddin, the veteran League leader of Jabalpur, had written to Jinnah about the dissensions in the party, seeking his intervention. Ayesha Jalal, *The Sole Spokesman, Jinnah, the Muslim League and the Demand for Pakistan*, Cambridge, 1985, p. 44 fn. Siddiqui's reelection to the Central Assembly was not liked by some in the provincial League, among them S.W. Rizvi of Raipur who, under pressure, withdrew from contesting Siddiqui. *Hitavada*, 26 Oct. and 31 Oct. 1945. Also Ibid., 10 Jan. 1946. MAPM, File 1/1942, FR, 1st half of Oct. 1942.
194. The League had accused the Momins of being Congress hirelings. HP File 18 April 1943, 2nd half of April 1943.

Abdul Qaiyum Ansari, Vice-President of the All India Momin Conference, sent a telegram to Gandhi and Rajendra Prasad in New Delhi saying that the Momins, constituting a large segment of the Muslim population in the country—four and a half crores—did not accept the League as representing the entire Muslim community. Momins demanded separate representation on all bodies. The Shia Conference also rejected the League claim of being the sole representative body of the Muslims. *Samarpit Ardhasati*, pp. 482, 483.

The President of the All India Momin Conference Dr. Zahiruddin, described the Momins as the Depressed Class of modern India. Coupland, *The Future of India*, p. 10.

195. *Hitavada*, 6, 8, 9, 21, 22, 27, 28 Feb. and 13 March 1946.
196. Ibid., also 21 Feb. 1946.
197. Ibid., 6, 8 Feb. 1946. Some Momins wanted the Provincial League to field at least two Momin candidates who numbered about 80,000 in the province. Ibid., 19 Jan. 1946.
198. Ibid., 22, 27 and 28 Feb. 1946.

90 per cent Muslim voters voted for Faruqui who won the Nagpur-Kamptee seat. However, educated Muslim voters, who disliked Faruqui, preferred absence from poll booths to defying the League leadership by supporting Faruqui's rival, Anisuddin Ahmad. *Hitavada*, 4 April 1946.

199. Ibid., 10 Jan. 1946.
200. The two other rebel Leaguers were Anisuddin Ahmad and Abdul Salam Khan (contesting for the Chhindwara Muslim reserved constituency).

Ibid., 2 and 10 March 1946. Asghar Ali, President of the Nimar District Muslim League, was expelled from the party. Ibid., 23 March 1946.

Muslims of Akola refused to say Id prayers led by the Pesh Imam, Khan Bahadur Mirza Rahman Beg, for he had not given up his government title and had stood against the official League candidate. He was also expelled from the League for three years. Local Muslims elected another Posh Imam. *Hitavada*, 4 Sep. 1946. He had contested the Akola seat as an Independent and lost. Reforms, File 94/4/1945, CP govt. to V.P. Menon, Secy. to the GG (Reforms), 23 July 1946.

201. In August 1946, wearing a Gandhi cap and a *khadi sherwani*, he joined Muslim gatherings, demanding a 'free land' for the Muslim community. He managed to become a member of the Nagpur District League Council with the help of Faruqui. *Hitavada*, 30 April and 17 Aug. 1946.
202. Ibid., 20 Oct. and 11 Nov. 1945. However, just before the election, Iftikar Ali and Burhan-ul-Mulk buried the hatchet, the former agreeing to support the latter against two non-League Muslims, one a Shia and the other a Momin. Ibid., 23 March 1946.
203. HP File 18 Sept. 1945, FR, 2nd half of Sept. 1945.
204. *Hitavada*, 30 Oct. 1945. The board's chairman was Maulavi Chiraguddin of Sagar, and convenor-cum-secretary was Maulavi Maqbul Ahmad of Seoni, Dr M. Hasan of Wardha was member of the board. Ibid., 11 Dec. 1945.
205. Ibid., 16 Jan. 1946.
206. Reforms (Deposit), 1945, File 99/45, R.P. Kodanda Rao, Servants of India Society, Nagpur, to V.P. Menon, Secy. Reforms Dept., 26 Sept. 1945. *Hitavada*, 30 Aug. 1945.

207. Reforms File 94/4/1945, CP govt. to Menon, 25 July 1946.
    HP File 18 Dec. 1945, FR, 1st half of Dec. 1945. Khaksars were a divided group on the eve of the elections, many of them at Jabalpur and Amravati having joined the League while many others staying away from and challenging the League.
208. Asghar Ali defeated Hifazat Ali who was the first Muslim Minister in 1922.
209. Asghar Ali, after winning the election, declared that he was a follower of the League and a firm believer in Pakistan, and so his success should not be regarded as the League's defeat. However, the election tribunal upheld the election of Hifazat Ali, who was declared elected in place of Asghar Ali. *Hitavada*, 11 and 21 April 1946.
210. HP File 18 Dec. 1945, 1st half of Dec. 1945.
211. Some Momin leaders like Abdul Hamid Ansari insisted that the League was the only representative organization of the Muslims. *Hitavada*, 9 Nov. 1945.
212. M.K. Siddiqui contested for the Wardha-Chanda seat and Maqbool Ahmad contested for the Balaghat-Bhandara-Seoni seat. Reforms, File 94/4/1945, CP government to V.P. Menon, Secy. to GG (Reforms), 23 July 1946. The party position after the elections was: Congress 94; Muslim League 13; Independent 1; SC Federation 1, League Independent 1, European 1, Hindu Mahasabha 1. *Hitavada*, 21 April 1946. See also Reforms File 94/4/1945, CP govt. to Menon, 21 Oct. 1946.
213. In the Commerce constituency, Muslims were one-third of the voters. The University constituency was won by Dr M. Hasan against Kedar and D.T. Mangalmurty, once colleagues in the People's Party. *Hitavada*, 18 Jan. 1946.
214. Deshpande, 'Militant Nationalism', p. 201 fn.
215. Palkar, *Hedgewar*, pp. 376–7. Khare also referred to the differences between the RSS and the Mahasabha. He was close to both. *My Political Memoirs*, Nagpur, 1959, pp. 215-16.
216. *Hitavada*, 18 July, 1946.
217. Ibid., 8 May 1946. It was rumoured that the Congress would sacrifice Dr Hasan to accommodate a Leaguer in the ministry. Ibid., 1, 2 May 1946. Dr Hasan became the Health Minister in the cabinet but after about a year resigned his post due to differences with the Premier, Ravishankar Shukla.
218. MAPM, File 18/1946–47, DC Amravati to Commr. Berar, 5 April 1947.
219. Ibid.
220. Mansergh, ed., vol. III, Document no. 62, referring to Shukla's statement.
220a. HP File 18 March 1945, FR, 2nd half of March 1945.
220b. HP File 18 March 1944, FR, 1st half of March 1944. *Hitavada*, 27 Feb, 6 Sept., 10 Oct. 1946.
221. Penderal Moon, ed., *Wavell, the Viceroy's Journal*, London, 1973, p. 484. In communal riots in Sept–Nov. 1946, only three lost their life and thirteen were injured in the province, the figures being the lowest in India except

in Sind and Baluchistan. Mansergh, vol. IX, p. 102. During the great Calcutta killings (Aug. 1946), communal relations in the province were 'peaceful but not cordial'. Ibid., p. 49.

222. *Hitavada*, 15, 23, 30 Aug. 1946.
223. Ibid., 17, 21, 23 Aug. 1946. Section 144 was declared as a precautionary measure.
224. *Hitavada*, 18 July 1946.
225. Ibid., 5 May 1946.
226. Ibid., 16, 23, Oct. 1946.
227. Ibid., 7 July 1946.
228. Ibid., 2 Nov. 1946.
229. Ibid., 12 Feb. 1947.
230. MAPM, File 18/1946–47, DC Akola to Commr. Berar, 14 Nov. 1946; File 1/1946, DC Buldana to Commr. Berar, 20 June 1946.
231. Speaking on the Independence resolution moved by Premier Shukla in the Assembly, Rauf Shah feelingly stressed Muslim loyalty to India, their country. *CPLA*, vol. IV, 6 Oct. 1947, pp. 9–10.
232. V. Shankar, 'Mishraji as I have known him', *Samarpit Ardhasati*, p. 108.
233. MAGAD, File 29/1947 (Secret); MAPM, File 32/1947, 16-17/1948. The government set up camps for 85,000 refugees. *CPLA*, vol. II, no. 2 Sept. 1946, p 3.
234. MAPM, File 15/54/1947, SDO Gondia to CS, 25 Oct. 1947.
235. *Hitavada*, 14, 25 Jan. 1947.
236. Muslims formed nine per cent of the Berar population. MAGAD, File 29/1947.
237. MAGAD, File 10/1946, DSP Amravati to DM Amravati, 6 no. 1946. *CPLA*, 11 Nov. 1946, p. 792.
238. MAPM, File 10/1946, Watson to Commr. Berar, 7 Nov. 1946.
239. MAPM, File 10/1946, Amravati District Muslim League's Report to the Provincial League, 28 Oct. 1946.
240. Ibid.
241. Ibid., *Hitavada*, 2 Nov. 1946. The Mandal had close association with the Hindu unity movement in Berar. It also gave financial assistance to the Congress Civil Disobedience Movement besides organising volunteer corps for all India Congress meeting. MAPM, File 2(724)/1939–40, DSP Amravati to DM Amravati, 1 Aug. 1940.
242. SP 280079, File 71/1947.
243. *Hitavada*, 5, 9, 20 Nov. 1946. Gandhi asked Shukla to reply to the League charges. SP 280079, File 71/1947, Shukla to Gandhi, 26 Feb. 1947.
244. Ibid.
245. Mansergh, *The Transfer of Power*, vol. IX, p. 376, Policy in India, Memorandum by the Secretary of State, 18 Dec. 1946. Muslims welcomed the agreement hoping that the Nizam's Agent at Amravati would help promote the Muslim cause in general. HP File 18 Nov. 1936, FR, 2nd half of Nov. 1936.
246. Khan Bahadur Nawab Abdullah Khan, editor, *Islamic Mail*, Lucknow,

took initiative in the matter. His letters to G.S. Khaparde of Amravati, Khaparde Papers, VIth File, pp. 385–416.

247. Ibid., Correspondence between Abdullah and Khaparde, June–July 1918.
248. Ibid., p. 389, Tambe to Khaparde, 12 June 1918; also pp. 395–8, Tambe's letters to Khaparde, 23, 25, 30 June and 5 July 1918.
249. R.J. Moore, *The Crisis of Indian Unity, 1917–1940*, Oxford, 1974, pp. 28–32.

In 1934, Sir Samuel Hoare, the Secy. of State, said that the people of Berar were the Nizam's subjects while discounting any possibility of Berar's retrocession to the Nizam. *Parliamentary Debates Indian Affairs Commons, 1934–35*, vol. 2, Columns 2028–9.

250. MAPM, File 3/1945, FR, 1st half of Jan. 1945.
251. Ibid., 1st half of Feb. 1945.
252. MAPM, File 3/1945, FR, 1st half of Feb. 1945. Aney wanted Berar's separation from the CP and then either its merger with the Bombay Presidency or its formation as a separate province. MAPM, File 1(76)/1941, FR 30 April 1941.
253. MAPM, File 3/1945, FR, 1st half of Feb. 1945. The Mahasabha wanted the removal of all 'constitutional fiction' of the Nizam's authority over Berar. *Hitavada*, 30 May 1946.
254. MAPM, File 3/1945, FR, 1st half of Jan. 1945.
255. Ibid., 2nd half of Jan., 2nd half of April 1945.
256. Ibid., 2nd half of Jan. 1945.

Deshpande, a native of Fatterkheda in Buldana, was a college teacher in Nagpur. He had taken a prominent part in the Hyderabad Satyagraha in 1938–39. MAPM, File 7(724)/1942, DC Buldana to Trivedi.

257. MAPM, File 3/1945, 2nd half of Jan. 1945.
258. MAPM, File 3/1945, FR, 1st half of Feb. 1945. Some Congressmen even attended a Muslim League meeting at Khamgaon to discuss the arrangements for the Prince's reception. They condemned the Mahasabha agitation and urged the government to take stern action against the Mahasabha activists. HP File 18 March 1944, FR, 1st half of March 1944.
259. MAPM, File 3/1945, FR, 1st half of April 1945.
260. Ibid., 2nd half of March 1945.
261. MAPM, File 3/1945, FR, 2nd half of March 1945, 1st half of April 1945.
262. Ibid., File 638/1947, Report on the visit of Sir Mirza Ismail to Berar in April 1947.
263. Ibid., DC Akola to Commr. Berar, 30 April 1947.
264. MAPM, File 638/1947.
265. Ibid.
266. Ibid., DC Amravati to Commr. Berar, 30 April 1947.
267. MAPM, File 638/1947, Bahl to CJW Lillie, Commr. Berar, 30 April 1947. Police report described the Mandal as 'an organization of sufficient significance' but having 'nothing communal about it'. SP 280072, Report of Asst. to DIG Police Special Branch, CPB, 29 May 1939.
268. MAPM, File 63B/1947, Lillie to P.S. Rao, Secy. PM, 2 May 1947.

Mirza Ismail in a public speech said 'Berar has been and is an integral part of Nizam's dominion' and 'true to the traditions of his House and his duty as the sovereign, feels towards the Beraris the same responsibility as for those in other parts of the realm.'

269. MAPM, File 16-18/1947.
270. Deshmukh, a leader of the Shetkari Sangh, joined the Congress in December 1945, on the eve of the elections. *Hitavada*, 6 Dec. 1945.
271. Deshmukh, like most other Berar leaders, wanted Berar's separation from the CP to end the latter's domination. He criticized the Hindi-speaking Mahakoshal leaders for exploiting the 'sons of the soil of Berar'. He opposed the Berar's return to the Nizam. *CPLA*, vol. IX, 2 Feb. 1935, pp. 480–1.
272. MAPM, File 63B/1947, Letters of Bahl and Lillie.
273. Ibid.
274. Ibid., DC Amravati to Commr. Berar, 30 April 1947
275. Ibid.
276. In 1948 Deshmukh requested the government to give his Shivaji Education Society a portion of the annual rental (Rs. 25 lakh) which the British government had given to the Nizam from 1902 to 1946 for his cession of Berar. In his letter (27 Aug. 1948) Deshmukh referred to Patel disapproving of his (Deshmukh's) receipt of financial assistance from the Nizam for his educational programme. Deshmukh disclaimed any political motivation underlying the assistance he had received from the Nizam's government, dismissing the 'most malicious and essentially untrue allegation against me'. MAPM, File 16-22/1948.
277. Mansergh, *The Transfer of Power*, vol. X, p. 325, Bourne to Lord Mountbatten, Viceroy, 18 April 1947; p. 57, Pethick-Lawrence, Secy. of State, to Mountbatten, 31 March 1947; p. 461, C. Corfield, Political Advisor to Crown Representative, to Mountbatten, 22 April 1947.
278. Ibid., p. 532, Mountbatten to Earl of Listwell, Secy. of State, 1 May 1947.
279. MAPM, File 15-54/1947; File 32/1947. *CPLA*, 6 Nov. 1947, p. 11.
280. Ibid., File 16-18/1947.
281. Ibid., Dept. Notes.
282. MAPM, File 16-18/1947.
283. The Razakars were the Hyderabad militia deployed to prevent the state's integration with the Indian Union; the Razakars spread terror in the neighbouring areas by provocative anti-Hindu action. Ultimately by police action (armed measures) Hyderabad's merger with the Indian Union was effected.
284. MAPM, File 15-C/1947, Lillie to Rao, 2 July 1947.
285. Ibid.
286. *Samarpit Ardhasati*, pp. 489–96, 536.
287. Ibid.
288. In the Assembly Shukla said that Muslims, only 4.6 per cent of the population (1941 census), held 10 per cent of the gazetted posts, 11 per cent of the subordinate ministerial posts and 18 per cent of the sub-

ordinate executive posts. They held about 30 per cent posts in the police department.

Between Dec. 1944 and June 1946, of the 71 men appointed Inspectors of civil services, there were 11 Muslims and 57 Hindus.

However, Shukla disclaimed any intention to apply 'communal consideration' either in recruitment or retrenchment from public services. *CPLA*, 25 Feb. 1947, pp. 11, 23–4; 27 March 1947, p. 11.

289. Ibid.

290. MAPM, File 17-58/1949, Shukla's Notes, 11 June, 24 Sept. 1947.

291. Ibid., Departmental Notes, June 1947. D.K. Mehta, the Home Minister concurred with the officers. Mehta's Note, 23 July 1947.

291a. *CPLA*, 8 Oct. 1947, p. 10. Muslim National Guards then numbered 10,802.

291b. Md. Ibrahim Khan Fana (1905–94) of Nagpur, a Congressman turned Leaguer, migrated to Pakistan where, in Karachi, he died. Abdus Salam Faruqui, a Nagpur pleader and a prominent Leaguer, also went away to Pakistan and became a High Court Judge there. Siddiqui Ali Khan (1902–74) became political Secretary to successive Prime Ministers of Pakistan, Liaquat Ali Khan, Khwaja Nazimuddin, Hasan Suhrawardy and Muhammad Ali Bogra. He was Pakistan's High Commissioner to Ceylon and Ambassador to Sudan. Sharafuddin Shail, *Nagpur Ka Muslim*, pp. 172–8, 194. Abdus Sattar Faruqui, the League MLA (Nagpur-Kamptee), became a Congressman after 1947, working in close concert with Maharashtrian leaders, Y.B. Chavan, Kannamwar and Sheshrao Wankhede. Momin Mahiuddin, *Momin Ansari Biradari ki Tahzibi Tarikh* (in Urdu), Bombay, 1994, p. 648. Rauf Shah (1878–1954) came away from Pakistan, lived his last days and died in India. Qazi Allauddin, *Tazkira-i-Mushahir-i-Berar* (in Urdu), Amravati, 1982, p. 222.

Many League offices were wound up shortly after Independence. Interview with Zaheer Warsi of Kamptee, 27 Sept. 1998.

292 MAPM, File 52/1948, V.S. Jha, DPI, to Secy. Ed. Dept., 11 Dec. 1947.

293. *CPLA*, vol. IV, 6 Nov. 1947, p. 12. Siddiqui Ali Khan's autobiography, *Be Tegh Sipahi*, pp. 390-1. MAPM, File 52/1942. Sarafraj Khan, Head Master, Anjuman High School, Khamgaon, was a prominent League leader. The school received aid from the Nizam's government. Ibid.

294. MAGAD, File 29/1947 (Secret). Muslims formed about 40 per cent of the Berar police. In the District Emergency Force (Constabulary), they were 45 per cent and the Hindus 41 per cent, the rest being Sikhs and Christians. MAGAD, File 38/1947.

295. A Congress MLA complained against S.M. Hussain, Naib Tahsildar, Boregaon, as being a League sympathiser, H.S. Kamath, Commr. Berar, wanted him to be compulsorily retired. Ibid.

296. Ibid., File 30/1947, M.K. Kher, Addl. Secy. PM, to IGP, 20 Oct. 1947, T.A. Bambawale, IGP to H.S. Kamath, 3 Nov. 1947.

The government drew up a list of all influential Muslims 'who were likely to turn traitors' and needed to be jailed. Military authorities visited

Wasim and took down names of all/police officers. Ibid, S. Mushran, DC Akola, to Kamath, 18 Oct. 1947. See also MAPM, File 15C/1947.

297. MAGAD, File 30/1947, S. Mushran to Kamath, 15 Nov. 1947.
298. Ibid., District officers' letters to Commr. Berar, Oct.–Nov. 1947.
299. RSS (39,000 members), Azad Hind Dal (8000), Hindustan Red Army (1470), Veer Bajrang Dal or Rashtra Dal (2500), Rashtra Seva Dal (1797) (this organization was led by a Muslim, Suleman Khan Pathan), Rashtra Yuvak Sangh (800), Samata Sainik Dal and Shivaji Dal were Hindu voluntary organizations.

    Muslim National Guards (7,337) and Khaksars (467) were two important Muslim voluntary organizations. There were fifteen such Muslim organizations *CPLA*, 18 March 1947, p. 641; 8 Oct. 1947, p. 10.
300. *Hitavada*, 28 Feb. 1947.
301. Many Hindu refugees from Punjab, Sind and Hyderabad moved about the Nagpur city narrating tales of Muslim atrocities on them. Some Muslims who returned to their homes in the CP and Berar from Hyderabad were strongly disliked by the enraged Hindus.

    All this needed the imposition of curfew and promulgation of Section 144 in Nagpur and the latter's extension for about two years after August 1947. The influx of refugees, the assassination of Gandhi in January 1948, the strong anti-Brahmin and anti-RSS feelings sweeping the country following the assassination of Gandhi, prolonged labour troubles and Communist agitations—all this created grave problems for local authorities in Nagpur justifying the imposition of Curfew and Section 144. Communal tension was acute in Aug. 1947 following reports of Muslim atrocities on Hindus in Bihar, Bengal and the Punjab, although no riots worsened the situation. MAPM, File 15-59/1947, 16-7/1948, 18/1946-7.
302. MAGAD, File 30/1947; Kamath to Mushran, 26 Oct. 1947. Mushran to Kamath, 16 Oct. 1947.
303. Ibid., File 28/1947, Kamath to Bahl, 21 Nov. 1947.
304. Ibid.
305. Interview with Zaheer Warsi, 27 Sept. 1998. Warsi, then an influential Muslim Leader, Yusuf Shariff and Abdus Sattar Faruqui went about Muslim localities to dissuade the local people from leaving India for Pakistan. Warsi and Faruqui were particularly active among the Momins. Muslim exodus to Pakistan was considerably prevented by the activities of these Muslim leaders.

CHAPTER VII

Conclusion

Communalism in the Central Provinces and Berar manifested, as elsewhere in the country, in the embattled relations between the local Hindus and Muslims was both a problem for regional politics and a challenging peril for societal peace. For years the province was rocked by the conflict of the two creeds, leaving a trail of fear and fury among their followers. As elsewhere in the country, religion in the CP and Berar became both a tool and victim of politics. Also, as elsewhere again, communal problem in the province was rooted in jousts for political power. It provided a passionate stimulus for both power wielders and power seekers.

However, the extent and intensity of communalism in the province—not its general character—varied from elsewhere due to factors typical of the region: its general political backwardness, its very small Muslim population, their prolonged political inertia, their leaders' utter mediocrity and the legacy of Hindu-Muslim amity bequeathed by the Bhonsle rulers of central India.

Beginning as a feeling among the social riffraffs, both Hindus and Muslims, communalism developed into a factor in regional politics though not a force ever. At first only a routine law and order problem for local peacekeepers to tackle, communalism grew from around the late 1920s into a majority-minority syndrome in the very process of the political development of the province. The acceleration of the process accounted for the intensification of the problem.

The genesis and growth, the assertion and institutionalization of communal distinctiveness and the resultant inter-communal embitterment was a heritage of the British colonial rule. In the Bhonsle period the social typicality of the Hindus and Muslims stood out through cross cultural influences and economic interdependence between them. There was no fear of either cultural absorption of the

Muslim minority into the majority Hindu fold or political domination of the one by the other. There was no scope for Hindu Muslim elite competition and conflict over sharing political prominence and power.

Communalism, representing cultural and religious exclusiveness, assumed a new social and political connotation when used by the colonial government to meet the nationalist challenge. It developed with the government's policy of check and balance as clearly indicated by its investing the miniscule Muslim community with an importance disproportionate to its strength in the local population and inspite of the political naivete of its leaders. The introduction of the communal electoral system, the preservation of the privileged position of the Muslims in respect of educational facilities, pubic employment and representation in legislatures and ministries convinced the Hindus that the government favoured the community.

British policy provided a distinct political outline to Hindu-Muslim religious discord which was coeval with the colonial rule, the earlier Bhonsle rule being free from it. With progressive Indianization of the administration and the growing impact of electoral politics on the public mind, when riots raged in the province, from only the religious feeling communalism acquired a political form. It created the problem of reconciling the security of the religious minority with the political dominance of the religious majority.

Muslims welcomed the communal electoral system as the government's recognition of the political distinctiveness of the community; Hindus resented it as a calculated blow on the emerging national unity against the colonial rule. Communal electoral system polarized the political equation between the Hindu and Muslim elites along religious lines, intensifying the on-going clash of creeds. The system institutionalised the political exclusiveness of the Muslim elite while sundering—though not immediately—the many deep socio-economic roots of the shared life of the Hindu and Muslim commoners.

The Hindu *Sangathana* Movement had a bearing on communalism in the province. The genesis of the movement was no doubt the reaction to what appeared to the Hindus as Muslims assertiveness, and on occasions aggressiveness, stimulated by pan-Islamism. It affected Hindu-Muslim societal relations but not quite served the intended political purpose of those who launched it and kept it going. Recurrent riots and competitive blood shedding by social ruffians worsened inter-communal relations at the mass level but yielded neither the Hindu Mahasabha nor the RSS any great political gain. Their increasing cadre strength was no real indication of their political clout; they could not rival the secular Congress in political power any more than they could stem the communal Muslim League influence among the Muslims.

Results of both the 1937 and 1946 elections confirmed that playing the Hindu communal card was no means to win Hindu votes, however effective the playing of Muslim communal card had proved to be for the League to win Muslim votes. In fact, the *Hindutva* Movement united the Muslims far more than the Hindus. It only rallied the high born Hindus—mainly the Brahmins—while the resultant reaction united the elements hostile to the high born Hindus. Muslims joining them and the government encouraging the development, the coalescence of anti-high born Hindu elements effectively countered the *Hindutva* Movement.

Riots correlated with the Hindu *Sangathana* Movement and the strong Muslim reaction to it had an important effect: though not politically united under any one party, Muslims now became psychologically far more united than before for self-defence and communal self-respect. The feeling lasted till the end of the British rule in the province despite the political division among the Muslim elite, sharpened by their conflicting personal ambitions. They became more dependent on the government to protect and preserve their interests. It was no small relief for the government to find that the loyalty of the Muslim leaders to their community was not above their allegiance to the government. Plums of patronage ensured the allegiance.

It was more external stimuli than internal impulsion that caused and influenced the course and character of communalism in the CP and Berar. The League's spell on the Muslims and its confrontation with the Congress had a decisive bearing on Hindu-Muslim relations. The Congress inability to influence the Muslims—except during 1916–22—contrasted with the League's success in drawing the Muslims to its fold and marginalizing the few Muslim groups who opposed it, the Khaksars and the Momins, for example. The desertion of the Congress by even the few Muslim leaders who were in it till the 1937 elections proved a great gain for the League. Above all, the League's call for a Muslim homeland accounted most for its pervasive popularity.

The League magnified the local grievances—real or imagined—into issues involving the very self-respect of the entire Muslim community in the country. League support to local Muslim leaders made them often unamenable to local control as easily as before, and the national League leadership's reaction to the steps taken by the provincial authorities rendered local problems at times insolvable. However, it must be added that the object of the government was not the eradication of communalism as such but prevention of any overt threat to public order. Many a time Muslim and Hindu rabble rousers went on their way notwithstanding the laws to prevent such actions. During war years, in particular, political necessity and the compulsion of sustaining an anti-Congress front obliged the government to ignore the activities of communal organizations which were anti-Congress and supportive of the government's war operations.

The League would not allow any cross-communal political alliances which marked the political life of the province till the party's ascendancy was confirmed in the late 1930s, even non-League Muslims being anathema to Jinnah. The League could convince the Muslims of the inverse relationship between exclusive cultural identity of the community and the inclusive nationalism of the Congress, a 'Hindu' party. Local Muslims were also impressed by the League propaganda that its conflict with the Congress was not just a contest between two political parties for power sharing but a struggle for survival of the minority against being politically swamped by the majority represented in the Congress. The persistent influence of the Hindu Mahasabha and the RSS in the Congress leadership smirched the party's image further among the Muslims. It validated the League's charges against the Congress and raised its stock among the Muslims.

The general Muslim avoidance of all Congress movements at the League's behest no doubt increased the latter's political clout but it also confirmed the general Hindu impression of the Muslims being unsympathetic to the national cause. Local League MLA's public declaration that they were Muslims first and then Indians marked the Muslims out as an 'anti-national' community—the more so when the Congress received overwhelming Hindu support to its opposition to the Pakistan scheme which was dear to every Muslim heart. No wonder, for some years after Independence, anti-Pakistan agitation of the Hindus had its fall-out in a general anti-Muslim sentiment nurtured by many Hindus in the province; the sentiment deepened with news of the Hyderabad Nizam's activities and Pakistan's misadventure in Kashmir.

However, unlike some other places in the country, the CP and Berar came out lightly of the tumultuous two years, 1946–7. This was due to the secular ideals held fast by the Congress leadership, the division in the local Muslim elite between the hawks and the doves and the general Muslim preference for reconciliation with the Congress rule to continuance of confrontation with it. The Congress government set up in 1946 maintained the British policy of keeping a tight rein on all communal groups. The general peace in the province in inter-community relations on the eve of Independence gave a lie to the League propaganda that the Congress rule was for the Muslims nothing but Hindu tyranny; it also established that communalism had all along been a political ploy of the League which only served the colonial government's interest in delaying the end of its authority.

After the merger of Bhopal and Hyderabad with the Indian Union, many Muslim evacuees returned to their homes in Berar districts where the anti-Muslim feelings were soon swamped by the general anti-Brahmin sentiment which Gandhi's assassination and the ban on the RSS intensified. The state of Andhra Pradesh made Hyderabad its capital and Madhya Pradesh, which followed, made Bhopal its capital. The two cities being associated with great days of Islamic rule, their elevation to the new status was gratifying to Muslim sentiments as it also confirmed the secular credential of the Congress government.

Communalism struck no deep social roots in the erstwhile Central Provinces and Berar as was borne out by the absence of serious communal violence in both MP and Vidarbha after 1947—although the latter soon formed a part of greater Maharashtra where such violence was neither few nor far between. The middle India region quickly relapsed into its accustomed state of political placidity.

Bibliography

PRIMARY SOURCES

Unpublished Material

Official Documents

Bundle Correspondence, Judicial	Madhya Pradesh Secretariat Record Room, Nagpur.
Civil Secretariat Records, Education Department	Madhya Pradesh Secretariat Record Room, Nagpur.
Foreign Political Consultations (Copies)	Madhya Pradesh Secretariat Record Room, Nagpur.
Nagpur Residency Correspondence (unindexed)	Madhya Pradesh Secretariat Record Room, Nagpur.
Nagpur Residency Records	Madhya Pradesh Secretariat Record Room, Nagpur.
Home (Political) A Proceedings	National Archives of India, New Delhi.
Home (Political) Deposit	National Archives of India, New Delhi.
Home (Reforms) Notes	National Archives of India, New Delhi.
Home Reforms	National Archives of India, New Delhi.
Home Reforms Deposit	National Archives of India, New Delhi.
Home (Political)	National Archives of India, New Delhi.
Home (Police), Part B Proceedings	National Archives of India, New Delhi (copies of these documents are available in the personal collection of Professor J.P. Mishra of Jabalpur and Dr K.S. Kshirsagar of Nagpur).

Records of the CP and Berar government in Political and Military Department, Home (Police) Department, General Administration Department, Elections Dept. — Maharashtra Archives, Nagpur.

Records of the DIG, CID, Intelligence and Special Wing, Bombay, Police Diaries: Abstract of Intelligence, CP — Maharashtra Archives, Mumbai.

Sinha Papers (Typed copies of official documents relating to nationalist movement in CP and Berar collected by Professor R.M. Sinha of Jabalpur) — Nagpur University Library.

Private Papers

Papers of Viceroy Lord Reading — National Archives of India.

Papers of Lord Halifax (Irwin) — National Archives of India.

Papers of Lord Linlithgow — National Archives of India.

Papers of G.S. Khaparde — National Archives of India, Maharashtra Archives, Nagpur, with Khaparde family at Amravati.

Papers of Dr B.S. Moonje — National Library, Calcutta. Copies also available in the personal collection of Dr K.S. Kshirsagar.

PUBLISHED MATERIAL

Newspapers

The Hitavada (on microfilm) — Nehru Memorial Museum & Library, New Delhi.

Report on Indian Newspapers Published in the CP and Berar — National Archives of India.

Official Reports and Other Publications

Indian Statutory Commission, vol. XIII, *Views of Local Government on the Recommendations of the Indian Statutory Commission, 1930* Calcutta, 1930; vol. XV, *Extracts from Official Oral Evidence* London, 1930; vol. XVII, *Selections from Memorandum and Oral Evidence by Non-Officials*, pt. II, London, 1930.

Indian Delimitation Commission, vol. I, *Report*, Delhi, 1936.

Report of the Indian Central Committee, Calcutta, 1929.
Indian Franchise Committee, vol. III, *Memorandum submitted by the Local Governments*, Calcutta, 1932; vol. V, *Selections from Memoranda and Oral Evidence*, Calcutta, 1932.
Indian Round Table Conference, vol. III, *Sub-Committee 3 (Minorities)*, Calcutta, 1931.
Report on the Working of the Reformed Constitution, Calcutta, 1928.
Report of the Indian Education Commission, Calcutta, 1883.
Indian Statutory Commission, Interim Education Report, Review of the Growth of Education in British India, London, 1930.
Constitutional Reforms, vol. IV, Opinions of Governments on Montagu-Chelmsford Report.
Report on the Reforms Enquiry Committee, 1924, Calcutta, 1929.
Parliamentary Debates, Indian Affairs, Commons, 1934–5, vol. 2.
Moral and Material Progress and Condition of India, 1926–7.
Memorandum on the Working of the Reformed Government in the Central Provinces and Berar, vol. I, *Memorandum*, Nagpur, 1930.

Gazetteers

The Imperial Gazetteer of India, vol. III, *Berar*, by W.W. Hunter, 1908.
______, vol. X, *Central Provinces*, 1908.
Central Provinces Gazetteer, by Charles Grant, 1971.
District Gazetteer: Amraoti, by S.V. Fitzerald and A.E. Nelson, 1911.
District Gazetteer: Buldana, by A.E. Nelson, 1910.
District Gazetteer: Chhindwara, by R.V. Russell, 1907.
District Gazetteer: Damoh, by R.V. Russell, 1906.
District Gazetteer: Jabalpur, by A.E. Nelson, 1909.
District Gazetteer: Nagpur, by R.V. Russell, 1908.
District Gazetteer: Narsingpur, by R.V. Russell, 1908.
District Gazetteer: Nimar, by R.V. Russell, 1908.
District Gazetteer: Saugar, by R.V. Russell, 1907.
District Gazetteer: Seoni, by R.V. Russell, 1908.
District Gazetteer: Yeotmal, by C. Brown and R.V. Russell, 1908.
Central Provinces Legislative Council Proceedings, 1915–35.
Central Provinces Legislative Assembly Proceedings, 1936–1949.
Annual Report on the Police Administration of the Central Provinces, 1894.
Reports on the Police Administration of the Central Provinces and Berar, 1920–1939.
Report on the Administration of the Central Provinces for 1862, by Richard Temple, Nagpur, 1923.
Report on the Administration of the Central Provinces, 1863–4 to 1901–02.
Report on the Administration of the Central Provinces and Berar, 1903–30.

Report on the Administration of the Central Provinces and Berar, 1920–40.

Report on the First Provincial Conference, CP and Berar, held at Nagpur on 22–23 April 1906.

A Scheme of Reforms of the CP and Berar Government submitted to the Secretary of State and the Viceroy, by the CP Deputation (1917); Scheme of Reforms submitted by the Graduates Association, Nagpur (1917).

A Scheme of Reforms submitted to the Secretary of State and Viceroy on behalf of Nagpur District Council (held at a meeting on 7 November 1917).

Papers connected with the Report of the Council's Committee, Calcutta, 1907.

Report of the Central Provinces Provincial Committee (Howell Committee) with Evidence taken before the Committee and Memorials submitted to the Education Commission, Calcutta, 1884.

Census Reports

Census of India, 1872, Central Provinces, Report.

_______, *1881*, vol. II, *Central Provinces, Report*, by R.H. Craddock.

_______, *1891*, vol. XI, *The Central Provinces and Feudatories*, pt. 1, *Report*, by B. Robertson.

_______, *1901*, vol. VII, *Berar*, pt. 1, *Report*, by A.D. Chinoy.

_______, *1911*, vol. X, *Central Provinces and Berar*, pt. 1, *Report*, by J.T. Marten.

_______, *1921*, vol. XI, *Central Provinces and Berar*, pt. 1, *Report*, by N.J. Roughton.

_______, *1931*, vol. XII, *Central Provinces and Berar*, pt. 1, *Report*, by W.H. Shoobert.

_______, *1941*, vol. VII, *Central Provinces and Berar, Tables*, by R.K. Ramadhyani, 1942.

_______, *1951*, vol. VII, *Madhya Pradesh*, by J.D. Kerawalla and H.N. Banerjee, 1953.

Report on the Nagpur State down to 1845, by George Ramsay, Nagpur, 1923.

Administration of the Nagpore Province by G. Plowden, Commissioner from 1855 to 1859, Nagpur, 1920.

The Settlement of the Affairs of the Ranees of Nagpore and the Course of Events after the Escheat of the State, Nagpur, 1920.

Escheat of the Nagpore State, the Arrangements for the Administration of the New Province and the Settlement of the Affairs of the Bhonsle Family, Nagpur, 1920.

The Report on the Territories of the Raja of Nagpore submitted to the Supreme Government of India by Richard Jenkins, Resident, 1827, Nagpur, 1923.

Supplement to the Report, Nagpur, 1925.

A Report on the Subah or Province of Chattisgarh by Major P. Vansagnew, 1820, Nagpur, 1922.

Vidya Mandir Scheme—A Way to the spread of free and compulsory mass education with a fixed period, Nagpur, 1938.

SECONDARY SOURCES

Abhyankar, Nana, *Vasishthechi Pani Arthat Narkesari Barrister Moreshwar Vasudev Abhyankar Yanche Charitra* (Marathi), Nagpur, 1965.

Ahmad, Jamiluddin, *Some Recent Speeches and Writings of Mr Jinnah*, Lahore, 1946.

Ahmad, Rafiuddin, *The Bengal Muslims, 1871–1906: A Quest for Identity*, 2nd edn., Delhi, 1988.

Allama, G., *Pakistan Movement, Historic Documents*, Karachi, 1967.

Allauddin, Qazi, *Tazkira-i-Mushahir-i-Berar* (Urdu), Amravati, 1982.

Ambedkar, B.R., *Pakistan or Partition of India*, Bombay, 1945.

Baker, D.E.U., *Changing Political Leadership in an Indian Province: The Central Provinces and Berar, 1919–1939*, Delhi, 1979.

_______, 'The Muslim Concern for Security: The Central Provinces and Berar, 1919–1939', in Mushirul Hassan, ed., *Communal and Pan-Islamic Trends in Colonial India*, New Delhi, 1981.

______, 'Foundations of Congress Raj in the Central Provinces and Berar, 1919–1937', in Jai Prakash Mishra, ed., *Researches in Social Sciences* (*Professor Amreshwar Avasthi Felicitation Volume*), Delhi, 1993.

Bhagat, M.E., 'Dalit Ideas and Leadership in Vidarbha' (Marathi), in P.L. Joshi, ed., *Political Ideas and Leadership in Vidarbha*, Nagpur, 1980.

Bhalerao, S.V., 'A Militant Hindu Nationalist: Dharmaveer Dr. B.S. Moonje (1872–1948)', in P.L. Joshi, ed., *Political Ideas and Leadership in Vidarbha*, Nagpur, 1980.

Birkenhead, Earl of, *Frederic Edwin Earl of Birkenhead, The Last Phase*, vol. II, London, 1935.

Bose, Bipin Krishna, *Stray Thoughts on Some Incidents of My Life*, Madras, 1923.

Bose, Subhas Chandra, *Netaji's Life and Writings*, pt. II, *The Indian Struggle, 1920–1934*, Calcutta, 1948.

Chatterton, Eyre, *The Story of Gondwana*, London, 1916.

Chopra, P.N., ed., *Towards Freedom*, New Delhi, 1985.

Coupland, Reginald, *The Constitutional Problem in India*, pt. III, *The Future of India*, Madras, 1944.

_______, *Indian Politics, 1936–42*, London. 1944.

C.P. Ministerial Crisis, Allahabad, 1938.

Datar, M.G., *Speeches and Statements of Dr. N.B. Khare*, Nagpur, 1943.

Deb, J.M., *Blood and Tears*, Bombay, 1945.

Deshpande, V., 'Militant Nationalism in Maharashtra, 1925–51', unpublished Ph.D. thesis, University of Jammu, Jammu, 1989.

Diwan, C.U., 'The Bahujan Samaj Movement in Vidarbha', in P.L. Joshi, ed., *Political Ideas and Leadership in Vidarbha*, Nagpur, 1980.

Fraser, A.H.L., *Among Indian Rajahs and Ryots: A Civil Servant's Recollections and Impressions of Thirty Seven Years of Work and Sport in the Central Provinces and Bengal*, London, 1912.

Gandhi, M.K., *Communal Unity*, Ahmedabad, 1949.

Gandhi, Rajmohan, *Patel*, Ahmedabad, 1990.

Glondevon, J, *The Viceroy at Bay: Lord Linlithgow in India*, London, 1971.

Government of Maharashtra, *Correspondence and Diary of G.S. Khaparde, 1897–1934*, vol. VII, Bombay, 1978.

Gwyer, Maurice and Appadorai, A, *Speeches and Documents in the Indian Constitution, 1921–47*, vol. I, London, 1957.

Hardas, Vina Balashastry, *Dr Balkrishna Sivaram Munje Yanche Charitra* (Marathi), Pune, 1966.

Hasan, Mushirul, ed., *Communal and Pan-Islamic Trends in Colonial India*, New Delhi, 1981.

Hooja, B., *A Life Dedicated: Biography of Govind Das*, Delhi, 1956.

Jagirdar, P.J., 'A Moderate of Moderates: Sir B.K. Bose', in P.L. Joshi, ed., *Political Ideas and Leadership in Vidarbha*, Nagpur, 1980.

Jalal, Ayesha, *The Sole Spokesman, Jinnah, the Muslim League and the Demand for Pakistan,* Cambridge, 1985.

Johari, Shubha, *Glimpses of Freedom Struggle: Politics in CP and Berar, 1927–39*, Nagpur, 1997.

Joshi, J.R., *Dr Kedar Yanche Charitra* (Marathi), Nagpur, 1956.

Joshi, P.L. ed., *Nagpur Nagar Sanstha Satabdi Granth* (Marathi), Nagpur, 1964.

Kamal, Khursheed, *A Documentary Record of the Congress Government, 1937–39 relating to Muslims under Congress Rule*, Islamabad, 1988, 2 vols.

Khaliquzzaman, Chaudhri, *Pathway to Pakistan*, Lahore, 1961.

Khane, B.D., 'Shahu's Crusade against Untouchability', in P.B. Salunkhe, ed., *Chhatrapati Shahu, the Pillar of Social Democracy,* Bombay, 1994.

Khaparde, B.G., *Shri Dadasaheb Khaparde Yanche Charitra* (Marathi), Pune, 1962.

Khare, N.B., *My Defence*, Nagpur, 1938.

______, *My Political Memoirs or Autobiography,* Nagpur, 1971.

Krishna, K.B., *The Problem of Minorities or Communal Representation.*

Kshirsagar, K.S., 'Dr N.B. Khare, Neo-Tilakite and Hindu Mahasabhite, 1880–1970', in P.L. Joshi, ed., *Political Ideas and Leadership in Vidarbha*, Nagpur, 1980.

Kshirsagar, K.S. and N.G.S. Kini, 'Neo-Tilakite: Narkesari Bar. M.V. Abhyankar, 1886-1935', in P.L. Joshi, ed., *Political Ideas and Leadership in Vidarbha*, Nagpur, 1980.

Landge, S., *Samsodhananjali* (Marathi), Nagpur, 1960.

Mansergh, Nicholas and Moon, Penderel, eds., *The Transfer of Power, 1942–47,* vols. VI, IX, X.

Mishra, B.B., *The Indian Political Parties*, Delhi, 1976.

Mishra, D.P., ed., *History of the Freedom Movement in Madhya Pradesh*, Nagpur, 1956.

Mishra, D.P., *Living an Era,* vol. I: *India's March to Freedom,* Delhi, 1975.

Mitra, H.N., ed., *Indian Quarterly Register, April–June 1924.*

Mitra, N.N. ed., *Indian Annual Register, 1919–46.*

Mojumdar, K., 'Chimur, 16 August 1942: Revolt at the grassroots', *Indo-British Review*, XVIII, no. 1, Madras, 1990.

_______, 'The Congress Ministry in the Central Provinces and Berar, 1937–39: The Communal Problem', in P.K. Mishra, ed., *Aspects of Indian History and Historiography*, New Delhi, 1996.

_______, 'Muslim Factor in the Politics of the Central Provinces and Berar (1880–1937)', *The Indian Archives*, New Delhi, XLVI, nos. 1–2, January-December 1997.

_______, 'Nagpur, 1920–23: The Changing Political Scene', *Journal of Indian History and Culture,* Chennai, September 1997.

Momin Mahiuddin, *Momin Ansari Biradari Ki Tahzibi Tarikh* (Urdu), Bombay, 1994.

Moon, Penderel, ed., *Wavell, The Viceroy's Journal*, London, 1973.

Moore, R.J., *The Crisis of Indian Unity, 1917–40*, Oxford, 1974.

Muslim Sufferings under Congress Rule (Fazlul Haq's Report), Calcutta, 1939.

Nathan, R, *Progress of Education in India 1897–98 to 1901–02, Fourth Quinquennial Review*, vol. II, Calcutta, 1904.

Neogi, M.B., 'Glimpses of Political Awakening in Nagpur', *Souvenir, The Indian National Congress, 64th session*, Nagpur, 1958.

Omvedt, Gale, 'Shahu Maharaj: Descendant of Shivaji, Protector of Non-Brahmins', in P.B. Salunkhe, ed., *Chhatrapati Shahu: The Protector of Social Democracy*, Bombay, 1994.

Padmasha, *Indian National Congress and the Muslims* (2nd edn.), New Delhi, 1985.

Page, David, *Prelude to Partition: The Indian Muslims and the Imperial System of Contral, 1920–1932*, New Delhi, 1982.

Palkar, N.H., *Dr Hedgewar* (Marathi), Pune, 1959.

Pande, Biswambharnath, 'Freedom Struggle in Madhya Pradesh', in *Samarpit Ardhasati: Pandit Dwaraka Prasad Mishra Abhinandan Granth*, New Delhi, 1970.

Pendke, Suhas, 'Leadership of Dr N.B. Khare', unpublished Ph.D thesis, Nagpur University, 1991.

Peshwe, V.M., 'A Synthesis of Tilak and Gandhi: Loknayak M.S. alias Bapuji Aney (1880–1968)', in P.L. Joshi, ed., *Political Ideas and Leadership in Vidarbha*, Nagpur, 1980.

Phillips, C.H. and Wainwright, M.D., eds., *The Partition of India, Policies and Perspectives, 1935–47*, London, 1970.

Pirzada, Syed Sharifuddin, *Foundations of Pakistan, All India Muslim League Documents*, 2 vols., Karachi, 1969.

Quddusi, M.Y., 'Some Freedom Fighters of Vidarbha', *Hitavada*, 20 August 1976.

Ram Gopal, *A Political History of Indian Muslims*, New Delhi, 1988.

Razak, Syed Abdur, *Swanesh Umari Khan Bahadur Badr-ud-din Ghulam Hussain Saheb* (Urdu), Nagpur, 1929.

Report of the Enquiry Committee appointed by the Council of the All India Muslim League to enquire into Muslim grievances in Congress Provinces (Pirpur Committee Report), Lucknow, 15 November 1938.

Reddy, C.R., *Congress in Office*, Madras, 1940.

Rizvi, Gowher, *Linlithgow and India: A Study of the British Policy and the Political Impasse in India, 1936–43*, London, 1978.

Russell. R.V. and Lal, Hira, *The Tribes and Castes of the Central Provinces of India*, vols. I and II (Indian edn.), Delhi, 1975.

Sahil, Muhammad Sharafuddin, *Nagpur Ka Muslim Maashara (Ahd-e-Bartaniya Mein, 1857–1947)*, Nagpur, 1997.

Saswadkar, P.L., 'Nagpur at the end of the 18th century', *Proceedings of the Indian History Congress*, 1969.

Savarkar, Vinayak Damodar, *Ratnagiri Parva*, vol. I, *1924–37* (Marathi), Bombay, 1972.

Sayeed, Khalid Bin, *Pakistan: The Formative Years*, Lahore, 1960.

Sejwalkar, T.S., *Nagpur Affairs*, vol. I, Nagpur, 1954.

Shankar, V., 'Mishraji as I have known him', *Samarpit Ardhasati*, New Delhi, 1970.

Shraddhanand, Swami, *Inside Congress*, Bombay, 1946.

Sharma, Kamlesh, *Role of Muslims in Indian Politics, 1857–1947*, New Delhi, 1985.

Sheshadri, H.V., ed., *R.S.S.: A Vision in Action*, Bangalore, 1988.

Shiva Rao, B., 'India, 1935–47', in C.H. Philips and M.D. Wainwright, eds., *Partition of India, Policies and Perspectives*.

Siddiqui Ali Khan, *Be Tegh Sipahi* (Urdu), Karachi, 1971.

Sinha, H.N., ed., *Selections from Nagpur Residency Records*, 5 vols.

Sinha, R.M., *Bhonsles of Nagpur, The Last Phase, 1818–1854*, New Delhi, 1967.

Tirtha, Swami Ramanand, 'D.P. Mishra and the Hyderabad Freedom Movement', *Samarpit Ardhasati*, New Delhi, 1970.

Tomlinson, B.R., *Indian National Congress and the Raj, 1929–1942: The Penultimate Phase*, London, 1976.

Wills, C.U., *The Raj Gond Maharajahs of the Satpura Hills, A Local History*, Nagpur, 1923.

———, *British Relations with the Nagpur State in the 18th century*, Nagpur, 1926.

———, *Early European Travellers in the Nagpur Territories*, Nagpur, 1930.

Wylie, F., 'Federal Negotiations in India, 1935–39 and After', in Philips and Wainwright, eds., *The Partition of India, Policies and Perspectives, 1935–47*, London, 1970.

Zaidi, A.M., ed., *The Demand for Pakistan*, New Delhi, 1978.

Zaidi, Z.M., 'Aspects of the Development of Muslim League Politics, 1937–47', in Philips and Wainwright, eds., *The Partition of India, Policies and Perspectives, 1935–47*, London. 1970.

Index